Toxic Waste and Environmental Policy
in the 21st Century United States

Toxic Waste and Environmental Policy in the 21st Century United States

Edited by DIANNE RAHM

McFarland & Company, Inc., Publishers
Jefferson, North Carolina, and London

363.7
Tox

10/02

Library of Congress Cataloguing-in-Publication Data

Toxic waste and environmental policy in the 21st century United
States / edited by Dianne Rahm.
        p.   cm.
    Includes index.
    ISBN 0-7864-1202-X (softcover : 50# alkaline paper) ∞
    1. Hazardous wastes— United States.   2. Radioactive wastes—
United States.   3. Environmental policy — United States.   I. Rahm,
Dianne.   4. Pollution   5. Industrial waste
TD1040.T687   2002
363.72'87 — dc21   2001007167

British Library cataloguing data are available

Manufactured in the United States of America

Cover image: ©2002 Art Today

McFarland & Company, Inc., Publishers
  Box 611, Jefferson, North Carolina 28640
    www.mcfarlandpub.com

Table of Contents

Introduction
by Dianne Rahm

The 21st century brings with it many challenges, not the least of which is dealing with the 20th century's legacy of toxic waste. The weapons that fought the Cold War, the facilities that manufactured those weapons, and the factories that fueled an economy of prosperity left behind a trail of pollution. One of the great challenges we now face is to find ways to clean up the toxic wastes left behind.

With the end of the Cold War, nearly half a century of sustained nuclear weapons production came to a halt. Not only had the country produced nuclear weapons during that period of time, but chemical weapons as well. With the fall of the Soviet Union, U.S. efforts shifted from building weapons to planning how the stockpiles might be drawn down. Several chapters in this volume address aspects of this large problem. W. Henry Lambright and Agnes Gereben Schaefer focus on the difficult issue of chemical and nuclear weapons disposal. Weapons control historically meant the manufacture of new weapons and the disposal of old weapons when they no longer fulfilled their purpose, and during the years of the Cold War, this process was shrouded in secrecy. With the end of the Cold War, however, these weapons control programs became open to public scrutiny. This openness, in turn, has resulted in an increasing number of domestic participants in the general process as well as amplified pressure from the international community for weapons control. Foreign policy actors such as the State Department, arms control officials, and the presidential administration in Washington are pushing to dispose quickly of weapons to meet international treaty deadlines. They frequently run into conflict with other groups wanting to slow the process down. Citizens at the national, state and local levels, especially environmental activists determined to stop a process they view as harmful, have had influence on not only the number of weapons destroyed but also the technologies used to dismantle them.

The weapons themselves are just one part of the toxic remains. The

1

facilities that were used to manufacture these weapons are another part of the legacy. Two chapters in this book look at the problems associated with the cleanup of a nuclear weapons complex. Rahm describes the complex and discusses the extent of environmental contamination. This complex, which started in the Second World War with efforts to build an atomic bomb and expanded rapidly in the Cold War, is of enormous size (about twice the size of Delaware) and the contamination at the major sites is extensive. With the end of the Cold War, attention focused on how to clean up the nuclear and chemical waste at the sites. The first challenge was to overcome the secrecy of the Cold War years and fully reveal the problem. By the early 1990s, Superfund sites were identified at all major nuclear weapons complex facilities and the cleanup work began. The disclosures have revealed an environmental problem and administrative challenge of enormous proportions.

Ahmedov provides a detailed discussion of the management processes at work in attempting to clean up one small part of a major site in the weapons complex. He examines the decision making surrounding the cleanup of Pit 9 at the Idaho National Engineering and Environmental Laboratory. The experiment with performance-based management contracts to clean Pit 9 attempted to create incentives to reduce costs and set objective performance criteria by which Department of the Energy (DOE) administrators could judge contractors' results. The failure of this strategy speaks to the difficulty of even seemingly minor cleanup efforts.

The complexity of decision making in toxic waste cleanups extends to the Environmental Protection Agency (EPA). Davis explores the interplay of federal field offices with headquarters in an attempt to explore their effectiveness in promoting cooperation between federal, state and local governments in the development and implementation of national policy objectives. Davis reviews the role of EPA field offices in their oversight of state efforts to implement federal policies. Regional EPA bureaucrats need to walk the fine line. They need to make field management decisions that show consistency with headquarters, but they also need to use independent discretion so that unique field conditions are considered. The balancing act of pleasing headquarters and dealing with site-specific problems in the cleanup of hazardous wastes, illustrates one of the challenges of toxic waste cleanup.

Simons and Winson also focus on the interplay of the states and the EPA. Their focus is on state brownfield programs which are a major shift away from the federally directed Superfund program as the vehicle for cleaning contaminated sites. Dissatisfaction with slow, expensive, and lawsuit-prone Superfund cleanups created the incentives for states to take the lead on cleanups. States experimented with both mandatory and voluntary programs for toxic waste cleanup. The voluntary brownfield programs are explored in this chapter. Simons and Winson suggest that these new programs may be the key to overcoming obstacles to difficult toxic waste cleanups.

Toxic waste cleanup is something that tends to invite community and local response. Unlike other environmental issues that tend to be more removed from direct community action, toxic waste gets local actors heavily involved. Falcone explores this from the level of the variety of actors involved in decision making for transport of nuclear and hazardous waste from one community, through many communities, to a final deposit site. Steelman and Carmin explore community-based solutions to toxic waste problems. Only in engaging the affected communities in the decision making can there be any equity in toxic waste remediation processes.

One of the great challenges of the 21st century will be the cleanup of the toxic wastes left behind in the 20th century. That cleanup will involve thinking carefully about weapons, weapons facilities, waste transport, government management, intergovernmental relations, and community relations. This volume begins a discussion of some key issues within each of these areas.

Chapter One

The Environmental Politics of Chemical and Nuclear Weapons Disposal

W. HENRY LAMBRIGHT AND
AGNES GEREBEN SCHAEFER

Introduction

The end of the Cold War has precipitated an increasing policy drive to move beyond the dismantling and long-term storage of chemical and nuclear weapons to their outright destruction. For example, the Chemical Weapons Convention, which was ratified by both the U.S. and Russia in 1997, called for signatory nations to destroy existing chemical weapon stockpiles as well as cease research, development and production activities. In addition, a number of agreements between the U.S. and Russia, including the START and Intermediate-Range Nuclear Forces (INF) treaties, have outlined sharp reductions in the nuclear stockpiles of both nations, and both countries have declared that several hundred tons of "surplus" nuclear weapons will be dismantled and destroyed. The shift from dismantlement and storage policy to disposal policy has created a significant new issue area whose political landscape reflects both the increasing synthesis of international and domestic policy as well as the increasing role of nongovernmental organizations (NGOs) in domestic and international politics.

While most policy participants can agree on the underlying principles of these international agreements, their implementation has proven to be difficult. This chapter focuses on implementation in the U.S. where the prime roadblock to demilitarizing Cold War weapons has been the intense controversy regarding disposal technologies. There is heated debate over which means are the safest and most environmentally benign. At the

center of the debate are the two agencies charged with the prime implementation tasks: the U.S. Army, as executive agent for the Department of
Defense, and the Department of Energy (DOE). The army and DOE have
been charged respectively with chemical and nuclear demilitarization and
have created programs for these purposes. Although federal implementers
of international arms control treaties, they have been met by considerable
resistance from states, environmentalists and local citizens concerned about
both the safety of the chosen methods of disposal for these weapons and
the economic implications of their communities being known as destruction sites for deadly wastes. The increasing politicization of both the chemical and nuclear demilitarization programs shows how global issues such
as arms control have become linked with local environmental issues, and
how disposal technology can become a fulcrum upon which controversy
turns.

In order to understand the political debate surrounding chemical and
nuclear weapons disposition in the U.S., it is necessary to examine the historical evolution of these two programs with attention to the actors involved
and their political strategies. While the chemical and nuclear demilitarization programs have historically been two of the most tightly and hier-
archically managed programs in government, this chapter examines how,
over time, control over the programs has become increasingly diffused as
the policies have become influenced by increasing numbers of domestic
actors as well as international pressures. The emphasis in this chapter is
on a comparison of the domestic and international political forces shap-
ing the policy environment of the two demilitarization programs and their
ability to implement particular disposal technologies. This analysis reveals
how pressures from foreign policy actors (e.g., State Department, arms
control officials, and even the President) to speed up demilitarization, can
come into conflict with counterpressures from domestic forces at the
national, state and local levels, including environmental nongovernmental organizations (NGOs), to slow down the process.

Theoretical Approach

In examining the historical evolution of these two demilitarization
programs, our analysis draws from several strands of academic literature.
First, it draws from the vast literature that deals with how the policymaking process becomes infused with differing perceptions of risk. Second, the chapter draws from the literature on the politics of science and
the role of technical experts in policymaking. Third, it draws on the grow-

ing literature on the increasing synthesis of domestic and international politics. These strands of literature provide a means to understand the incredibly complex political contexts of the U.S. chemical and nuclear disposal programs, and how arms control can devolve into an arena of environmental politics.

Risk Perception

The literature on risk is useful because it gets to the heart of the debate surrounding the technological choices for chemical and nuclear weapons destruction. The various stakeholders in both issues have very different perceptions as to what is an "acceptable" risk, and these differing perceptions have often created a stalemate in the policymaking process. The vast majority of the literature on risk is dominated by psychological studies that examine how we develop risk perceptions. Much of this research is driven by the quest to discover why we have developed a "culture of fear" (Furedi 1997). The dominant theoretical approach to these studies deals with the social construction of risk in terms of the interaction of values and attitudes, and the ways in which risks are framed (Nelkin 1989). This approach emphasizes that our values and attitudes predispose us to interpreting risk data in particular ways, and that this interpretation can often be reinforced by the way scientists or the media frame the risk. For instance, Peters and Slovic discovered that:

> affect associated with images of nuclear power was systematically related to a person's worldviews. How we feel about a risk seems to be determined in part by how management of that risk is set within the power structures of industry and government and how that type of management pattern relates to the individual's view of how the world should be organized [Peters and Slovic 1996, 1450].

Renn et al. argue that "social amplification" of risks occurs from "the interaction of psychological, cultural, social, and institutional processes that amplify or attenuate public experience of risk and result in secondary impacts" (Renn et al. 1992, 154). Taken as a whole, this literature provides valuable insights into the sources of risk perception construction and will be useful in interpreting the differing perceptions of risk in the two areas of weapons disposal policy that will be analyzed.

Another aspect of the risk literature that is relevant to this chapter is the extensive work that has been done on the issue of trust in the siting of nuclear and other hazardous waste facilities. Pijawka and Mushkatel point out that public opposition to the siting of hazardous waste facilities has been studied extensively, and that more recent studies have shown that the lack of public trust in government agencies is identified as a major cause of opposition (Pijawka and Mushkatel 1992).[1] This body of literature is significant because it offers insight into the lack of trust between the army and citizens living near particular chemical weapons disposal sites, and between DOE and citizens living near nuclear weapons disposal sites.

Finally, the most significant aspect of the risk literature deals with how risk perceptions are incorporated into the policymaking process. There is an extensive literature that examines the impact of risk assessment on the policymaking process. Waterstone offers a comprehensive comparative analysis of the incorporation of risk assessment and risk perception in a number of case studies (Waterstone 1992). Wandersman and Hallman argue that quantitative risk assessments are not enough because they are often too complex for people to comprehend. Instead, they argue that experts need to understand that the public is not necessarily acting irrationally if its risk perceptions do not match scientific estimates of risk, and that these fears are derived from underlying personal and value judgments (Wandersman and Hallman 1993). They also argue that policymakers need to be better trained to understand this discrepancy between scientific assessment and risk perception. Vaughan and Seifert not only acknowledge that the policy process cannot effectively incorporate risk analysis and risk assessment, but also offer several proposals that are relevant to the cases analyzed in this chapter. They argue that:

> the underlying reasons for disputes is a prerequisite for the effective implementation of a more participatory and democratic approach to risk management (Stern 1991), and for promoting a dialogue between various interest groups. A successful resolution of many controversies will necessitate strategies that acknowledge, reflect, and accommodate the variability within society in those beliefs and values that influence how risk problems are conceptualized [Vaughan and Seifert 1992, 131].

In addition to this literature related to risk in general, there is also an extensive and useful literature that examines how perceptions of technological risk are incorporated into the policy process. This work is significant because it is in this sense that risk has become a divisive factor in both of the cases that are examined. There is a very rich array of scholarly work which deals with both the public perception of technological risk,[2] as well as how technology is shaped by political and social forces.[3]

Overall, the literature on risk is significant to this chapter because it offers insight into how risk perceptions are formed, and how these perceptions can become entangled in the policy process. Such an analysis is particularly useful when analyzing the case of chemical weapons disposal because there has been extreme controversy over differing perceptions of risks associated with different disposal technologies, and there is a long legacy of distrust between the army and local citizens living near the disposal sites. Such conflict is only now beginning to take shape in the case of nuclear weapons disposal, so such an analysis may prove to be useful in deriving strategies to head off any escalation of this conflict.

The Politics of Science: Epistemic Communities and Participatory Decision Making

The second set of literature that is particularly useful in developing the theoretical framework of this chapter deals with the role of scientific and technical experts in the policy process. Jasanoff's seminal work on science advisors offers a comprehensive analysis of the problems associated with turning scientific knowledge into policy, and in trying to negotiate between placing scientific knowledge in a privileged political position and maintaining an open democracy (Jasanoff 1990). Barker and Peters offer an interesting comparative analysis of how expert advice is dealt with in different countries (Barker and Peters 1993).

Haas' work on "epistemic communities" is also relevant to the topics examined in this chapter. Haas defines an epistemic community as a professional group that believes in the same cause-and-effect relationships and in the truth tests to assess them, and that shares common knowledge. Most importantly, the community's domestic and international power resource is its authoritative claim to knowledge (Haas 1992). Haas argues that scientific experts can be an extremely effective group in bringing about international cooperation because they share a common knowledge (the scientific method) and their concern for the natural world transcends international borders (Haas 1990). In addition, scientists can easily gain access to (and often usurp) the decision-making process because they are needed by policymakers who do not understand highly scientific or technical issues.

Haas' work stands in contradiction to another aspect of the politics of science literature that examines the merits of new, participatory forms of scientific decision making. The use of participatory forms of decision making as a whole has increased under the assumption that including the stakeholders in the decision-making process will ultimately lead to a more effective outcome because the outcome will have been reached by consensus.[4] More importantly, though, this approach challenges Haas' notion that scientists should be in privileged political positions because of their expertise. It instead argues that the public should have a say in technological choices because they are the ones who are going to have to live with the consequences of those choices. In an article, Morrell analyzed these new forms of scientific decision making and came to the conclusion that they will only be effective if they are structured in a manner in which "the opinions offered by citizens do not become constitutive of them as persons. Otherwise, critical deliberation cannot help being directed at both a citizen's position and him or her as an individual" (Morrell 1999). This body of work is also significant to this chapter because it offers insight into the participatory decision-making process that has been initiated by the army to surmount the stalemate between it and its critics, and may offer insight into why DOE should or should not engage in a similar conflict resolution strategy.

The Synthesis of Domestic and International Politics

Traditional theoretical perspectives in the field of public administration have focused on domestic organizational factors in isolation from international pressures. Recently, though, a body of literature has emerged which challenges this traditional perspective and argues instead that domestic administrative structures must be placed within "the global administrative environment" as global pressures increasingly impact domestic bureaucracies (Welch and Wong 1998). Several authors note the changing power dynamics between domestic and international structures, and the need for domestic bureaucracies to accommodate to international pressures (Cleveland 1993; Farazmand 1998). The topics discussed in this chapter demonstrate that domestic programs cannot be isolated from international pressures and events.

International relations scholars have recognized that the interactions of nation-states can be analyzed at different "levels," most importantly, at the international systemic level or at the level of the individual nation-state. While some early international relations scholars dealt with the level-of-analysis issue with regard to very specific topics (i.e., the causes of war) (Waltz 1954), Singer's 1961 seminal article on the "level-of-analysis problem" redefined how scholars approached the analysis of international relations. Singer argued that the systemic and national state levels of analysis have different descriptive, explanatory, and predictive advantages and disadvantages, and the issue is not whether one level is "better" than another; rather, it is that "even if the case for one or another of the possible levels of analysis cannot be made with any certainty, one must nevertheless maintain a continuing awareness as to their use. We may utilize one level here and another there, but we cannot afford to shift our orientation in the midst of a study" (Singer 1961, 28). Singer's work infused the field with increasing analytical rigor and awareness of the implications of moving from one level of analysis to another.

In *Turbulence in World Politics: A Theory of Change and Continuity*, Rosenau adds to the levels of analysis debate by arguing that there has been a historical breakpoint at which a bifurcation of the macroglobal structures has occurred. He argues that the statecentric world has evolved into two nonhierarchically ordered and coexisting worlds of global politics: 1) the statecentric world composed of nation-states, and the multicentric world composed of subgroups, IGOs/INGOs, state bureaucracies and transnational actors (Rosenau 1990). In this new, more pluralistic evolution of world politics, Rosenau argues that world politics is defined by "micro-macro" linkages in which micro actors such as citizens, officials, and private people interact with macro actors such as states, subgroups, transnational organizations, leaderless publics and movements. "Focusing on the interactions between the levels enables one to get to the core of global life, to the ways in which large, impersonal forces at work in the world *both* derive from *and* influence the actions of people in coping with challenges and conducting their affairs" (Rosenau 1990, 143).

Rosenau's work breaks down the conceptual constraints imposed by the traditional realist and neorealist approaches to international relations by acknowledging that there is interaction between actors at different levels of analysis and that one level does not always determine the actions of actors at the other levels.[5] Therefore, Rosenau's perspective offers a very useful theoretical framework for this chapter's analysis of the interplay between the local demands of citizens living near weapons disposal sites, and international arms control objectives. International arms control agreements and local public mobilization mutually impact and redefine each other.

Chemical Weapons Demilitarization and Origins of the First Technological Debate

Twelve years before there was the international treaty to destroy chemical weapons, there was national policy. In 1985, as part of a Reagan administration package to develop new chemical weapons, there was legislation passed to destroy old obsolete weapons. There are some 30,000 tons of these weapons, including nerve and mustard gases, located at sites in eight states and Johnston Atoll, 700 miles south of Hawaii (Smithson and Lenihan 1996). The states are: Utah, Arkansas, Alabama, Oregon, Maryland, Indiana, Colorado and Kentucky. It was initially believed that "Chem Demil" would be a $1.7 billion program that could be completed by 1994 (Warren 1995).

The first technological choice, made in 1988 following three years of study, was to incinerate the weapons in a facility that would have to be created *de novo* on-site. It was considered both dangerous and politically infeasible to transport the weapons, many of which were volatile, across state borders (M. Owen, personal communication, May 7, 1997). The plan was to develop and test the facility at remote Johnston Atoll, and then replicate it at the eight sites in the U.S., starting with the largest site, Tooele, near Salt Lake City. The Environmental Protection Agency approved army plans, which had a design goal that the facility be 99.9999% safe in terms of release of toxic fumes (W. Busbee, personal communication, June 14, 1997).

The first challenge to baseline incineration (the name given the army technique) came from industry and Congress. An industrial contractor, General Atomics, proposed a technology called cryofracture. In baseline incineration, rockets and other munitions were disassembled by robotic and other devices prior to being burned (National Research Council 1996). In cryofracture, the weapons were frozen, making them brittle and breakable into small pieces prior to incineration (M. Owen, personal communication, May 7, 1997). Simpler, presumably less subject to breakdown, cryofracture appealed to key legislators who believed the army should investigate the technology (J. Wilson, personal communication, 1989). The army believed it already had done so prior to choosing baseline incineration.

In 1989, the army was well in to building a baseline incineration facility at Johnston Atoll. Meanwhile, it persuaded the state of Utah to issue an environmental permit to start building a replica at Tooele (Battelle Pacific 1994). State officials in Utah believed it was riskier to let the weapons sit, fester, and possibly explode than to accept baseline incineration. The state of Utah, however, held open the decision to operate the facility — which would be made only when its environmental and health officials were convinced that the technology was fully effective.

International Pressure

At this time, the Cold War was ending and U.S. foreign policy was rapidly shifting to a position of trying to prevent proliferation of chemical weapons and getting Russia to destroy its weapons. Also, Germany pushed hard to have U.S.-owned NATO weapons on its soil removed. While the removal of the weapons was scheduled to begin in 1992, environmental groups pressured German Chancellor Helmut Kohl to push for a speeding up of the timetable (Fisher 1990). President George Bush in 1989 agreed to Kohl's request and announced the goal to move the weapons to Johnston Atoll in late 1990 (U.S. General Accounting Office 1991).

The decision to remove the weapons from Germany (a foreign policy choice) impacted domestic decision making in the sense that the army now had to accelerate testing and verification of the technology at Johnston Atoll. When the army asked for money to implement the additional requirements for Chem Demil concerning Germany, Congress forced it to mount a cryofracture research and development program as the price of its agreement (Atwood 1989; Memo from Ms. Heffernan 1989).

Johnston Atoll's preparation was placed on a crash schedule. The army ultimately certified Johnston Atoll as "technically ready" to take the German weapons, and transport from Germany began in July 1990 (Fisher 1990). In reality, the readiness was questionable, and there were many breakdowns and glitches that opponents would later use as ammunition against baseline incineration. Meanwhile, costs of Chem Demil soared well beyond original estimates. In 1992, the estimate was that the stockpile would be destroyed by 2003 and the cost would be $8.6 billion (Memorandum to the Secretary of the Army 1993).

In 1993, the army certified to DOD and Congress that Johnston Atoll was now fully operational and full-scale destruction activities could commence. At the same time, the army got Congress to go along with terminating cryofracture, which had been shown to have unanticipated technical problems (M. Owen, personal communication, May 7, 1997). Moreover, cryofracture also ended in incineration and the technological debate was now about one incineration technique vs. another, not incineration vs. some nonincinerating alternative.

Confronting Mistrust and Differing Perceptions of Risk

By 1994, the political locus of Chem Demil was shifting to the state and local level. State officials in Utah were allowing construction of a baseline incineration plant, but no other state had come close to making such a decision. Army attempts to persuade state and local officials had in many cases been met by fear and anger. Some citizens living near the disposal sites were concerned that despite the army and NRC's reassurances, chemical agents would be released during the incineration process and that their families and the environment would be placed at risk. Unfortunately in some communities, there was a legacy of distrust that needed to be overcome due to past incidents about which the army had not been forthcoming. For instance, in Kentucky, Army personnel were disposing of "smoke pots" (canisters of smoke used to obscure troop movements in combat) when the wind carried the smoke into civilian territory and created health problems. The army initially denied any wrongdoing, and the community lost confidence in its credibility (M. Parker and B. Pehlivanian, personal communication, May 21, 1998). In addition, there were reports that testing of chemical weapons in the 1960s had killed up to 6,000 sheep at Dugway Proving Ground in Utah (Chemical Weapons Working Group 2000a). In general, trust was in short supply and it appeared that some local communities and the army had very different perceptions of acceptable risk.

While opposition to incineration could be found in all eight states, the greatest opposition was in Kentucky. Here, a new nongovernmental organization, the Chemical Weapons Working Group (CWWG), had come into being and was influencing its congressional representatives to slow down the army's attempts to push incineration in Kentucky and elsewhere. While the group began in Kentucky, it later became an umbrella organization for a coalition of smaller groups organized at each of the sites. Under the adept leadership of Craig Williams, the CWWG has become a powerful force with which the army has had to deal. CWWG established valuable strategic links to larger national organizations such as Greenpeace and the Sierra Club, and also created ties with similar organizations concerned with chemical weapons disposal in Russia, home to the world's largest arsenal of chemical weapons (Brooke 1997). CWWG has been very effective in using its congressional representatives as well as the courts to derail the army's incineration plans and force it to develop alternative nonincineration technologies for chemical weapons disposal.

Another state that strongly opposed incineration was Maryland. Here the opposition was focused in the Citizens Advisory Commission (CAC). In 1992, federal legislation authorized such groups, funded by the army, to advise governors on Chem Demil (Walker 1994). Each CAC consists of nine members (seven from the stockpile site region and two state officials with technical expertise). The intent of this legislation was to provide more of an opportunity for those living near the disposal sites to comment about the various disposal methods (U.S. Program Manager for Chemical Demilitarization 2000a). The Maryland CAC seized on a report by the National Research Council (NRC) in 1994 that said the Maryland and Indiana sites were suitable for a possible chemical neutralization technology followed by biological treatment or oxidation, since they had only bulk chemical materials stored on site. They did not have assembled weapons, including rockets, which the other sites had. The army claimed that only incineration would be effective with these chemicals. The NRC agreed, insofar as existing technology was concerned. However, the NRC saw neutralization as needing development and testing, but it agreed with the army generally on the risk question — that letting the chemicals sit and age was riskier than incinerating them (National Research Council 1994; U.S. General Accounting Office 1994). State officials and local citizens in Maryland disagreed with the army on the risk issue, and their lawmakers in Congress pressed hard for neutralization.

In 1996, the army's incineration plans regained momentum when Utah provided it with a permit to operate its Chem Demil facility in Tooele (U.S. General Accounting Office 1997). However, the army continued to feel pressure from incineration opponents in Maryland and Indiana who argued that they were in a very different situation than those sites that had assembled weapons, and therefore, the army should implement the most appropriate technology to their situation — in their opinion, neutralization. The army gave in and announced in 1997 that it would build neutralization facilities in Maryland and Indiana only (Plan Approved to Neutralize APG Mustard Agent 1997). The six other states were still slated for baseline incineration.

CWWG saw a break in the army's dike, however, and used its supporters in Congress to get an amendment attached to the 1997 Defense Authorization Bill to provide $40 million to conduct a pilot program to identify and demonstrate two or more alternatives to the incineration process that would destroy assembled weapons as well as chemicals. This program came to be known as the Assembled Chemical Weapons Assessment (ACWA) program. The baseline incineration and neutralization programs were organized under one army manager, ACWA under a different manager (U.S. Congress 1996). Both reported to an overall official, Ted Prociv, Deputy Assistant Secretary of the Army.

The ACWA program had a major impact on the army's ability to implement baseline incineration at the sites that had assembled weapons. The incineration plant in Utah continued to operate (albeit with some glitches) and in 1997, state officials in both Oregon and Alabama agreed to issue the army a permit to build an incineration facility (Prociv, 1997). Officials in Arkansas said they would follow suit — but did not do so until 1999. The acquisition of these permits was only a partial victory for the army, however. Incineration opponents in Kentucky and Colorado were determined to hold out until the ACWA program found alternative technologies to baseline incineration. The ACWA program provided the vehicle by which the CWWG and its allies in the various states hoped to derail the army's incineration plans, and, in fact, undo decisions already made in the proincineration states.

Meanwhile, the army also felt pressure from federal arms control officials, including the National Security Council, to get on with Chem Demil (M. Sullivan, personal communication 1998). The U.S. was engaged in serious negotiations on a Chemical Weapons Convention (CWC) to head off development and proliferation of these kinds of weapons. How could the U.S. preach to Russia, Iraq and other countries if it did not provide an example? The United States demonstrated leadership when it ratified the CWC in 1997. The treaty set a new deadline for Chem Demil of ten years following ratification, or 2007. Under the CWC, the State Department was officially put in charge of implementation, and it placed pressure on the army to adhere to the 2007 deadline.

Participatory Decision Making

In an effort to end the logjam with Chem Demil (even the proincineration states were moving extremely slowly, and Kentucky and Colorado were not moving at all) the ACWA program turned to a third party, the Keystone Center (Assembled Chemical Weapons Assessment Program Office 1998b). Keystone was adept at getting opposing parties around a table to work out their disagreements. Thus began a series of meetings, known as "the Dialogue," involving the various stakeholders in the issue. These stakeholders included members of the affected communities surrounding the disposal sites, state environmental officials, representatives from industry (who were providing the alternative disposal technologies), and various officials from the army and DOD. While the different stakeholders all agreed that chemical weapons should be destroyed, the task of the Keystone Center was to overcome the bitter disagreements over how to go about destroying them. Hence, the stakes were high.

The army, in an unprecedented move, allowed the Dialogue participants to set requirements for a new technical system (Assembled Chemical Weapons Assessment Program Office 1998a). Various companies proposed designs that would meet those criteria. By July 1998, after several months of meetings, the Dialogue process had moved to a point where the states had agreed to certain technical requirements for an alternative technology. The Dialogue determined that six companies had designs that could qualify. Prociv, however, told the Dialogue participants at the July meeting that the army had money for testing only three. The meeting turned tense and adversarial. While the primary outcome was to agree to continue talking, it was clear that the bond of trust had been damaged. Some participants believed the army had been disingenuous in its commitment to the Dialogue process (Lambright 1998).

During the following year, the CWWG continued to try to reverse (or at least forestall) the decision to build incineration facilities. In particular, the group filed an environmental justice lawsuit against the state of Arkansas, claiming that the construction of an incinerator in Arkansas would disproportionately impact minorities and people of low income (Chemical Weapons Working Group 1999a).[6] The CWWG also worked hard to reopen the decision to test all six alternative technologies. The group mobilized its congressional allies from Kentucky and pushed for an amendment to the FY 2000 Military Construction Appropriations Bill to prohibit any funds from being expended on any Chem Demil facility in Kentucky until all six of the ACWA approved technologies had been evaluated (Chemical Weapons Working Group 1999b). Finally, in June 1999, after obtaining an internal DOD memo, the CWWG wrote the Secretary of the Army calling for Prociv's removal. While stating support for the "ACWA process," CWWG alleged that Prociv had lied about not having enough funds to demonstrate all six alternative technologies (Chemical Weapons Working Group 1999c). Following an investigation, the Pentagon announced that all six of the alternative technologies that were chosen by the Dialogue would be tested. In October 1999, it was announced that Prociv would resign. However, the whole incident fueled the mistrust between DOD and army officials and incineration opponents.

In April 2000, the army announced that the U.S. had met and surpassed the April 29, 2000, disposal milestone of the Chemical Weapons Convention. While the treaty calls for signatory countries to have destroyed 1 percent of their stockpile and nonstockpile chemical material by this deadline, the army announced that the U.S. had destroyed over 15 percent (U.S. Program Manager For Chemical Demilitarization 2000d). This is primarily because after ten years of operation, the facility at Johnston Atoll had destroyed 94 percent of the weapons stockpiled there. It was expected to begin closure activities in January 2001 (U.S. Program Manager For Chemical Demilitarization 2000c). Another milestone was reached in

October when the army announced that 50 percent of the chemical weapons stored at the Tooele Chemical Agent Disposal Facility (TOCDF) had been destroyed (U.S PMCD, 2000b). That was the good news.

The bad news was that the pace of destruction was slow at virtually all of the other disposal sites. The debate continues, amidst lawsuits and public protests at virtually every site. Colorado and Kentucky continue to refuse to accept the risks associated with incineration. Testing of alternative technologies also continues and permits have been issued for pilot neutralization plants. In addition to these controversies, it appears that the army will face even more opposition. In September 2000, it reiterated that incineration should be considered for the disposal of stockpiled weapons at the eight sites discussed above, and in addition, that the incinerators at the eight sites should be considered for the disposal of "non-stockpile" chemical material such as chemical agent testing kits, bulk agents and munitions. While the army's plan is not to ship nonstockpile material from out of state, some citizens are concerned that this will open up the door for the transport of this material over long distances (Chemical Weapons Working Group 2000b). This does not bode well for the disposal process. In a report issued in May 2000, the GAO found that because an acceptable method of disposal has not been found at all of the disposal sites, it was unlikely that the U.S. would destroy 100 percent of its stockpile by the 2007 deadline required by the CWC (U.S. General Accounting Office 2000). Unless the differences over environmental risk can be bridged, it appears that the U.S. may violate a treaty that it has made a symbol for post–Cold War arms control policy.

Chem Demil thus reveals how public concerns about risk, scientific uncertainties about alternatives to incineration, and the conflicting pressures of global arms control and local protest can come together in controversy. Everyone wants to get rid of chemical weapons, most of which are militarily obsolete and dangerous. The issue is not whether, but how, and so far local interests, which are focused and active, have had the advantage over more diffuse international interests in arms control.

The Case of Nuclear Demilitarization

The end of the Cold War has also had a significant impact on the way in which the United States deals with its nuclear arsenal, particularly plutonium, an exceedingly dangerous material. While nuclear deterrence is still a primary defensive strategy in the post–Cold War era, the race to produce more weapons has been replaced by the need to dismantle a large portion of the nuclear weapons arsenal in accordance with the requirements of international agreements with Russia. Perhaps the most telling departure from Cold War policies came in September 1998 when the United States and Russia agreed to "remove by stages approximately 50 metric tons of plutonium from their nuclear weapons programs, and to convert this material so that it can never be used in nuclear weapons" (Joint Statement of Principles For Management and Disposition of Plutonium Designated as No Longer Required for Defensive Purposes 1998). This declaration to destroy "surplus" nuclear material has moved the dialogue between the United States and Russia from one that focused on simply dismantling nuclear weapons and storing the fissile material, to one which now emphasizes outright conversion and disposal of the fissile material. The question is how can this be done in the safest and most environmentally benign manner.

The issue of nuclear weapons disposal is in many respects more complex than chemical weapons disposal because the waste includes fissile material (of which plutonium is the prime example) that can be reused for both military and commercial purposes. Therefore, the technological debate surrounding nuclear weapons destruction has been heightened by proposals that call for disposing of military fissile materials in commercial reactors. Unlike the case of chemical weapons disposal, "Nuclear Demil" blurs the line between the military and civilian sectors. Viewed one way, it offers the opportunity to make swords into plowshares; viewed another way, it opens a Pandora's box of nuclear proliferation.

While the production and dismantling of nuclear weapons was tightly managed by DOE with relatively little outside interference during the Cold War, the new and growing mission to dispose of these weapons and their component parts is proving to be a much more complicated task, owing in large part to the increased number of policy participants. The implementation phase of Nuclear Demil, as a formal program, is shorter than that of Chem Demil. However, the policy debate over nuclear weapons disposal actually started before that of Chem Demil and has involved the president as a decision maker.

In order to understand the present technological debate surrounding plutonium disposal, one must first examine some technological aspects of the disposal process as well as several key policy decisions that were made during the Cold War. Plutonium is virtually nonexistent in nature, and is manufactured as a consequence of burning uranium 238 in a thermal nuclear reactor. Therefore, nuclear power plants produce plutonium as a by-product in "spent nuclear fuel," but in order to extract the plutonium, it must be chemically separated out of the spent fuel through a process known as "reprocessing" (Berkhout 1991). Since the separated plutonium can then be used to make a nuclear weapon, reprocessing technology is carefully guarded. However, in addition to its military applications, reprocessing technology also has significant commercial value because the separated plutonium can also be "recycled" back into the fuel cycle by mixing it with uranium oxide to produce mixed-oxide (MOX) fuel for commercial nuclear reactors. This recycling-MOX technology may also be a viable option for disposing of the fissile components of nuclear weapons.

Technological Choice and International Constraints

During the Carter administration, the U.S. government decided to defer indefinitely recycling as a technological option for the disposal of civilian nuclear waste.[7] At this time, the primary concern was that recycling plutonium and producing MOX for civilian reactors would allow too many people to have access to the material and would create an intolerable proliferation risk. From this point on, high-level nuclear waste was to be stored on-site until a long-term storage facility could be built.

While the U.S. rejected the option to recycle plutonium, it did not dismiss the option to "immobilize" spent nuclear fuel in glass or ceramic logs and then store them in a deep geological repository. Immobilization was perceived to be a better technological choice in disposing of nuclear waste because it did not present the same proliferation risks as did recycling of plutonium. Over the next 30 years, the United States would build immobilization plants at the DOE Savannah River Site in South Carolina and West Valley, New York (Kramer 1994). The U.S., in promoting immobilization and direct disposal, became the leading opponent in the world to developing and applying recycling technologies. Meanwhile, other countries (particularly France and Great Britain) made great technological strides in the recycling of plutonium, developing MOX for commercial purposes (Blowers et al. 1991).

As tensions between the United States and the Soviet Union began to dissipate in the latter 1980s, several arms control agreements outlined major reductions in the nuclear arsenals of both countries. In 1987, the United States signed the Intermediate-Range Nuclear Forces (INF) Treaty that called for the dismantling of all intermediate range nuclear missiles (those with a range between 1,000 kilometers and 5,500 kilometers) (Ziegler 1997). In 1991, the United States signed the first Strategic Arms Reduction Treaty (START), which called for a reduction of its long-range nuclear weapons from 12,000 to 9,000 in number (Ziegler 1997). In 1991, President

Bush also took unilateral action to eliminate all tactical weapons, which resulted in the dismantling of almost 4,000 warheads in a four-year period (McCormick and Bullen 1998). While these treaties outlined specific reductions, they only stipulated that the weapons should be disassembled and the fissile material placed in interim storage until a permanent method of disposal could be developed. The question of how to dispose of the fissile material still remained, although the U.S. continued publicly to speak only of long-term storage or immobilization followed by burial at a geological repository.

With the signing of the START II treaty in 1993, which meant further nuclear demilitarization, pressure continued to mount to find a permanent solution to the disposal problem. START II called for an additional reduction of thousands of warheads, bringing U.S. numbers down to 3,500 or less (McCormick and Bullen 1998). In 1994, Congress responded to the increasing pressure by establishing a formal Office of Fissile Materials Disposition within the Department of Energy. Previous ad hoc activities were replaced by a new organization and program for Nuclear Demil. The office was charged with technical and management activities aimed at providing for the "safe, secure, environmentally sound, and inspectable future storage" of weapons-usable fissile material (U.S. Department Of Energy-Office of Fissile Materials Disposition, 1999).

Reopening the Technological Debate

In March, 1995, President Clinton made the dramatic announcement that the United States would withdraw 200 tons of "surplus" fissile material (including 50 tons of plutonium) from the U.S. stockpile and that it would never again be used to build a nuclear weapon (Agreement Between the Government of the United States of America and the Russian Federation on Scientific and Technical Cooperation in the Management of Plutonium that has been Withdrawn from Nuclear Military Programs 1998). This announcement was extremely significant because it meant that it was no longer acceptable to simply store the fissile materials from dismantled weapons. Instead this material would be converted so that it could not be reused in future nuclear weapons. In effect, Clinton was moving from a policy of long-term storage to one of disposal.

President Clinton's announcement coincided with a National Academy of Sciences (NAS) report that evaluated potential disposal options and concluded that two technological possibilities were most feasible. NAS proposed a "dual track approach." It included: 1) the existing immobilization option, which consisted of mixing weapons-grade plutonium with radioactive waste, encasing it in glass or ceramic logs, and then burying it in a geological repository; and 2) a variation of the recycling option, which consisted of mixing the weapons-grade plutonium waste with uranium oxide, thus producing MOX fuel. The MOX fuel would then be burned in a reactor before being disposed of as high-level nuclear waste (National Academy of Sciences 1995). The NAS report had serious implications because it potentially challenged the Carter administration decision to abandon recycling technologies, and it opened up the possibility that military nuclear waste would be used in civilian nuclear reactors.

The NAS report sparked intense controversy over the desirability, feasibility, and safety of the immobilization and MOX options and spurred DOE to conduct its own assessment of the environmental and proliferation risks of the two technologies. In January 1997, Energy Secretary Hazel O'Leary announced that DOE would pursue the dual-track approach. DOE also released its final programmatic environmental impact statement (U.S. Department of Energy 1997b) and its final assessment of the proliferation risks of each of the technologies (U.S. Department of Energy 1997a). While the NAS report had sparked the debate over the disposal options, the decision by DOE transformed the NAS recommendations into official policy.

Government officials argued that MOX would only be used to dispose of military plutonium and not civilian waste, and that therefore, the 1997 decision was consistent with the government's opposition to plutonium recycling technologies. However, critics of the MOX option argued that it opened the door to the reversal of a 20–year-old policy not to develop recycling technologies for civilian use. They claimed that it would inevitably lead to a permanent option because the nuclear industry would realize they could make a profit from the country's need to dispose of its nuclear weapons (Holdren and Moore 1997). Some felt that the U.S. action conveyed a new sense of legitimacy to multiple uses of plutonium and that it would expedite exactly what the U.S. feared — proliferation of nuclear material.

The motivating factor behind the Clinton administration's decision was Russia. The Russian government made it very clear that it would not immobilize its stockpile of weapons waste, but instead would take advantage of its waste either by recycling it back into its own civilian nuclear complex or selling the material to other countries for their civilian nuclear industry (Cochran et al. 1995). Secretary O'Leary said the MOX plan "keeps the Russians at the table with us. Russians are not yet comfortable with the immobilization project." She also added that Russia views plutonium as an energy asset rather than a liability (Allen 1996). In sum, the

Russian government perceived plutonium as a valuable resource, whereas the United States has historically regarded it as a threat. The Clinton administration determined it could not influence Russian policy regarding MOX and the ultimate disposal question in Russia unless it participated in the MOX technological arena (Lippman 1996; U.S. Department of Energy 1997b).

The Debate Over Risk

DOE's decision to favor both the immobilization and MOX approaches raised many of the same issues that were debated during the Carter administration when the recycling option was abandoned. Of primary importance was the increased possibility that plutonium could one day move from the military sector to the civilian sector in the U.S. As the new policy inched closer to implementation, an increased number of stakeholders began to get involved, and as in the case of Chem Demil, DOE's choices of disposal technology were challenged by a variety of nongovernmental organizations who had differing perceptions of risk from those of policymakers.

The immobilization option has received the endorsement of many environmental groups in the United States because they argue that this option will be safer both to the public and the environment. In particular, some environmental groups have argued that the immobilization option will entail less transportation of the nuclear material and will therefore minimize the risk of a potential accident (Greenpeace 1996). The United States does not have a plant to produce MOX fuel (Plutonium: Two-Track Approach Allows Pu Burning and Vitrification, 1996). Therefore, such fuel would need to be exported to other countries for MOX fuel processing until one can be built in the U.S. The United States has looked at options to send shipments to either Europe (Airozo 1996) or Canada (Hobson 1996), although they have since been dismissed.[8] The possibility of transporting plutonium out of the U.S. raises serious environmental questions and is politically challenging. Proponents of immobilization also argue that MOX will lead to an increased risk of proliferation because there may be security problems with burning the fuel in commercial reactors. They argue that, "the U.S. is regarded internationally as the leading opponent of closed fuel cycles and plutonium use, and its authority will suffer if it chooses to develop and fund a large-scale MOX infrastructure" (Lyman and Leventhal 1997). The proponents of immobilization firmly believe that it is less risky to humans, the environment, and the country

to immobilize the military plutonium rather than to recycle it back into
fuel for commercial reactors.

In contrast, some proponents of the MOX option argue that it is better than the immobilization option because MOX can convert dangerous
military plutonium into a benefit to society by generating electricity with
it in a manner that is safe to the environment and to human health. They
point out the fact that several countries (including France and Britain)
have recycled plutonium successfully for years (Grier and Spotts 1996).
Proponents of MOX also argue that recycling military plutonium would
not lead to a commercial market for the fuel because it is much cheaper
to make fuel for civilian reactors from low enriched uranium and will
remain so for many decades (Holdren and Moore 1997). Finally, some proponents of the MOX option argue that it is riskier to alienate the Russians
by delegitimizing the MOX option (their preferred method of disposal)
than to give the option credibility. By giving credibility to MOX, the dialogue regarding disposal will at least remain open.

The debate over the safety and feasibility of the immobilization and
MOX options has been extremely scientific. Unlike in the case of chemical weapons disposal, which is dominated by grassroots local and national
environmental organizations, the case of nuclear weapons disposal is dominated by well-organized, highly scientific organizations that have organized at the national and transnational levels. These groups, including the
Nuclear Control Institute, Greenpeace, and the Natural Resources Defense
Council, have a longstanding involvement in nuclear issues and have
become very knowledgeable about their scientific complexities. These
groups have been very effective in using their own scientists to counter
their opponents' claims and to engage in a scientific debate over which
technology is safest.

Another organization, Physicians for Social Responsibility (PSR), has
used its reputation as a very credible scientific organization comprised of
doctors to further its position. PSR joined a coalition of environmental
and antinuclear groups that proclaimed its "vigorous opposition" to the
MOX disposal option (Lippman 1996). "The most influential and wealthy
supporters of this plan are the ... companies that design and make nuclear
reactors," said Daryl Kimball, director of nuclear programs at PSR
(Vartabedian 1996). The group also appealed directly to President Clinton to abandon the possibility of using MOX technology to dispose of plutonium (Physicians for Social Responsibility, 1996). They believe it is a
threat to human health.

Public Involvement

DOE has begun to be confronted with new opposition as it tries to implement the MOX option. Unlike the case of Chem Demil, where public opposition moved from the local level to the national level, public opposition to MOX has first come from national and transnational organizations and has only recently trickled down to the local level as DOE has selected the sites where it will test and carry out MOX. Since the technological debate has been largely scientific up until this point, the organizations that have become involved in it are highly versed in its complex science. The challenge now is to relay these complexities to the local communities that will be impacted by the MOX option.

In June 1998, DOE announced that its Savannah River Site in Aiken, South Carolina was the preferred site for the mixed oxide fuel fabrication facility (U.S. Department of Energy 1999). In December, DOE also announced that Savannah River was its preferred site for a proposed pit-disassembly and conversion facility that would take apart the fissile cores of nuclear weapons and convert the metal into plutonium oxide powder to be added to the MOX fuel (Haddock 1999). This decision created some controversy since the only disassembly plant in the country is located at the Pantex Plant near Amarillo, Texas (U.S. Congress Office of Technology Assessment 1993; Williams 1999). DOE argued that having the pit-disassembly plant and MOX fabrication plant in one location would eliminate some of the transportation risks involved in the process. However, the pits that are currently stored at the Pantex Plant would still need to be transported to the Savannah River Site. While the selection of Savannah River received the endorsement of the local community (due to the economic implications), the news was not so well received by other communities along the potential transportation route. In particular, the state of Georgia considered legislation asking DOE to concentrate its efforts on cleaning up the Savannah River Site rather than increasing its mission (Williams 1999).

The selection of sites has sparked increasing public opposition. In March 1999, DOE announced that it had awarded a contract with Duke Engineering & Services, COGEMA Inc., and Stone & Webster to "provide mixed oxide fuel fabrication and reactor irradiation services in support of the department's mission to dispose of surplus weapons plutonium" (U.S. Department of Energy 1999). At the same time, DOE announced that the MOX fuel produced at the Savannah River Plant would be irradiated at six existing commercial light water reactors at three sites: Catawaba in York, South Carolina; McGuire in Huntersville, North Carolina (near

Charlotte, NC); and North Anna in Mineral, Virginia (near Richmond) (U.S. Department of Energy 1999).

As Secretary O'Leary observed in 1996, "to make this policy work, there will need to be public engagement" (Passell 1996). However, some have questioned whether DOE has made enough of an effort to engage the public. In April 1999, a coalition of eight environmental, peace, and scientific organizations wrote to Secretary of Energy Bill Richardson citing their objection to DOE's plans to hold only one public meeting (held in Washington, DC) on the decision to irradiate MOX fuel at the three sites. The coalition argued that, "the communities around these reactor sites have a great deal at stake in these decisions, and deserve an opportunity to voice their opinions on the MOX proposal. It is also important to solicit input from stakeholders most directly impacted by the MOX plan, and make it easy for them to be heard by holding hearings in their communities" (Group Letter to DOE on MOX Hearings). A June 1999 petition signed by a broad coalition of international and domestic organizations also accused DOE of failing to "include the input of communities living near reactors that are proposed for MOX fuel irradiation" (Institute for Energy and Environmental Research 1999).

While the debate surrounding technological choice in the Nuclear Demil case has been primarily waged on scientific grounds and has been dominated by national organizations up to this time, DOE's selection of MOX reactor sites has begun to generate public debate at the local level. As one local newspaper editorial proclaimed, "If you are like us, you may have no idea what MOX stands for. We have learned only recently about this new development and what it means for our communities" (Clark and Boniske 1999). As DOE continues to take steps to implement the MOX option, it appears that it will continue to be opposed by national and transnational organizations which have now begun to enlist the support of some of the local communities that will be most impacted by this new disposal technology.

In addition to growing local opposition to MOX, the consortium involved in implementing the MOX option has been fragile. In April 2000, Virginia Power pulled out of the consortium and cancelled its plans to irradiate MOX fuel at its North Anna plants (Nuclear Control Institute 2000). Virginia Power claimed that it was not a profitable operation and it did not "fit their strategy" (Haddock 2000).

The START II treaty was ratified by the Russian Duma in April 2000, forcing the U.S. government to actually implement the arms reductions called for in that document. In addition, in June 2000, U.S. President Clinton and Russian President Putin signed an agreement that called for each country to destroy 34 metric tons of weapons plutonium (Sciolino 2000). This will undoubtedly place even more pressure on DOE to move ahead with MOX testing. International pressures have been the determining factor in disposal technologies in the nuclear demilitarization program. The question remains whether these technologies will be acceptable to local communities. Eventually, DOE will have to make a decision to follow a strategy similar to the army's recent attempts to incorporate the different stakeholders into the decision-making process or to try to keep them at bay while it implements its preferred method of disposal.

Conclusions

As the previous cases illustrate, the chemical and nuclear demilitarization programs have become increasingly complex and politicized. The end of the Cold War has been the catalyst for international agreements that go beyond simply dismantling and storing chemical and nuclear weapons, and instead mandate their outright destruction so that they can never again be used as weapons of mass destruction. At the beginning of the 21st century, the chemical and nuclear demilitarization programs resemble hazardous waste disposal controversies more than they do traditional national security issues. They illuminate how issues of risk, the interplay of scientists and opposing stakeholders, and the merging of domestic and international politics can influence the course of policy. While both cases deal with weapons disposal, there are important differences in terms of the array of actors and their roles in the policy process.

In both cases, the demilitarization programs have had to confront differing perceptions of what is "acceptable risk." The notion of "acceptable risk" in these two cases has also been intermeshed with concerns over environmental risks, risks to human health, and risks associated with the proliferation of chemical and nuclear weapons. Therefore, different stakeholders in the two issues have very different perceptions of what is "acceptable," depending on their priorities. International arms control experts place a priority on preventing proliferation and abiding by international treaties; local citizens on the other hand, place a priority on minimizing risks to human health and the environment.

Since making its initial technological choice (baseline incineration), the army has had to repeatedly defend that choice against opposition. First, it was challenged by Congress and industry who advocated cryofracture as an alternative. This controversy was settled on technical grounds when it was determined that cryofracture was not a viable technology. The sec-

ond challenge to the army's preferred disposal technology came from citizens in Maryland and Indiana who lived near disposal sites that stored
bulk chemical agents as opposed to assembled munitions. They were concerned that baseline incineration might not be the safest and most appropriate technology to dispose of this type of weapons material. These
concerned citizens seized on the expert opinions of the NRC who claimed
that neutralization technology may in fact be viable and safe for the disposal of bulk agents.

When the army accepted neutralization as an alternative technology
to baseline incineration, the question of what is acceptable risk was thrown
wide open. Incineration opponents living near disposal sites that were
slated for incineration now began to question why alternative technologies were not being explored for assembled weapons; they began to question why they should be left with what they felt was the army's more
dangerous technological choice if the sites in Maryland and Indiana were
going to use safer alternative technologies. Incineration opponents realized that it would take time to develop alternative technologies for the disposal of assembled munitions, but they clearly felt that the risk of storing
the weapons was less dangerous than incinerating them. While baseline
incineration may in fact be as safe as the army's scientific experts claim,
the important point is that it is not *perceived* to be safe. Incineration opponents instead point to the potential for the release of toxic chemicals during the incineration process and are determined to protect their children
and the environment from its perceived threats.

The issue of risk has also been a factor in the nuclear demilitarization
program. However, international pressures have played a more prominent
role in determining risk in this program than in the chemical demilitarization program. During the Cold War, the United States' primary concern was to stop the proliferation of nuclear weapons and this was a
deciding factor in abandoning recycling as a method of disposing of civilian nuclear waste. The U.S. instead decided that nuclear waste would be
stored directly near nuclear facilities. While there was controversy over the
environmental and human health risks associated with this decision, they
were perceived by arms control experts to be less dangerous than the risk
of proliferation.

As the Cold War came to an end and the United States and Russia
signed several treaties that called for the disposal of nuclear weapons, the
Clinton administration felt that it was forced to revisit the issue of how
to dispose of nuclear waste — only in this case the question was not how
to dispose of civilian nuclear waste, but nuclear weapons. In 1997, the
administration announced that it would reexamine the possibility of

recycling military plutonium into nuclear fuel to be burned in commercial nuclear reactors. This was seen as a strategic move to keep the Russians engaged in a dialogue regarding nuclear weapons disposal. This decision sparked a highly scientific debate concerning which technology was safer to humans and the environment, and which minimized the risk of proliferation. On the one hand, nongovernmental organizations with technical expertise such as Greenpeace and the Nuclear Control Institute claimed that the use of commercial reactors to dispose of military plutonium would open up the door to a commercial market, increase the risk of proliferation, and endanger the environment and human health. On the other hand, some argued that the MOX option posed little threat to the environment, and that it was the best way to convince Russia to dispose of its nuclear weapons (Plutonium: Two-Track Approach Allows Pu Burning and Virtrification). Clearly the driving factor in U.S. policy regarding nuclear weapons disposal up until recently has been the international context, rather than the site-related controversy, as with Chem Demil.

The role of scientific expertise in each of the cases has also been different. In the chemical weapons demilitarization case, the army found that it was going nowhere in trying to convince incineration opponents that incineration was indeed a safe technology. The opinion of "experts" did not make much of a difference in persuading incineration opponents to change their position. When the army was forced by Congress to develop and test alternative technologies to incineration, it took a very novel approach to head off some of the opposition that it had experienced in trying to implement incineration. The army allowed local citizens to actually participate in developing the requirements for the alternative technologies. If the public had a say in what they considered "safe," perhaps the implementation process would go more smoothly, with less local opposition. While this experimental participatory decision-making mechanism has yet to complete its task, it has certainly been successful in managing conflict and in bringing together scientific and technical experts with concerned local citizens. The result has been that local citizens have become extremely proficient and knowledgeable about the technical aspects of the issue area and their concerns have received attention since the outset of the alternative disposal technology development. The Chem Demil case demonstrates that the inclusion of lay people may at times be more effective than relying on an epistemic community to move policy forward.

In the case of nuclear weapons disposal, the debate over which disposal technology is "safer" (MOX versus immobilization) has been highly scientific. The controversy has been dominated by scientists and by nongovernmental organizations with technical expertise. Unlike the issue of chemical weapons disposal, which is dominated by local and national NGOs, the NGOs involved in nuclear weapons disposal are primarily national and transnational, have been involved with the nuclear waste issue for years, and have established scientific credibility within the issue area. Now that the MOX disposal sites have been chosen, there is increasing local interest in the technological choice and its potential risks. The national and transnational NGOs have embarked on the task of educating local communities about the disposal options and trying to mobilize them around a subject that is in many ways arcane and difficult to understand. The *perceived* risks of MOX versus immobilization are much harder to discern than those of incineration versus some undetermined "safer" technology. Incineration technology is a rather straightforward technology and easy to understand — MOX and immobilization are not. Since the dispute surrounding nuclear weapons disposal remains at the level of scientific debate, MOX and recycling advocates will need to distill the highly scientific nature of the controversy in order to mobilize local communities. Now that local citizens have become stakeholders in the issue, they will also seek to wrest a measure of control over decision-making from scientists. If DOE chooses to keep local communities at bay and not include them in the decisionmaking process regarding MOX, it risks confronting the same opposition that the Army has come up against in its efforts to implement incineration.

The cases of chemical and nuclear weapons disposal are thus particularly noteworthy because they illustrate many policy trends taking shape in the post–Cold War era. These include the infusion of environmental concerns into issues of national security, the convergence of national and international politics, and the use of participatory decision-making mechanisms to avert or mitigate conflict. While hazardous waste disposal controversies are not new, it is significant that two *weapons* disposal controversies resemble them. With the veil of national security lifted, the army and DOE are discovering that they cannot implement arms control treaties without the cooperation of local communities. The goal of disposing of these weapons hinges on bridging the divide between the different stakeholders. What was once international arms control has now meshed with domestic environmental policy.

The authors wish to acknowledge support from the National Security Program of the Maxwell School, Syracuse University and the School of Advanced International Studies, Johns Hopkins University. The DOD provided, through the National Security Program, funds in the preparation of case studies of the federal management of Chem Demil for an executive education-training program at Maxwell and Johns Hopkins' School of

Advanced International Studies. In addition, the authors wish to acknowledge support from the Center for Environmental Policy and Administration (CEPA) for providing funds that enabled additional research to be undertaken on both the chemical and nuclear demilitarization programs. Finally, the authors with to acknowledge support from the U.S. Department of State through a Hubert Humphrey Doctoral Dissertation Fellowship in Arms Control, Nonproliferation and Disarmament awarded to Ms. Schaefer. The DOD and U.S. Department of State, in particular, are not responsible for any views expressed in this article.

Endnotes

1. Kasperson, Roger, et al. (1992) echo these findings in "Social Distrust as a Factor in Siting Hazardous Facilities and Communicating Risks." *Journal of Social Issues* 48 (4): 161–187.

2. See Pilisuk, Marc, et al. (1987). "Public Perception of Technological Risk." *The Social Science Journal* 24 (4): 403–413. Also see Freudenberg, William, and Susan Pastor (1992). "Public Responses to Technological Risks: Toward a Sociological Perspective." *The Sociological Quarterly* 33(3): 389–412.

3. See Pool, R. (1997) *Beyond Engineering: How Society Shapes Technology.* New York: Oxford Press. Also see Kraft, Michael, and Norman Vig, eds. *Technology and Politics.* Durham: Duke University Press.

4. This argument is also intimately tied to arguments related to democratic theory. See Dryzek, John (1996). "Political Inclusion and the Dynamics of Democratization." *American Political Science Review* 90 (1): 475–487.

5. Robert Putnam examines the interrelationship between domestic and international politics in his article entitled "Diplomacy and Domestic Politics: the Logic of Two-Level Games." Putnam argues that negotiators often have to deal with counterpressures from international objectives and domestic constituencies. See Putnam, Robert (1988). "Diplomacy and Domestic Politics: the Logic of Two-Level Games." *International Organization* 42 (3): 427–460. The cases this chapter examines differ from the scenarios examined by Putnam because there was no objection from the organizations involved to the ratification of the international agreements; rather, their objection was over *how* to dispose of the weapons. The debate over technological choice was not addressed at all by the international agreements and was not considered a barrier to their implementation since they had been ratified.

6. The CWWG also filed an environmental justice lawsuit against the construction of an incinerator in Alabama (CWWG, 1997).

7. See U.S. Congress, U.S. House of Representatives, Committee on Interior and Insular Affairs, Subcommittee on Energy and the Environment (1977), "Proposals Affecting Use of Plutonium as a Reactor Fuel," Washington: U.S. Govern-

ment Printing Office; (1976), "Recycling of Plutonium," Washington: U.S. Government Printing Office.

8. The Russians are seriously considering exporting some of their military plutonium to Canada to recycle it into Canadian CANDU reactors. The first test shipment from Russia arrived in September 2000 and created opposition from Canadian environmental groups who are concerned that Canada will turn into a plutonium dumping ground.

References

Adler, Emanuel. 1992. "The Emergence of Cooperation: National Epistemic Communities and the International Evolution of the Idea of Nuclear Arms Control." *International Organization* 46 (1): 101–145.

Agreement Between the Government of the United States of America and the Government of the Russian Federation on Scientific and Technical Cooperation in the Management of Plutonium that has Been Withdrawn from Nuclear Military Programs. 1998. http://twilight.saic.com/md.

Airozo, Dave. 1996. DOE to Renew Bid to Test MOX at AECL Facility this Summer. *Nucleonics Week*, 12 December. Lexis-Nexis on-line database.

Allen, Vicki. 1996. U.S. to Scrap Surplus Plutonium. *Reuters North American Wire*, 9 December.

Assembled Chemical Weapons Assessment Program (ACWA) Office. 1998a. *Dialogue on Assembled Chemical Weapons Assessment*. Aberdeen, MD: U.S. Department of Defense.

Assembled Chemical Weapons Assessment Program (ACWA) Office. 1998b. *Ground Rules for Dialogue on Assembled Chemical Weapons Assessment*. Aberdeen, MD: U.S. Department of Defense.

Atwood, D. 1989. *Letter to Senator John Warren*. Washington, DC: U.S. Department of Defense.

Barker, Anthony, and B. Guy Peters, eds. 1993. *The Politics of Expert Advise: Creating, Using and Manipulating Scientific Knowledge for Public Policy*. Pittsburgh, PA: University of Pittsburgh Press.

Battelle Pacific. 1994. *Community Viewpoints of the Chemical Stockpile Disposal Program: Tooele Army Depot Site Report*. Washington, DC: Northwest Laboratories.

Berkhout, Frans. 1991. *Radioactive Waste: Politics and Technology*. London: Routledge.

Blowers, A., D. Lowry, and B. Solomon. 1991. *The International Politics of Nuclear Waste*. New York: St. Martin's Press.

Brooke, J. 1997. Chemical Neutralization is Gaining in War on Poison Gas. *New York Times*, 7 February.

Chemical Weapons Working Group. 1997. Environmental Justice Complaint Filed Against Alabama for Approving Chemical Weapons Incinerator. http://www.cwwg.org/PR_12.18.97alejcomplaint.html.

Chemical Weapons Working Group. 1999a. Letter to Secretary of the Army Calling for Prociv's Resignation. http://www.cwwg.org/calderaletter.html.

Chemical Weapons Working Group. 1999b. Pine Bluff Citizens File Environmental Justice Complaint Against Army Incinerator. http://www.cwwg.org/pr_06.29.99ejar.html.

Chemical Weapons Working Group. 1999c. Sen. Bill McConnell's "Don't Build Anything Technology-Specific in Kentucky Until You Test All Six Alternatives" Amendment. http://www.cwwg.org/amendment.html.

Chemical Weapons Working Group. 2000a. Army Report Recommends that Chemical Weapons Incinerators be Considered for Disposal of "Non-Stockpile Weapons." http://www.cwwg.org/pr_09.15.00nsreport.html

Chemical Weapons Working Group. 2000b. Chem-Weapons Disposal Chronology. http://www.cwwg.org/Chronology.html.

Clark, B., and K. Boniske. 1999. Should Weapons-Grade Plutonium Be Used in Nuclear Reactors? *The Herald* (Rock Hill, SC), 29 March.

Cleveland, Harlan. 1993. *Birth of a New World: An Open Moment for International Leadership.* San Francisco: Jossey-Bass.

Cochran, T., R. Norris, and O. Bukharin. 1995. *Making the Russian Bomb: From Stalin to Yeltsin.* Boulder: Westview Press.

Farazmand, Ali. 1998. Globalization and Public Administration. *Public Administration Review* 59 (6): 509–522.

Fisher, Marc. 1990. U.S. Starts Pullout of Chemical Arms. *Washington Post*, 27 July.

Furedi, Frank. 1997. *Culture of Fear: Risk-Taking and the Morality of Low Expectation.* London: Cassell.

Greenpeace USA. 1996. Broad Opposition to DOE Proposal to Use Weapons Plutonium for Commercial Nuclear Power Reactor Fuel. 10 December. Greenpeace USA: Washington, DC.

Grier, Peter, and Peter Spotts. 1996. Plan to Use Military Plutonium at Civilian Plants Stirs Debate. *Christian Science Monitor*, 10 December.

Group Letter to DOE on MOX Hearings. http://www.nci.org/c42199.htm.

Haas, Peter. 1992. Introduction: Epistemic Communities and International Policy Coordination. *International Organization* 46 (1): 1–35.

Haas, Peter. 1990. *Saving the Mediterranean: The Politics of International Environmental Cooperation.* New York: Columbia University Press.

Haddock, B. 1999. Activists Oppose MOX Plan. *Augusta Chronicle*, 25 February. http://augustachronicle.com/stories/022599/tec_066–5784.000.shtml.

Haddock, B. 2000. Virginia Utility Abandons MOX Project. *Augusta Chronicle*, 8 April. http://augustachronicle.com/stories/040800/met_066–4792.000.shtml.

Holdren, John, and Mike Moore. 1997. Work with Russia. *Bulletin of the Atomic Scientists* 53 (42): 42.

Institute for Energy and Environmental Research (IEER). 1999. Statement of Non-Governmental Organizations on Plutonium Disposition. http://www.ieer.org/ieer/comments/pu-disp/ngostmt.html.

Jasanoff, Sheila. 1990. *The Fifth Branch: Science Advisors as Policymakers.* Cambridge, MA: Harvard University Press.

Joint Statement of Principles for Management and Disposition of Plutonium Designated as No Longer Required for Defense Purposes. 1998. http:// twilight.saic.com/md.

Kramer, David. 1994. Grumbly Says Agency Will Seek Funding for Pilot Vitrification Plants. *Inside Energy,* 21 November. Lexis-Nexis On-line Database.

Lambright, W.H. 1998. *Searching for a Safer Technology: Army-Community Conflict in Chemical Weapons Destruction (CS 1298-11).* Syracuse, NY: Maxwell School of Citizenship and Public Affairs.

Lippman, T. 1996. U.S. Faces Hurdles in Implementing Plutonium Disposal Plan. *Washington Post,* 16 December.

Lyman, Edwin, and Paul Leventhal. 1997. Bury the Stuff; Disposal of Weapons-Grade Plutonium. *Bulletin of the Atomic Scientists,* 13 March. Lexis-Nexis online database.

McCormick, James, and Daniel Bullen. 1998. Disposing of the World's Excess Plutonium. *Policy Studies Journal* 26 (4): 682–702.

Memo from Ms. Heffernan. 1989. *Chemical Demilitarization Program.* Washington, DC: U.S. Department of Defense.

Memorandum to the Secretary of the Army. 1993, January 19. *Significant Accomplishments: 1989–1992.* Washington, DC: Department of Defense.

Morrell, Michael. 1999. Citizens' Evaluation of Participatory Democratic Procedures: Normative Theory Meets Empirical Science. *Political Research Quarterly* 52 (2): 293–322.

National Academy of Sciences. 1995. *Management and Disposition of Excess Weapons Plutonium: Reactor-Related Options.* Washington, DC: National Academy Press.

National Research Council. 1994. *Recommendations for the Disposal of Chemical Agents and Munitions.* Washington, DC: National Academy Press.

National Research Council. 1996. *Review and Evaluation of Alternative Chemical Disposal Technologies.* Washington, DC: National Academy Press.

Nelkin, D. 1989. Communicating Technological Risk: the Social Construction of Risk Perception. *Annual Review of Public Health* 10: 95–113.

Nuclear Control Institute. 2000. Virginia Power Quits Plutonium "MOX" Fuel Program. 7 April. http://www.nci.org/pr4700.htm.

Passell, Peter. 1996. U.S. Set to Allow Reactors to Use Plutonium From Disarmed Bombs. *New York Times,* 22 November.

Peters, Ellen, and Paul Slovic. 1996. The Role of Affect and Worldview as Orienting Dispositions in the Perception and Acceptance of Nuclear Power. *Journal of Applied Social Psychology* 26 (16): 1427–1453.

Physicians for Social Responsibility (PSR). 1996. Physicians Call on President Clinton to Abandon Plans to Re-Use Military Plutonium. http://www.psrus.org/plutonium.htm.

Pijawka, K. David, and Alvin Mushkatel. 1992. Public Opposition to the Siting of

The High-Level Nuclear Waste Repository: The Importance of Trust. *Policy Studies Review* 10 (4): 180–194.

Plan Approved to Neutralize APG Mustard Agent. 1997. *Baltimore Sun*, 23 September.

Plutonium: Two Track Approach Allows Pu Burning and Vitrification. 1996. *Nuclear Waste News* 16 (49), 12 December.

Prociv, Theodore. 1997, March 11. *Testimony: Dr. Theodore Prociv, Deputy Assistant to the Secretary of Defense for Chemical and Biological Matters.* U.S. House of Representatives, Committee on National Security, Subcommittee on Military Readiness. Washington, DC: U.S. Government Printing Office.

Renn, Ortwin, et al. 1992. "The Social Amplification of Risk: Theoretical Foundations and Empirical Applications." *Journal of Social Issues* 48 (4): 137–160.

Rosenau, James. 1990. *Turbulence in World Politics: A Theory of Change and Continuity.* Princeton, NJ: Princeton University Press.

Sciolino, Elaine. 2000. Clinton in Moscow: The Overview. *New York Times*, 5 June 2000.

Singer, J.D. 1961. The Level-of-Analysis Problem in International Relations, in Klaus Knorr and Sidney Verba (eds.), *The International System.* Princeton, NJ: Princeton University Press.

Smithson, A., and M. Lenihan. 1996. The Destruction of Weapons Under the Chemical Weapons Convention. *Science & Global Security* 6: 79–100.

Stern, P. 1991. Learning through Conflict: A Realistic Strategy for Risk Communication. *Policy Sciences* 24: 99–119.

U.S. Congress. 1996. *National Defense Appropriations Act for Fiscal Year 1997: Public Law 104–208.* Washington, DC: U.S. Government Printing Office.

U.S. Congress, Office of Technology Assessment. 1993. *Dismantling the Bomb and Managing the Nuclear Materials.* Washington, DC: U.S. Government Printing Office.

U.S. Department of Energy. 1999. Energy Department Selects Private Sector Team to Help Dispose of Surplus Plutonium. *DOE News*, March 22. http:www.ch.doe.gov/pres/032299.htm.

U.S. Department of Energy. 1997a. *Final Nonproliferation and Arms Control Assessment of Weapons-Usable Fissile Material Storage and Excess Plutonium Disposition Alternatives.* Washington, DC: U.S. Department of Energy.

U.S. Department of Energy. 1997b. *Record of Decision for the Storage and Disposition of Weapons-Usable Fissile Materials: Final Programmatic Environmental Impact Statement.* Washington, DC: U.S. Department of Energy.

U.S. Department of Energy-Office of Fissile Materials Disposition. 1999. *What Is Our Mission?* Washington, DC: U.S. Department of Energy.

U.S. General Accounting Office. 1991. *DOD's Successful Effort to Remove U.S. Chemical Weapons from Germany.* Washington, DC: U.S. Government Printing Office.

U.S. General Accounting Office. 1994. *Chemical Weapons Destruction: Advantages and Disadvantages of Alternatives to Incineration.* Washington, DC: U.S. Government Printing Office.

U.S. General Accounting Office. 1997. *Chemical Weapons and Materiel: Key Factors Affecting Disposal Costs and Schedule.* Washington, DC: U.S. Government Printing Office.

U.S. General Accounting Office. 2000. *Chemical Weapons Disposal; Improvements Needed in Program Accountability and Financial Management.* Washington, DC: U.S. Government Printing Office.

U.S. Program Manager for Chemical Demilitarization (U.S. PMCD). 2000a. Citizens Advisory Commissions. http://www-pmcd.apgea.army.mil/main/CSDP/PI/cac.html

U.S. Program Manager for Chemical Demilitarization. 2000b. Halfway Point Reached. http://www.pmcd.apgea.army.mil/main/CSDP/IP/PR/2000/200010/20001012/index.html

U.S. Program Manager for Chemical Demilitarization. 2000c. Ten Year Anniversary in the Chemical Weapons Disposal Program. http://www-pmcd.apgea.army.mil/main/CSDP/IP/PR/2000/200006/20000606/index.html

U.S. Program Manager for Chemical Demilitarization. 2000d. United States Exceeds Chemical Weapons Convention Expectations; U.S. Commitment to Treaty Backed by Strong Performance. http://www.pmcd.apgea.army.mil/main/CSDP/IP/PR/2000/200004/20000428/index.html

Vartabedian, Ralph. 1996. Plutonium Disposal Plans Trigger Environmentalists' Ire; Hazardous Waste: Energy Department's Proposal Either to Bury the Substance or to Burn It Is Called a SOP to Nuclear Power Industry. *Los Angeles Times*, 10 December.

Vaughan, Elaine, and Marianne Seifert. 1992. Variability in the Framing of Risk Issues. *Journal of Social Issues* 48 (4): 119–135.

Walker, Robert. 1994. *Testimony: Robert Walker, Assistant Secretary of the Army, United States Army.* U.S. Senate, Committee on Armed Services, Subcommittee on Nuclear Deterrence, Arms Control and Defense. Washington, DC: U.S. Government Printing Office.

Waltz, Kenneth. 1954. *Man, the State and War.* New York: Columbia University Press.

Wandersman, Abraham, and William Hallman. 1993. Are People Acting Irrationally?: Understanding Public Concerns About Environmental Threats. *American Psychologist* 48(6): 681–686.

Warren, David. 1995, July 13. *Testimony: David Warren, U.S. General Accounting Office.* U.S. House of Reps., Committee on National Security, Subcommittee on Military Procurement. Washington, DC: U.S. Government Printing Office.

Waterstone, M. 1992. *Risk and Society: The Interaction of Science, Technology, and Public Policy.* London: Kluwer Academic Publishers.

Welch, Eric, and Wilson Wong. 1998. Public Administration in a Global Context: Bridging the Gaps of Theory and Practice between Western and Non-Western Nations. *Public Administration Review* 58 (1): 40–49.

Williams, D. 1999. State Lawmakers Preparing Anti-MOX Fuel Measure. *Savannah Morning News*, 26 February. http://www.savannahmorningnews.com...22699/LOCxgrsavannahriversite.html.

Ziegler, David. 1997. *War, Peace, and International Relations.* New York: Longman.

Chapter Two

Environmental Contamination and the Nuclear Weapons Complex

DIANNE RAHM

Introduction

With the end of the Cold War, nearly half a century of sustained nuclear weapons production came to a halt. U.S. efforts shifted from bomb building to planning how the stockpiles might be drawn down and dealing with the Cold War's domestic environmental legacy. The years of nuclear weapons manufacture left behind an enormous volume of dangerous radioactive waste. The Department of Energy (DOE) managed the Nuclear Weapons Complex in secrecy and was exempt from adherence to the nation's environmental laws during the years of the Cold War. By the mid–1980s, however, Congress stipulated that DOE bring the Nuclear Weapons Complex into compliance with U.S. environmental statutes.

Overseeing the environmental remediation of the Nuclear Weapons Complex will be one of the foremost government management challenges of the coming century. The goals of environmental "cleanup" are the stabilization and long-term ecological isolation of the nuclear waste now present at all sites in the complex. This is a formidable task given safety, health, and ecological concerns surrounding the most lethal and long-lived materials on the planet.

This chapter focuses on the site-based administrative challenges associated with fulfilling the congressional mandate of bringing the U.S. Nuclear Weapons Complex into environmental compliance. It begins with a brief description of the Nuclear Weapons Complex along with the legislative and budgetary policy framework. Drawing on data collected by means of personal interviews, site tours, and published and unpublished material, the chapter describes the nature of the problem at the five most

contaminated sites in the complex — Hanford, Savannah River, Rocky
Flats, Oak Ridge Reservation, and Idaho National Engineering and Environmental Laboratory. Four key factors that heavily influence each site's
progress toward the goal of environmental compliance are discussed: the
degree of environmental difficulty; stakeholder relationships; organizational transformation; and national politics.

Methods

The sites of the Nuclear Weapons Complex discussed in this paper,
as well as several other sites, were visited between 1997 and 1999. These
include Hanford, Idaho National Engineering and Environmental Lab,
Oak Ridge, Rocky Flats, Savannah River, Fernald, and Mound. The Pinel-
las Plant was visited in 1994. During these visits, structured interviews
with 54 individuals were completed. These individuals included a mix of
DOE, Environmental Protection Agency (EPA), and state government
officials; contractors; and members of citizen advisory boards.

A three-part interview protocol was followed. Part one asked questions regarding mitigation decisions and remedial actions undertaken. Part
two asked for information about the various actors involved. The last section allowed the interviewee to comment on the relative success or failure
of the cleanup process.

Content analysis of the text of the interviews revealed several repeated
factors and related subfactors of widespread interest to interviewees,
although their opinions regarding these might diverge. Each site in the
study was subsequently systematically analyzed based upon these factors
and subfactors. This manner of treatment allowed the sites to be compared within a series of standard categories rendered important by individuals spread across the entire complex.

Background

The U.S. Nuclear Weapons Complex is comprised of approximately
75 sites spread across the United States (U.S. General Accounting Office
1995a). The complex was begun in 1942 when the three original Manhattan Project sites were created: Oak Ridge, for uranium enrichment; Hanford, for plutonium production; and Los Alamos, for research, design, and
production of the first atomic weapons (Eubank 1991; Rhodes 1988). An
emphasis on redundant facilities, to ensure that nuclear weapons production

would not be disrupted, resulted in substantial growth of the complex during the years of the Cold War. By the late 1980s, production facilities occupied about twice as much land as the state of Delaware and employed over 90,000 people (Cochran et al. 1990).

In the late 1980s, environmental and safety concerns led to the temporary closure of numerous sites in the complex, and with the end of the Cold War, these closures became permanent. While U.S. public policy calls for a small national nuclear production capacity to be maintained, most facilities within the Nuclear Weapons Complex are in the process of shifting from a mission of bomb production to one of bomb dismantling and environmental restoration (Season 1997).

Superfund, the program most associated with toxic waste cleanup, was established by the Comprehensive Environmental Response, Compensation, and Liability Act of 1980 (CERCLA). The initial legislation focused on industrial sites; however, in 1986 the Superfund Amendments and Reauthorization Act (SARA) mandated that federal government units identify Superfund sites located on federal lands, and they were consequently identified at all major facilities within the Nuclear Weapons Complex. The Federal Facilities Compliance Act of 1992 further required that progress reports be submitted to Congress in 1993, 1994, and 1995 giving detailed information on the development of site treatment plans. The subsequent disclosures have revealed an environmental problem and administrative challenge of enormous proportions.

The Department of Defense (DOD) and DOE are responsible for most of these federal facilities. Cost estimates for cleanup provide a rough indicator of the extent of safety, ecological, and human health problems. In 1996, DOD estimated its total cleanup costs at $39 billion which, while a large sum, pales in comparison to DOE's anticipated costs for cleaning its Nuclear Weapons Complex facilities. DOE's 1996 cost assessment ranged from $230 billion to $360 billion, depending on the level of cleanup attained (U.S. General Accounting Office 1996a). In 1996, DOE lowered its cost estimate range to between $189 billion and $265 billion (U.S. Department of Energy 1996), and again in 1998 once again lowered it to $147 billion, based upon an accelerated cleanup scenario (DOE 1998). The Federal Facilities Policy Group, established jointly by the Office of Management and Budget (OMB) and the Chair of the Council on Environmental Quality (CEQ), however, estimated a staggering $400 billion cleanup cost for the department (Federal Facilities Policy Group 1995; U.S. General Accounting Office 1996b).

The Problem

As the above discussion illustrates, cost estimates for the cleanup vary widely, but by any accounting, it will not be cheap (Wildavsky 1998). The five most polluted sites in the complex — Hanford, Savannah River, Rocky Flats, Oak Ridge Reservation, and Idaho National Engineering and Environmental Laboratory — will consume 70 percent of the cleanup budget (U.S. Department of Energy 1995). This fact renders understanding and solving the problems at these five sites of critical public policy importance. I now turn to a brief description of some of the pressing environmental problems at each of these sites.

Hanford. Occupying a sizeable 560 square miles of land in eastern Washington, Hanford produced plutonium for the building of the earliest plutonium-based atomic bombs; during the Cold War, it produced about two-thirds of the nation's plutonium. During the peak years of activity in the late 1950s and 1960s, Hanford ran nine nuclear reactors and several chemical separation plants. Production slowed in the late 1960s, and by 1971 eight of Hanford's nine reactors were closed. Its last production reactor, N Reactor, was shut down temporarily in February 1988 directly after the Chernobyl accident, as it was of the same design and engineers feared a similar accident (Reicher and Scherr 1990). The temporary shutdown became permanent in 1989. In that year, DOE, the Washington State Department of Ecology, and the U.S. Environmental Protection Agency (EPA) signed the Tri-Party Agreement which outlines the plans to clean Hanford.

Hanford is the most contaminated site in the complex, and over 1,400 individual waste sites have been identified there. Much of the contamination is from its nine reactors, which are located on the shore of the Columbia River. Reactor operations contaminated the buildings and the soil surrounding the reactors, and the dumping of small amounts of radioactive elements into the River was considered a typical part of normal reactor operations. During the Cold War, however, there was great pressure to increase the production of plutonium. As a consequence, reactor operations were intensified and reactor effluent discharges increased. Fuel cell ruptures, caused when uneven heating split open the aluminum jackets covering the fuel rods, dramatically increased the flow of radioactive elements to the Columbia River. These ruptured fuel cells and other contaminated materials were subsequently buried in what today are called "burial grounds." These unlined pits holding radioactive materials are in numerous locations across the site. Today, sediments of the Columbia River are contaminated with plutonium (Gerber 1992) and strontium 90 levels detected in parts of the Columbia River are 560 times higher than EPA safe standards (Reisnikoff 1990). Contaminated groundwater also endangers the Columbia. The DOE estimates that between 1945 and 1991, 350 billion gallons of contaminated wastewater was discharged directly onto the ground near the reactors. This produced a radioactive groundwater plume that is moving toward the Columbia River (U.S. Department of Energy 1997c).

The Columbia River is also threatened by K Basins — Olympic swimming pool-sized cooling ponds for spent nuclear fuel. Eighty percent of DOE's nationwide inventory, or about 2,300 tons of spent fuel, is stored in K Basins. (Spent fuel is the highly radioactive plutonium laden uranium fuel that results from nuclear reactor activity. It is generated in civilian energy production as well as in military efforts to produce weapons-grade plutonium. Spent fuel was the desired product for the military because the plutonium could be chemically stripped off and used in weapons. Spent fuel is not useful in civilian energy producing reactors and needs to be reprocessed for reuse.) The spent fuel stored in K Basins is corroded and crumbling. This is extremely problematic since K Basins have a history of leakage (15 million gallons leaked in the late 1970s, and 94 thousand gallons in 1993). If K Basins were to leak again, the contaminated water full of corroded spent fuel residue would be a severe threat to the soil and the Columbia River (Westinghouse Hanford Company 1996).

Hanford's tank waste, regulated by the Washington State Department of Ecology under Resource Conservation and Recovery Act (RCRA) authority, presents the site's largest safety and disposal challenge. Hanford's chemical separation plants produced 55 million gallons of high-level radioactive liquid waste that is stored in underground tanks arranged in formations called "tank farms." These tank farms are buried about ten feet below ground near the center of the site. Hanford has 177 tanks with capacities ranging from about 50,000 to one million gallons each. Sixty-nine tanks have leaked — releasing more than 1 million gallons of high-level radioactive waste (Westinghouse Hanford Company 1995). These leaked wastes have been confirmed to have reached the groundwater and are now migrating toward the Columbia River (Wald 1998).

The tank waste presents serious safety hazards. Concern about tank safety prompted the passage of the Wyden Amendment (Section 313 of PL 101-510) which created Watchlist tank categories and required a review of DOE's operation and management of these tanks. Fifty tanks were denoted Watchlist tanks because they require special treatment and handling to prevent explosion (Westinghouse Hanford Company 1995).

Some of the major cleanup challenges at Hanford can be traced to poor management of the tank waste over the years. For instance, in an attempt to create more room for waste during the high producing Cold War period, chemicals were added to the tanks to separate the radioactive metals from the liquid contents. The tanks were then made to boil to reduce the liquid volume thus creating room for more waste. Frequently, material was added to the tanks without keeping proper records. The result is that the tank contents have become an unknown mix of chemicals and radioactive waste. The contents of the waste in any one tank vary from side to side and from top to bottom so vastly that it has thus far proved impossible to extract a reliable sample from a tank that accurately characterizes the contents (Hileman 1996). Without such a sample, stabilization and disposal of the waste at a nuclear waste repository is extremely problematic (Bowsher 1989; U.S. General Accounting Office 1996b).

Another major obstacle stands in the way of stabilizing and ecologically isolating the tank waste. The waste in the tanks is, in large part, no longer liquid. Because of materials added over the years and efforts to evaporate off the liquid contents, the waste now exists in various solid forms (i.e., sludge and salt cake). It is thought that pumping the waste from the tanks, which is necessary if the waste is to be stabilized, can be accomplished only after the waste is reliquefied. Once the waste is liquefied, however, compromised tanks presently containing sludge and salt cake will again leak. The discussion now centers on what "allowable leakage" the regulators will permit.

Savannah River. The Savannah River Site (SRS), covering 310 square miles near Aiken, South Carolina, was built during the 1950s to assist Hanford in the production of plutonium and to produce tritium (a radioactive gas used in warheads to increase the magnitude of the nuclear explosion). To support this effort, SRS ran five reactors as well as two chemical separation plants, and produced about 36 tons of plutonium between 1953 and 1988 (U.S. Department of Energy 1997a). Because it performed comparable operations to Hanford, the contamination and legacy waste are similar.

Unlike Hanford, which has no active mission except site cleanup, SRS is engaged in on-going production. SRS continues to produce plutonium for special purposes; for instance, it supplied NASA with the plutonium it needed for the Cassini mission. SRS also recycles tritium from weapons that have been taken out of service and reloads it into active weapons. The site continues to use its chemical separation plants to stabilize its remaining inventory of plutonium-bearing materials and to convert highly enriched uranium from retired weapons to low-enriched uranium that can be converted to civilian reactor fuel (U.S. Department of Energy 1997a). These current activities produce an on-going stream of radioactive waste and toxic chemicals.

The contamination at SRS is extensive with 486 identified or potential cleanup areas (U.S. Environmental Protection Agency 1997a). SRS has a large quantity of nuclear waste that includes 34 million gallons of high-level tank waste. The aging underground storage tanks holding the site's high-level waste are at risk for leakage but, unlike Hanford's tank waste, the Savannah River site's high-level waste has been managed well over the years. SRS has been able to sample the tanks and characterize the waste stream, and it planned to stabilize this waste by vitrifying it in its Defense Waste Processing Facility (DWPF). This facility, which began operations in March 1996, is the largest radioactive waste vitrification plant in the world (American Ceramic Society Bulletin 1996). (Vitrification is a process that stabilizes nuclear waste by mixing it with molten glass. The resulting hardened glass mixture, while still radioactive, is in a stabilized form that can be more easily disposed of in a nuclear waste isolation facility.) The initial process SRS selected to remove the waste from the tanks, however, failed to work, and Savannah River is now seeking an alternative process that might be used (U.S. General Accounting Office 1999a).

Oak Ridge. The Oak Ridge Reservation, like SRS, has an ongoing production mission. Located on 55 square miles in eastern Tennessee, Oak Ridge was initially established for uranium enrichment (also called isotope separation) as part of the Manhattan project. The reservation is now composed of three major plant complexes: Oak Ridge National Laboratory (ORNL), the Oak Ridge Y-12 plant, and the East Tennessee Technology Park (formally the K-25 gaseous diffusion plant). ORNL is an operational lab focusing on energy research and development (R&D). The Y-12 plant's original mission was electromagnetic isotope separation, but its current functions now include dismantling nuclear weapons as well, providing support to other DOE programs. K-25, which used the gaseous diffusion method of isotope separation, was closed in 1985 when its functions were supplanted by the facilities in Paducah and Portsmouth (U.S. Environmental Protection Agency 1997b).

Current site activities continue to produce radioactive and chemical waste, and past activities left behind extensive contamination of both the land and facilities. The site contains 294 on-site contamination areas. Pollution has migrated off site to surrounding land areas as well as to the Poplar Creek and from it to the Clinch and Tennessee Rivers. Mercury and other heavy metals, organic compounds, and radioactive elements poison the on-site groundwater, surface water, and soil. During the 1950s and

1960s, DOE estimates that 733,000 pounds of mercury were released into the soil around Y-12; an additional 170,000 pounds of mercury are lodged in the sediments of Poplar Creek. Mercury and radioactive elements have been found in sediments of the Clinch and Tennessee Rivers as far as 118 miles downstream from Oak Ridge (U.S. Environmental Protection Agency 1989a).

Idaho National Engineering and Environmental Laboratory. Geographically the largest site in the complex, the Idaho National Engineering and Environmental Laboratory (INEEL) was established in 1949 to augment the efforts of those working on research reactors at Hanford. Then called the National Reactor Testing Station, it built, tested, and operated various reactors and fuel processing plants. Fifty-two test reactors were built at INEEL — the largest concentration of nuclear reactors in the world. In 1974 the site was renamed Idaho National Engineering Laboratory as a reflection of the expansion of its engineering activities to nonnuclear areas and, more recently, the site again changed names to emphasize its environmental mission (U.S. Environmental Protection Agency 1989b).

The vast 890 square mile site is located in the semiarid sagebrush desert area of southern Idaho, near Idaho Falls. INEEL has eight primary facility areas that include Argonne National Laboratory (West), Idaho Nuclear Technology Engineering Center, the Naval Reactor Facility, the Radioactive Waste Management Complex, and the Test Reactor area. INEEL performs a number of ongoing functions. Three Mile Island's damaged spent fuel is stored on the site, and radioactive waste is stored and treated there in preparation for shipment out of the state. Advanced technologies for nuclear power systems are tested on site, and off-site spent nuclear fuel and radioactive waste are received and stored there. Prior to 1992, spent fuel was reprocessed on site, so part of the waste management function includes monitoring high-level waste from on-site chemical separation activities. By agreement with the state of Idaho (discussed more below), by 2035 the site is expecting to receive up to another 1,133 shipments of spent nuclear fuel from off-site locations. The site also supports development of naval nuclear propulsion and carries out testing, examination, and spent fuel management activities. These activities are operated separately from the rest of INEEL and involve the active participation of the Department of the Navy (Idaho National Engineering and Environmental Laboratory 1998b).

Contamination resulting from these activities is substantial and of special concern due to the location of an environmentally sensitive aquifer. The site is positioned above the Snake River Plain Aquifer, which is the largest aquifer in Idaho and one of the richest in the country. It is the primary source of water for the state's agriculture, which is dependent upon irrigation because of nonsubstantial rainfall amounts. Regardless of this environmentally sensitive resource, about 17,000 tons of radioactive materials were directly injected into the Snake River Plain Aquifer from the test reactor area before deep injection was halted. The land surrounding the test reactors also contains numerous unlined ponds that hold contaminated cooling tower water, solvents, acids, and radioactive elements. Solvents near the waste management area have moved into the aquifer and long-lived radioactive elements have migrated to the groundwater (U.S. Environmental Protection Agency 1989b).

Rocky Flats. Unlike the other sites so far described, the Rocky Flats Environmental Technology site is not located on a large tract of land that is geographically remote. Rocky Flats is a compact 11 square mile site located just 16 miles northwest of Denver, Colorado. When it was first opened, it was isolated in the rural flat just below the foothills of the Rocky Mountains but population growth in the area over time has resulted in housing suburbs being built within a few miles of the site. Indeed, Rocky Flats has been called the most dangerous site in the U.S. Nuclear Weapons Complex because it is surrounded by two million people living within a 50 mile radius (Johnston 1989b). Built in 1952, Rocky Flats manufactured plutonium triggers for nuclear weapons during its productive life of 40 years.

Rocky Flats was listed as a Superfund site in 1989, although the presence of off-site plutonium contamination was affirmed as early as 1979. In that year, the Department of Housing and Urban Development (HUD) instituted a policy whereby applicants for an FHA mortgage wishing to purchase land within ten miles of Rocky Flats would have to sign an advisory notice. This notice described "various levels of plutonium contamination of the soil" and the threat of "accidental release of radioactive materials" from the plant (Rocky Mountain Peace Center 1992).

The contamination of the site is substantial. Rocky Flats currently stores 14 tons of plutonium, both weapons grade and in liquid form. The liquid plutonium is stored in deteriorating tanks that pose a severe safety and environmental threat. The buildings, soil, and groundwater of the site are contaminated with plutonium, uranium, and americium as well as with toxic chemicals. The potential exists for the radioactive elements in the soil to become airborne in the strong prevailing winds that blow off the mountains and toward the city of Denver. A concern also exists that plutonium in the soil will wash into two streams that flow on either side of the site's main production area (U.S. Environmental Protection Agency 1997c). A number of criticality safety infractions have occurred on site.

(These are situations whereby accidental self-sustaining nuclear reactions can occur due to mishandling of nuclear materials.) These infractions of safety codes raise concerns regarding the appropriateness with which the site's nuclear material is being handled (Rocky Flats Citizens Advisory Board 1996).

Rocky Flats differs from most other sites in the nuclear weapons complex in that the cleanup decisions there do not contain provisions for permanently allocating a part of the site to be a waste repository. Instead, perhaps due to the close proximity to population centers, the future land-use decision was to remove all waste material from the site and to environmentally restore it as well as possible (Eddy 1998). The cleanup level to be attained is an issue that may involve repeated exercises of revised risk decision making. The current plan calls for the production center of the Rocky Flats site to be zoned industrial and the rest of the land to be declared open space. This decision is already coming into dispute as population growth in the urban area creates demand for land for residential housing. As the suburbs press closer and closer to the site, residential standards for allowable radiation exposure are already being debated.

Factors Affecting Progress Toward Meeting Environmental Compliance Obligations

What factors are important for determining how smoothly and how quickly a site in the Nuclear Weapons Complex will move toward the goal of compliance with U.S. environmental statutes? I wish to suggest four key factors that help to explain progress sites make — the degree of environmental difficulty, stakeholder relationships, organizational transformation, and national politics. In the discussion that follows, each of these factors is described in more detail. Illustrations drawn from the five sites are provided.

The Degree of Environmental Difficulty. The key issue in determining the degree of environmental difficulty is the remedy selected. Accepted site mitigation plans fall somewhere between pristine cleanup and a large variety of lesser remedies. These lesser remedies do not seek to restore the site to its prebomb manufacturing state, but rather to isolate and stabilize waste so that the contamination already present does not migrate further. If a site adopts a land-use plan that includes on-site disposal of low-level waste with limited off-site shipment of other waste, these decisions may lower costs and speed remediation efforts (while at the same time they may also lower the level of on-site cleanup attained). The case of Rocky Flats shows that this is not always possible, however, due to other constraints. The population pressures coming from a growing Denver make total removal of waste the future land-use plan of choice. Whether or not Rocky Flats will be successful in achieving this goal of total removal remains to be seen. What is clear is that this future land-use decision massively increases Rocky Flats' degree of environmental difficulty.

The degree of environmental difficulty is also determined by the extent, type, and volume of waste or environmental contamination present. These, in turn, dictate the complexity of the science and technology needed to fashion an acceptable mitigation strategy. Some types of waste can be effectively dealt with using off-the-shelf technology. Other types of contamination still have no available solution and will require substantial R&D before arriving at an adequate remedy.

As the case of Hanford so clearly shows, the extent, type, and volume of contamination deeply effect progress toward environmental restoration. All other things being equal, it would be reasonable to expect sites like Hanford, with large volumes of waste to manage and a high degree of environmental contamination, to take longer and be more costly to mitigate. However, as the failure of Savannah River's plan to drain its fewer, smaller (in total volume), and better managed high-level waste tanks shows, nuclear waste cleanup is a tough problem. Cleaning a thimbleful can prove just as intractable as cleaning a million-gallon tank, if the technology to do the job does not yet exist.

How adept site managers are in providing for adequate levels of R&D, integrating new technologies into their site remediation plans, and in deploying the most effective cleanup technologies will impact progress toward compliance. For instance, an innovative aspect of the Savannah River site is its heavy emphasis on developing technology. Most of this development takes place in the Savannah River Technology Center (SRTC) which is the site's applied R&D lab focusing on solving the site's technological challenges as well as on transferring technologies developed on site to the private sector (U.S. Department of Energy 1997b). SRS has integrated these technological innovations into its site remediation plan and effectively deployed them. For example, it has been successful in substituting aboveground concrete vaults as permanent storage repositories for the site's low-level waste. These vaults are considered superior to inground storage, such as the on-site low-level waste repository being using at Hanford, because they function significantly better to assure permanent isolation of waste from the environment (U.S. Department of Energy 1997a).

The planning and integration of cleanup technologies at a site in large part is the responsibility of the site's contracted management company. In this regard, how effectively DOE site managers influence contractors' cleanup approaches, especially privatization approaches designed to leverage private sector R&D funds, and monitor the cleanup process, will strongly influence progress toward compliance. INEEL's unhappy experience with the privatization of Pit 9, a failed attempt (now under litigation) to privatize the cleanup of nuclear waste, demonstrates that privatization strategies are risky. Hanford is currently planning to privatize the vitrification of its high-level waste, and Oak Ridge has entered into an agreement with British Nuclear Fuels Limited (described more completely later) to clean its K-25 plant using a privatization scenario.

The degree of difficulty is an obvious first factor that might explain a site's cleanup progress, but it is not the only factor. Indeed, even small technical problems can be rendered far less likely to be solved if a site lacks or poorly addresses other critical factors.

Stakeholder Relationships. The first of these other critical factors involves interaction with stakeholders. Myriad actors are involved in a site's activities but two large groups may be readily distinguished. One consists of other units of government (local and state governments, other federal bureaus such as EPA, different command levels within the same bureau such as DOE headquarters and other field offices, and the courts). Included here are also those acting in the stead of a government unit (private contractors). The other group consists of those members of the public who are directly affected by the site and the unaffected but generally attentive public (sovereign tribes, community members, citizen advisory boards, environmental groups, site workers, unions, and the media).

Environmental legislation adds to the complexity of stakeholder interactions in several ways. It gives overlapping authority to different levels of government and bureaus, which frequently results in conflicting standards and regulations. Working with dual regulators is difficult, but the situation is made much easier if there are good interagency and intergovernmental relationships in place.

Environmental regulations also mandate that external actors (state governments as well as citizens) be involved in meaningful ways in the decision-making process for future land-use planning and site mitigation. Involving the community and governmental units in constructive ways is difficult if they harbor suspicion toward DOE or the site's contracted management company.

It is more often the case than the exception for high levels of mistrust to exist between a site and many of its stakeholders. This mistrust stems, in large part, from the long history of releases of harmful substances into the environment where they subsequently affected, or are feared to have affected, surrounding communities. Hanford's "Green Run" is an early example (Magnuson 1988).

The Green Run was the name given to a December 1949 incident of atmospheric contamination caused when officials at Hanford, in an effort to see if they could speed up the production of plutonium, deliberately used "green" or unseasoned fuel for a test. Aging fuel for 60 to 90 days eliminates fast-decaying radionuclides from smokestack vapors while green fuel emits high volumes of radioactive gasses. Knowing this, and being advised by the meteorologists that weather conditions were unsuitable for rapid dissipation of the expected high volumes of radioactive vapors, managers at Hanford went ahead with the Green Run anyway. Weather conditions concentrated the contamination in the local population area as well as in the surrounding fields used for dairy cow grazing. Elevated concentrations of radiation in local milk were subsequently observed (Gerber 1992).

It might be argued that actions such as the Green Run, while not in any way desirable, could be somewhat explained and perhaps even justified by the urgency of the Cold War. But as recently as 1998, officials at Hanford once again were being held in public disdain for their callous treatment of people. The 1998 event concerned the exposure of workers to toxic waste as a result of an accident. Reports in the newspaper suggested that workers were initially denied access to health screening by Hanford officials (Wald 1998). This recent event resulted in the Washington State Department of Ecology issuing fines against Hanford for safety violations that led to the accident.

Intergovernmental relations between the Hanford, the state of Washington, and EPA are extremely strained largely because Hanford has missed multiple cleanup milestone dates as stipulated in the tripartite agreement. The most recent missed milestone involves both K basins (under EPA regulation) and the tanks (under state RCRA authority). The state of Washington and the EPA notified DOE in June 1998 of their intent to file a joint lawsuit. Negotiations leading to a new schedule of milestones averted the legal action. Nevertheless, Hanford's poor community and intergovernmental relations complicate efforts and divert them away from the central problem — cleaning up the site.

Rocky Flats also possesses a devastatingly poor record of intergovernmental relationships best depicted by the Federal Bureau of Investigation (FBI) raid on the site. On June 6, 1989, after months of covert nighttime surveillance, 70 FBI agents entered unannounced through the gates of Rocky Flats to seize records they believed would prove criminal acts taken on the part of officials at the site. This unprecedented action was ordered by the Justice Department after surveillance revealed deliberate violation of environmental laws (McAllister 1989). These allegations included the secret nighttime operation of an unsafe incinerator that Rocky Flats' officials claimed to have been shutdown, as well as the dumping of toxic chemicals into surface water bodies used for residential drinking water. The following September, the plant's contracted operator, Rockwell International, notified DOE that it could not make nuclear triggers if environmental laws had to be followed. DOE promptly replaced Rockwell with EG&G, another contracted site manager; however, in November 1989, the site was temporarily shut down because of these safety concerns (Johnston 1989a; Rocky Mountain Peace Center 1992).

Perhaps most telling about the great leeriness the FBI had for Rocky Flats are the actions of its agents while they were on site investigating the case. Not trusting Rocky Flats' personnel to adequately oversee the agents' exposure to radiation and toxic chemicals, the FBI brought along its own monitoring devices to assure the safety of its people (Wald 1989). When news of the FBI raid was reported in the local paper, these poor intergovernmental relations immediately had a marked deleterious impact on public attitudes toward Rocky Flats. Why should the public have confidence in it when another agency of the government could not? This atmosphere of mistrust and suspicion remains, dampening the willingness of the public to sign off on any proposed cleanup action without extensive scrutiny and oversight.

Rocky Flats and Hanford both clearly illustrate the importance of maintaining smooth stakeholder relationships. Sites might move to cleanup completion even in the face of poor community and intergovernmental relations, but it is obvious that the pace would be slowed. More importantly, the sites lose powerful allies (who might offer assistance with the political process) when they are alienated from the citizens and their fellows in government.

Organizational Transformation. When the Nuclear Weapons Complex closure orders were given, a substantial part of DOE's mission shifted from production of nuclear weapons to environmental restoration. This mission shift created organizational tensions within DOE. Almost overnight, it moved from being the hero of the Cold War to being the nation's worst polluter (U.S. General Accounting Office 1995b). This department, once dominated by the Cold War culture of secrecy, is now required to behave openly and with full public disclosure. The change in mission required that DOE, with its history of absolute technological independence, submit to the regulation not only of EPA but of the states as well. All of these factors weigh heavily, but one more adds significantly to the burden. Successful achievement of the new environmental mission often is a mixed blessing for it inevitably means some level of career disruption and job loss. Nevertheless, DOE's organizational transformation and the ability of sites within the complex to fully adopt the environmental mission are crucial to the likely success of complex cleanup.

Hanford is a site that reveals this organizational dynamic. Many of those at Hanford have not yet fully accepted the end of their production mission. Hanford vied for consideration as a site to be a permanent repository for the nation's radioactive waste. With the decision to make Yucca Mountain the nation's nuclear disposal site, Hanford then strove for the reopening of its Fast Flux Reactor to become the nation's sole site producing tritium for the weapons complex. DOE eventually decided to privatize that function, awarding the contract to a civilian nuclear power plant. Part of the desire for a production mission certainly stems from the isolated location of the site and the fact that Hanford is the major employer for the local population — job losses at Hanford are not easily replaced — but much of the desire rests with Hanford's failure to adopt environmental restoration as a mission of value and priority.

Not all the sites are having difficulty with the new organizational mission. The Savannah River Technology Center is a fine example of successful organization transformation. Before the end of the Cold War the center concentrated on R&D to support the site's nuclear production mission. With the shifting national priorities, the site has adapted to the new reality. Now the work focus is on processing nuclear materials, environmental restoration, processing and stabilizing waste, and producing technologies for decontamination and decommissioning of nuclear facilities (U.S. Department of Energy Savannah River Operations Office 1997b).

INEEL is another example of sound organizational transformation. INEEL's long range plans call for "a sustainable future for the site and its employees ... through a central focus on the environment, such that the INEEL will be looked at as THE (emphasis in original) national environmental laboratory with viable solutions to the nation's complex environmental problems" (INEEL Long Range Plan Summary 1998). INEEL's plan is to continue waste management operations until all spent fuel is sent off site while phasing in the new environmental mission at the same time.

For Oak Ridge, the potential loss of jobs is a major issue and in many ways, the driving force behind organizational transformation. Like Savannah River for South Carolina, Oak Ridge is a major employer in the state of Tennessee. For that reason, Oak Ridge has concentrated heavily on the "reindustrialization" of the former Cold War production facilities. This effort entails luring industries to come to Oak Ridge to make use of idle or excess facilities and to gain advantage from its technological base. To this end, the K-25 site was renamed the East Tennessee Technology Park and its more than three million square feet of production area was made available to interested firms (Thomas 1998).

The rub, of course, is that most sections of the site are still heavily contaminated both with radionuclides and toxic chemicals. To overcome this obstacle, Oak Ridge has adopted a novel approach. A $238 million plus scrap contract was let to British Nuclear Fuels Limited (BNFL) to decontaminate several areas of the K-25 site. BNFL is permitted by the contract to take ownership of all materials salvaged at the site (including tons of precious metals and electrical equipment). DOE estimated this contract to cost $600 million less than what it would cost the government and its existing contractors to decontaminate the site. After decontamination, the facility can be rented to interested companies. If successful, this will not only bring in rental income but provide jobs as well (Powers 1997; Thomas 1998). Oak Ridge is also unique for its attempts at creating a capacity (and jobs) for recycling contaminated material. The DOE demonstration project to recycle radioactively contaminated carbon steel (RCCS) was awarded to Oak Ridge in November of 1996. The project directs Oak Ridge to decontaminate and release carbon steel material for general use. The material which cannot be decontaminated is to be fabricated into one-time-use containers for disposal of low-level waste generated by DOE's Environmental Management program (Nuclear News 1997).

The importance of true organizational transformation cannot be underestimated. Without dedication to the cleanup mission and strong leadership fully devoted to the environmental restoration, a site faces enormous obstacles on its path to cleanup.

National Politics. This factor is the least under the control of the individual sites. Nevertheless, four political consequences are particularly important to each site's progress. First, the national political process controls each site's resources, both budgetary and human. Second, the political process governs the completion and availability of national repositories such as the Waste Isolation Pilot Plant (WIPP) and Yucca Mountain for the permanent isolation and off-site shipment of designated waste from the complex. Third, the political process controls the level of ongoing investment in environmental R&D vital to the development of new and improved technologies. Finally, the political process is intimately linked to maintaining a national dedication to complex remediation at the maximum feasibly attainable level.

Budget estimates running into the $400 billion range and congressional uncertainty to allocate funds for projects with no clear foreseeable ending point, have resulted in reconsideration of the level of mitigation needed to be attained and the time frame within which environmental remediation occurs. For most sites in the complex, concern over cost constraints has resulted in replacing hopes of fuller environmental cleanup and off-site transport of all waste with the alternative of on-site disposal of at least some of the site's waste. Accelerated cleanup strategies are also proposed to reduce the cost of mitigation by replacing years of full site safety and oversight funding with the less costly function of stewardship of waste disposed on site. Accelerated cleanup is also thought to be a legitimate political tool to leverage money from Congress while at the same time assuring stakeholders of funding for at least some level of present cleanup.

Rocky Flats has been successful in several aspects of political activities. Its budget increased under the administration of DOE Secretary Pena (a Colorado resident). Rocky Flats was able to adopt the accelerated cleanup plan proposed by DOE headquarters and in this fashion was able to secure increased funding. Recent reviews of the progress made by Rocky Flats under its accelerated cleanup program, however, question whether it will meet its target date of 2006 for fast cleanup and closure (U.S. General Accounting Office 1999b). Even if it is able to do what needs to be done for on-site closure, many of its materials and wastes wait for off-site storage. The recently opened WIPP is now receiving some waste streams; however, current levels of shipments of radioactive materials from Rocky Flats to final repositories are insufficient to meet the 2006 deadline.

Hanford, by contrast, has been remarkably unsuccessful in dealing with the challenges of politics. Hanford's budget is in decline, owing in part to the lack of ability to show Congress that significant cleanup progress is being made at the site. While DOE is prohibited from directly lobbying Congress for appropriations, sites in the complex have been financially successful thanks to the lobbying skills of their contractors. This has not been the case at Hanford. Distance from the main seat of government may also explain the low issue salience Hanford seems to have in the nation's capital. Problems abound, solutions are lacking, and so Hanford is convenient to omit from center place on the agenda.

Politics comes into play on the complexwide level to assure a national solution to a national problem. Most site mitigation plans call for some shipment of waste to either WIPP or Yucca, and sites have entered into legal agreements with the states that specify dates by when shipments must occur. However, the sites cannot possibly meet these milestones without national repositories where they might send their waste. INEEL is perhaps the best example of this. In 1995, DOE, the navy, and the state of Idaho signed a settlement agreement resolving lawsuits filed by the state of Idaho against DOE. The main issue was the transport of waste into the state without offsetting shipments out of the state. While residents close to INEEL considered this practice good job insurance, Governor Batt echoed the sentiment of the rest of the state in filing the actions. The court ordered that all shipments of waste to INEEL be halted until an agreement was fashioned. By this settlement, DOE agreed to remove all spent nuclear fuel from the state by 2035 and all long-lived nuclear waste by no later than 2018. The navy agreed to make no more than 575 future shipments of spent fuel to Idaho, and Idaho agreed to accept these shipments. This agreement makes INEEL particularly dependent on the establishment of a national nuclear waste repository. Without such a repository, INEEL will miss settlement milestones, putting it in violation of the court agreement and subjecting DOE to pay the state of Idaho penalties of $60,000 a day.

Hanford also is fully dependent on access to a national waste repository eager to receive its myriad wastes, but the site brings an interesting problem into the scenario. Hanford holds so much volume of waste that present schedules for shipments to current and planned repositories mean that it will be "temporarily" holding this waste stream far into the future. Adjustments to the national shipment schedule would have to occur for Hanford to make any faster progress. The federal government is having a tough enough time just getting the repositories open and accepting waste. The idea of rethinking planned shipments to accommodate Hanford holds little political feasibility.

All sites could benefit from better cleanup technologies. Savannah River and Hanford, though, are completely dependent on the development of improved technologies so that they can handle their worst problem — the tank waste. Without significant advances in statistical methods (for tank characterization) and robotics (for remote waste removal) the tanks remain a problem with no technically viable solution. Adequate money to fund this R&D, and the willingness to request proposals in the field of nuclear waste cleanup, need to come from the national government.

Washington politics have a vast impact on all sites in the complex. Very little cleanup can be undertaken without adequate and stable budgets and a national political will to continue to provide the resources, including secure national repositories to receive shipment of waste and R&D to develop improved technologies. It is important that the cleanup of the U.S. Nuclear Weapons Complex remain a federal-level issue. It could be all too easy to allow the issue to become one that each state or region where a complex site is located has to face alone. This would be a terrible injustice to the states and regions concerned as well as a tragic mistake, for the problem is too large to permit a piecemeal solution.

Conclusions

This chapter has presented an overview of the policy and administrative problems associated with fulfilling the congressional mandate that DOE facilities come into compliance with environmental laws. The environmental conditions of the worst five sites in the U.S. Nuclear Weapons Complex — Hanford, Savannah River, Rocky Flats, Idaho National Engineering and Environmental Laboratory, and Oak Ridge — illustrate that stabilizing and ecologically isolating the waste now contaminating weapons complex lands will take many years of substantial and sustained effort.

The enormity of the environmental problems is reflected by the astronomical cleanup cost projections. Whether the actual costs correspond to the low estimates or the high end, the cleanup of the complex will be one of the most expensive public works projects ever undertaken by the United States. For the environmental remediation to be successful, attention needs to be devoted not only to the scientific and technical aspects of the cleanup, but also to dealing effectively with stakeholders, forging genuine organizational transformation, and obtaining the benefits of a supportive political structure.

REFERENCES

American Ceramic Society Bulletin. 1996. SRS Showcases Work in Vitrification. *American Ceramic Society Bulletin* 75 (8): 26–27.

Bowsher, Charles. 1989. *Comptroller General's 1989 Annual Report.* United States General Accounting Office.

Cochran, Thomas B., Dan W. Reicher, and Jason Salzman. 1990. The U.S. Nuclear Warhead Production Complex. In *Hidden Dangers: Environmental Consequences of Preparing for War,* edited by Anne H. Ehrlich and John W. Birks. San Francisco: Sierra Club Books.

Eddy, Mark. 1998. Pena Promises Fast Cleanup. *Denver Post,* 8 August.

Eubank, Keith. 1991. *The Bomb.* Malabar, Florida: Kreiger Publishing Company.

Federal Facilities Policy Group. October 1995. *Improving Federal Facilities Cleanup.* Report of the Federal Facilities Policy Group. Council on Environmental Quality and Office of Management and Budget.

Gerber, Michele Stenehjem. 1992. *On the Home Front: The Cold War Legacy of the Hanford Nuclear Site.* Lincoln and London: University of Nebraska Press.

Hileman, Bette. 1996. Energy Department Has Made Progress Cleaning Up Nuclear Weapons Plants. *Chemical and Engineering News,* July 22: 14–20.

Idaho National Engineering and Environmental Laboratory Facilities. 1998. *INEEL Primary Facility Area Descriptions. http://www.inel/gov/mpas/facility_intro. html.*

Idaho National Engineering and Environmental Laboratory Long Range Plan Summary. 1998. *Long Range Plan Summary. http://www.inel.gov/about/l-rsummary.html.*

Johnston, David. 1989a. Criminal Investigation Is Begun at Arms Plant. *New York Times,* 6 June.

Johnston, David. 1989b. Weapons Plant Dumped Chemicals into Drinking Water, F.B.I. Says. *New York Times,* 10 June.

Magnuson, Ed. 1988. They Lied to Us: Unsafe, Aging U.S. Weapons Plants are Stirring Fear and Disillusion. *Time Magazine.* 31 October: 60–65.

McAllister, Bill. 1989. Charges of Illegal Storage, Pollution Probed at Nuclear Arms Plant. *Washington Post,* 7 June.

Nuclear News. 1997. DOE Sets Policy, Selects Oak Ridge as Lead Site. *Nuclear News* 40 (1): 1.

Powers, Mary B with Debra K. Rubin and Sherie Winston. 1997. DOE Procedures Amid Controversy. *Engineering News Record* 239(5): 2.

Reicher, Dan W., and S. Jacob Scherr. 1990. The Bomb Factories: Out of Compliance and Out of Control. In *Hidden Dangers: Environmental Consequences of Preparing for War,* edited by Anne H. Ehrlich and John W. Birks. San Francisco: Sierra Club Books.

Resnikoff, Marvin. 1990. The Generation Time-Bomb; Radioactive and Chemical Defense Wastes. In *Hidden Dangers: Environmental Consequences of Preparing for War,* edited by Anne H. Ehrlich and John W. Birks. San Francisco: Sierra Club Books.

Rhodes, Richard. 1988. *The Making of the Atomic Bomb.* New York, London, Toronto, Sydney, and Tokyo: Simon & Schuster.

Rocky Flats Citizens Advisory Board. 1996. Status Report: Rocky Flats Cleanup Activities. *Rocky Flats Citizens Advisory Board Newsletter— The Advisor.*

Rocky Mountain Peace Center. 1992. *Citizens's Guide to Rocky Flats: Colorado's Nuclear Bomb Factory.* Rocky Mountain Peace Center.

Season, Harry T. 1997. Status of Dismantlement of Nuclear Weapons. *Dismantlement and Destruction of Chemical, Nuclear and Conventional Weapons* edited by Nancy Turtle Schulte. Dordrecht, Boston, London: Kluwer Academic Publishers.

Thomas, Lois Reagan. 1998. A New Vision. *Knoxville News-Sentinel,* 18 January.

U.S. Department of Energy. 1995. *Estimating the Cold War Mortgage: The 1995 Baseline Environmental Management Report.* U.S. Department of Energy, Office of Environmental Management. DOE/EM-0232.

U.S. Department of Energy. 1996. *The 1996 Baseline Environmental Management Report.* U.S. Department of Energy, Office of Environmental Management. DOE/EM-0290.

U.S. Department of Energy Savannah River Operations Office. 1997b. *Fact Sheet: Savannah River Technology Center.* DOE Savannah River Operations Office.

U.S. Department of Energy. 1997C. *Linking Legacies: Connecting the Cold War Nuclear Weapons Production Processes to Their Environmental Consequences.* U.S. Department of Energy, Office of Environmental Management. DOE/EM-0319.

U.S. Department of Energy. 1998. *Accelerated Cleanup: Paths to Closure.* U.S. Department of Energy, Office of Environmental Management. DOE/EM-0342.

U.S. Department of Energy Savannah River Operations Office. 1997a. *Fact Sheet: Savannah River Site.* DOE Savannah River Operations Office.

U.S. Environmental Protection Agency. 1989a. *NPL Site Narrative at Listing. Site Description for Oak Ridge Reservation.* U.S. Environmental Protection Agency, Office of Emergency and Remedial Response. *http://www.epa.gov/oerrpage/ superfnd/web/oerr/impm/products/ npl/nar1239.htm.*

U.S. Environmental Protection Agency. 1989b. *NPL Site Narrative at Listing. Site Description for Idaho National Engineering Laboratory.* U.S. Environmental Protection Agency, Office of Emergency and Remedial Response. Available from *http://www.epa.gov/oerrpage/ superfnd/web/oerr/impm/products/npl/ nar1231.htm.*

U.S. Environmental Protection Agency. 1997a. *National Priorities List. Site Description for Savannah River Site.* U.S. Environmental Protection Agency, Office of Emergency and Remedial Response. Available from *http://www.epa.gov/oer-rpage/superfnd/web/oerr/impm/products/nplsites/0403485n.htm.*

U.S. Environmental Protection Agency. 1997b. *National Priorities List. Site Description for Oak Ridge Reservation.* U.S. Environmental Protection Agency, Office of Emergency and Remedial Response. *http://www.epa.gov/oerrpage/ superfnd/web/oerr/impm/products/nplsites/0404152n.htm.*

U.S. Environmental Protection Agency. 1997c. *Rocky Flats Plant (DOE) Fact Sheet.* U.S. Environmental Protection Agency.

U.S. General Accounting Office. 1995a. *Department of Energy: National Priorities Needed for Meeting Environmental Agreements.* GAO/RCED-95-1.

U.S. General Accounting Office. 1995b. *Department of Energy: A Framework for Restructuring DOE and Its Missions.* GAO/RCED-95-197.

U.S. General Accounting Office. 1996a. *Environmental Protection: Issues Facing the Energy and Defense Environmental Management Programs.* Testimony before the Subcommittees on Military Procurement and Military Readiness, Committee on national Security, House of Representatives. Statement of Victory S. Rezendes, Director, Energy, Resources, and Science Issues, Resources, community, and Economic Development Division. GAO/T-RDED/NSIAD-96-127.

U.S. General Accounting Office. 1996b. *Federal Facilities: Consistent Relative Risk Evaluations Needed for Prioritizing Cleanups.* GAO/RCED-96-150.

U.S. General Accounting Office. 1999a. *Process to Remove Radioactive Waste from Savannah River Tanks Fails to Work.* GAO/RCED-99-69.

U.S. General Accounting Office. 1999b. *Accelerated Closure of Rocky Flats: Status and Obstacles.* GAO/RCED-99-100.

Wald, Matthew. 1989. Colorado Weighs Jobs and Arms Plant Danger. *New York Times,* 21 June.

Wald, Matthew. 1997. Caught Between Risks of Haste and Hesitation. *New York Times,* 29 September.

Wald, Matthew. 1998. Admitting Error at a Weapons Plant. *New York Times,* 23
    March.
Westinghouse Hanford Company. 1995. *Tank Waste Mitigation System.* A report
    prepared for the Department of Energy, Richland Operations Office.
Westinghouse Hanford Company. 1996. *K Basins.* A report prepared for the Depart-
    ment of Energy, Richland Operations Office.
Wildavsky, Ben. 1998. Looming Liabilities. *National Journal* 30 (3):102–105.

Chapter Three

The Privatization of Nuclear Waste Cleanup: A Case Study of DOE's Pit 9

SEVIM AHMEDOV

Introduction

Created in 1977 from several diverse agencies, the Department of Energy (DOE) manages the nation's nuclear weapons complex and conducts research and development on both energy and basic science. DOE operates an elaborate network of facilities, its core being the Nuclear Weapons Complex — a collection of 17 major facilities in 13 states that design, develop, test, produce, and now dismantle the U.S. vast nuclear arsenal (U.S. Department of Energy 1997a). About half of DOE's resources are devoted to the Nuclear Weapons Complex, an allocation that reflects both the buildup of these weapons through the 1980s and, more recently, the rapidly escalating cost of nuclear waste management and environmental restoration (U.S. Department of Energy 1997b). Budgeted at about $18 billion for 1998, DOE has nearly 20,000 federal employees and 140,000 contract workers (U.S. General Accounting Office 1995a).

The end of the Cold War has placed DOE at a critical juncture in its history. The department's original core missions — to develop and test nuclear weapons, conduct basic energy research, and set national energy policy — are being replaced by fundamentally new challenges in environmental cleanup. DOE is burdened with an environmental legacy consisting of more than 36 million cubic meters of nuclear waste spread throughout the DOE complex (U.S. Department of Energy 1997b) with conservative remediation cost estimates ranging between $250 and $350 billion (U.S. General Accounting Office 1998a). Unequivocally, this presents one of the most serious problems faced by DOE and the nation in general. The U.S. won the Cold War; today, a daunting environmental price is waiting to be paid.

Although as early as 1948, scientists involved with the nuclear weapons complex raised serious questions about its waste management practices (U.S. Atomic Energy Commission 1948), the imperatives of the arms race ignored those concerns and largely pushed control of environmental contamination out of the DOE's policy agenda. The established organizational structure fulfilled the Cold War priorities of designing, building, and testing nuclear weapons secretly and quickly. When production was the primary mission, one large contractor was responsible for virtually all services at each plant site, and that contractor was protected from most financial risks by the terms of the contract.

In the last decade, DOE has found that responding to its changing missions and new priorities within existing institutional structures is a challenging task. In 1994, its Contract Reform Team, which was established to identify basic contracting weaknesses and determine fundamental improvements, reported that DOE needed to make major changes to its unique contracting system to accomplish its changing missions. The team's basic premise was that DOE's contracting suffered from an over-reliance on cost-based contracts (i.e., allowing private contractors to manage and operate billion-dollar facilities with minimal direct federal oversight, yet reimbursing them for all costs regardless of their actual achievements), a lack of well-defined performance criteria and measures, and weaknesses in oversight (U.S. Department of Energy 1994). The team made more than 45 recommendations, including a call for more performance-based management contracts, new incentives to reduce costs, increased use of fixed-price contracts, and more objective performance criteria by which DOE's administrators could judge results. The team also urged that contracts be opened to competition more frequently (U.S. Department of Energy 1994).

On August 26, 1994, DOE signed its first fixed-price subcontract and initiated a new privatization strategy in accordance with recommendations reflecting its changing institutional environment. As a pilot project, Pit 9 was to demonstrate the advantages of the new strategy. Lockheed Martin emerged as the finalist from the competitive process and offered to clean up the pit for the fixed price of $200 million. DOE agreed to pay only for actual remediated waste, thus shifting the risk to the private company. DOE estimated its cost savings at about $135 million (U.S. General Accounting Office 1997a) and Lockheed Martin took a first stab at the lucrative $35 billion annual nuclear services market (British Nuclear Fuels 1998).[1] DOE was assured that Lockheed Martin possessed the needed technology and expertise to complete the project. Or, as one of the company's managers put it: "We sent a rocket to Mars, we can clean a pit."

Nevertheless, to date, not a single ounce of waste has been removed from Pit 9, and the contractual parties are entangled in a litigation process. Based on the case study methodology, this chapter reconstructs the chain of events that constituted the subcontract decision-making and implementation processes.

The urgency and uncertainties associated with building the world's first atomic bombs led to special arrangements that allowed DOE's predecessors to rely extensively on the contractors' expertise to manage and operate a vast network of weapons facilities. Contractors have worked under these arrangements for nearly 50 years and have created an enormous nuclear weapons production capability. However, DOE has exercised poor contract oversight of its management and operation (M&O) contractors (U.S. General Accounting Office 1994, 1995a, 1996c, 1998a). Although, the agency has acknowledged these weaknesses and made attempts to improve its practices by launching a broad range of initiatives over the last several years, the Pit 9 experience shows that DOE continues to struggle with the process of realigning itself to meet the new challenges.

The initial attitude that Pit 9 exemplified — i.e., streamlining the contractual strategy and shifting performance responsibility to the contractor — has been confronted by the realization that DOE has to find a middle way, one that combines a utilization of private and public resources for nuclear waste disposal projects. This requires cultural changes in the way DOE conducts the nation's business.

The development of the atomic bomb and the subsequent establishment of a complex network of nuclear weapons facilities was a great managerial achievement that pulled together enormous public and private resources. Dealing with the environmental legacy of that endeavor requires an even more skillful managerial feat. Although DOE has failed the first test, there are some indications that the final result may be different.

Privatization in the Department of Energy Context Historical Background and Overview

One cold morning in December 1989, workers at the Rocky Flats Plants in Colorado loaded a plutonium "trigger" for a nuclear warhead into a tractor trailer bound southeast for the Pantex Plant near Amarillo, Texas. Hardly anyone realized then that the nuclear weapon built with this plutonium trigger would be last one made in the United States for the foreseeable future (U.S. Department of Energy 1996). According to Thomas P. Grumbly, Assistant Secretary for Environmental Management at DOE, at that point the U.S. reached halfway in "closing the circle on the splitting of the atom" (U.S. Department of Energy 1996, ix).

The starting point for the circle was the first chain reaction conducted by Enrico Fermi which was followed immediately by the Manhattan Project and the explosion of the first atomic bombs. In the ensuing years of the Cold War and the nuclear arms race between the United States and the Soviet Union, the U.S. developed a vast research, production, and testing network that came to be known as "the nuclear weapons complex." The enormity of the project can be revealed by only two numbers. The nuclear weapons complex employed more than 100,000 contractor personnel at any one time, and from the Manhattan Project to the present, the U.S. has spent approximately $300 billion[2] on nuclear weapons research, production and testing[3] (U.S. Department of Energy 1997b).

With the enactment of the Atomic Energy Act of 1946, nuclear weapons development and production was placed under the control of the newly established civilian Atomic Energy Commission (AEC).[4] AEC developed and managed a network of research, manufacturing, and testing sites, focusing the efforts of these sites on stockpiling an arsenal of nuclear weapons. In the late 1940s and early 1950s, during a period of great expansion of the nuclear weapons complex, most of these functions were consolidated into a complex of large, centralized, government-owned production facilities (Hewlett and Duncun 1969). In 1975, the AEC was abolished by the Energy Reorganization Act and replaced by two new federal agencies: the Nuclear Regulatory Commission (NRC), which was charged with regulating the civilian uses of atomic energy (mainly commercial nuclear power plants), and the Energy Research and Development Administration (ERDA), which was responsible for the nuclear weapons complex. In 1977, the Department of Energy Organization Act created a cabinet level agency, the Department of Energy, and transferred ERDA's duties to this new entity (Fehner and Holl 1994). To this date, DOE continues to oversee the nuclear weapons complex. To administer the DOE's waste management, environmental remediation, and environmental compliance activities, the Secretary of Energy consolidated these function in 1989 into the Office of Environmental Management (EM). The Office of Environmental Management assumed a majority of these responsibilities, and the budgets to implement them, from functions previously exercised by the Office of Defense Programs, and, to a lesser degree, from the Offices of Nuclear Energy and Energy Research (Gosling 1994).

Nuclear Weapons Production
Stages and Waste Generated

Nuclear weapons production in the United States was a complex series of integrated manufacturing activities executed at multiple sites across the country. These processes can be generally grouped into eight major categories: uranium mining, milling, and refining[5]; isotope separation (enrichment) of uranium, lithium, boron and heavy water[6]; fuel and target fabrication for production reactors[7]; reactor operations[8]; chemical separations[9]; component fabrication[10]; weapon operations[11]; and research, development and testing (RD&T).[12]

Every step in the production of materials and parts for nuclear warheads generated waste[13] and other by-products. Every gram of plutonium, each reactor fuel element, every container of enriched uranium, and each canister of depleted uranium has radioactive waste associated with it. For example, the graphite bricks used by Enrico Fermi for his primitive reactor at the University of Chicago were buried as radioactive waste at the Palos Forest Preserve in Cooke County, Illinois. The acid used to extract the plutonium for the first nuclear test explosion in the Alamogordo desert of New Mexico is now high-level waste stored at the Hanford Site in Washington state (U.S. Department of Energy 1996).

The waste is classified in several categories, depending on the hazards it poses, the length of time it remains radioactive, or its source. The primary waste and by-product categories are defined as: spent fuel, high-level waste, transuranic waste, low-level waste, (also known as 11e2 by-product material[14]). Waste is measured in terms of its volume (cubic meters) and its radioactivity content (curies[15]). In 1997 DOE estimated that its total waste legacy includes 36 million cubic meters of waste. Overall, 89 percent of that volume is 11e(2) byproduct material and 9 percent is low-level waste; the remaining waste categories only comprise about 2 percent of the waste legacy. The distribution of radioactivity in the waste, however, is very different. Radioactivity in high-level waste is 94 percent,[16] 5 percent in low-level waste, and only about 1 percent of the radioactivity is found in the remaining waste categories. By volume, about 68 percent of the 36 million cubic meter waste is due to nuclear weapons production activities, and the remaining 32 percent to nonweapons activities.

In terms of radioactivity, overall the waste legacy contains 1.01 billion curies. By radioactivity content, 89 percent of the waste is due to nuclear weapons production, less than 1 percent to activities supporting the Naval

Nuclear Propulsion Program (NNPP), and 11 percent is attributed to other nonweapons programs. By radioactivity content, 86 percent of the waste legacy came from chemical separations for nuclear weapons production. The remaining 3 percent attributed to weapons production resulted primarily from RD&T (1.4 percent), and fuel and target fabrications (0.9 percent) (U.S. Department of Energy 1997b).

Approaches to the Environmental Legacy of the Cold War

All of the major facilities in the U.S. Nuclear Weapons Production Complex were shut down in the late 1980s. The end of production was quite sudden and largely unexpected. Incidents of mismanagement and contamination at U.S. nuclear weapons sites led to a series of federal investigations into safety and environmental practices. These investigations pointed out that most of the DOE's weapons plants, built several decades ago, were at or near the end of their design life and unable to comply with current environmental and safety standards and regulations. Many operations were therefore discontinued while alternatives for weapons production were being considered. At about the same time, the Cold War began winding down, and in 1991 the Soviet Union collapsed, bringing the nuclear arms race between the two superpowers to a sudden halt (U.S. Department of Energy 1996).

In view of these new developments, DOE found its mission drastically changed. Initially established to respond to the energy crises of the 1970s and to win the Cold War, today DOE has to deal with the environmental legacy of that conflict.

From the beginning stages of the nuclear age, scientists involved with the weapons complex raised serious questions about its waste-management practices. Shortly after the establishment of the AEC, its 12-member Safety and Industrial Health Advisory Board reported that "the disposal of contaminated waste in present quantities and by present methods ... if continued for decades, presents the gravest of problems" (U.S. Atomic Energy Commission 1948, 67). The imperatives of the nuclear arms race, however, demanded that weapons production and testing be given priority over waste management and the control of environmental contamination. Today DOE and the U.S. face daunting institutional and technical challenges in dealing with the environmental legacy of the nuclear weapons complex. Over the last several years, the total estimated cost of the DOE cleanup has risen from about $100 billion in 1988 to $230 billion, with a higher end estimate of $350 billion in 1996 (U.S. General Accounting Office 1996a).

The challenge for DOE is found not only in the lack of effective cleanup technologies for radioactive substances that will be hazardous for thousands of years; not only in the lack of full understanding of the potential health of prolonged exposure to materials that are both chemically toxic and radioactive; not only in making the institutional transition from nuclear weapons production to environmental cleanup *–the challenge is found in all these problems, and solving them under serious fiscal constraints.* DOE, as all government agencies, is operating in an ambiguous ideological environment shaped by the public's distaste for increased taxes and, concurrently, its desire for greater government involvement in solving pressing social problems. As a result, DOE is expected "to do more with less."

Privatization Options

Over the last 40 years, DOE and its predecessor agencies principally have used management contractors to accomplish work because of the security required for the production of nuclear weapons. In terms of procurement, this became almost exclusively a "make" rather than a "buy" decision. With the end of the Cold War, the need for security in making products or providing services has lessened significantly. Reflecting this change is DOE's engagement in increased privatization initiatives in recent years (U.S. Department of Energy 1995). These initiatives draw their justifications from several key reform efforts in line with DOE's mission-restructuring strategy. The first such effort was the "Contract Reform Initiative" which was completed in February 1994, and its report to the secretary outlined how performance-based contracting could result in dramatic savings to the taxpayer and increased productivity within the DOE. This report set the stage for an ongoing contract reform effort that is now pervasive throughout the department. In April 1994, DOE published its strategic plan, designed to refocus the department on the new challenges facing the nation. The strategic plan identified five business lines: industrial competitiveness, national security, energy resources, environmental quality, and science and technology. Finally, the strategic alignment initiative, announced in May 1995 as a complementing element of National Performance Review (NPR), provided the roadmap to a leaner DOE by redirecting resources to better meet core mission functions. All these initiatives recognized the potential for increased use of privatization as one means of reducing the cost of DOE activities.

DOE defines privatization as the "process of contracting for products and services from commercial sources with specialized competencies when these products have historically been provided by the DOE or its Management Contractor" (U.S. Department of Energy 1995, ix). Most broadly defined, privatization substitutes, in whole or in part, private market mechanisms for the traditional government role as employer, financier, owner, operator, or regulator of a product or a service (U.S. Department of Energy 1997a). This definition admits a wide variety of actions, from contracting out the delivery of services under governmental specifications to complete divestiture of activities or assets. The common objective underlying all these actions, however, is "to remove the agency from those activities that are not inherently governmental functions[17] or core business lines; to improve the management of remaining activities; to reduce the cost of doing business; and to shift greater performance and financial risk to the private sector" (U.S. Department of Energy 1997a, 1-1).

Privatization, according to DOE serves two primary purposes as a management tool. First, at a strategic level, it helps an organization focus on those work activities that represent its core expertise, skill or value-added offering. Second, at a tactical level, privatization is a means of reducing costs by ensuring that work activities are performed by the most productive, cost-effective means (U.S. Department of Energy 1997a).

Although privatization can take many forms, generally those initiatives in DOE can be grouped into three major types: divestiture of functions, contracting out, and asset transfers.

Although the distinction is blurry in some circumstances, divestiture of functions differs from simple asset transfers in both scope and impact. A functional divestment strategy involves transfer of the operation as a whole to the private sector as opposed to a simple transfer of real or personal property. More specifically, it represents an effort to transfer an entire ongoing operation to private-sector ownership and management in those cases where the operation's potential value in the private marketplace depends on maintaining the operation as a coherent commercial entity. Thus, while the operation may include assets such as real estate, equipment and materials, it also may include both managerial and wage employees who operate within a recognized managerial system. In contrast with contracting out, divestiture of functions is not predicated on the government being a customer for the newly privatized entity. While the new commercial company may count the government among its customers in some cases, the intent of functional divestiture is weighted more toward removing the government from an activity altogether rather than procuring the same level of services from private sources to increase efficiency and reduce cost (U.S. Department of Energy 1997a). Some recent examples of divestiture include the National Institute for Petroleum and Energy Research (NIPER) in Bartlesville, Oklahoma; the Western Environmental Technology Office (WETO) in Butte, Montana; and Elk Hills Naval Petroleum Reserve (NPR) in Kern County, California.

The asset transfer involves the sale or other transfer of real or personal property (e.g., sale of precious metals in DOE inventory). An asset sale, lease or donation implies little or no government involvement after transfer and affects property more than individuals (although employees engaged in maintaining assets may be affected). The asset inventory of DOE falls into four categories: (1) real property (e.g., land, buildings, facilities); (2) personal property (e.g., machines, equipment which are not part of a building or structure); (3) personal property in the forms of nuclear materials; and (4) personal property in the form of nonnuclear materials (e.g., metals, chemicals). The land holdings of DOE encompass more than 2.4 million acres[18] with 20,700 specialized facilities, 1,600 laboratories, 89 nuclear reactors, 17,000 pieces of large industrial or construction equipment, 130,000 tons of chemicals,[19] 270,000 tons of scrap metal, 246 million barrels of crude oil and 58 trillion cubic meters of natural gas, as well as enriched uranium and 17,000 radioactive sources used in research, industry, and medical treatment (U.S. Department of Energy 1996). In its first asset sale, which occurred in 1995, DOE netted $3 million from the sale of surplus gold, silver, and other precious materials (U.S. General Accounting Office 1995b). DOE completed a number of asset sales in 1996, including a $3.1 million sale of normal uranium, a $5.2 million sale of timber, and an $800,000 sale of gas turbine generators. In addition, DOE currently plans to dispose of much of the excess enriched uranium by transferring it to the U.S. Enrichment Corporation to produce fuel for commercial nuclear reactors. In addition, it is considering plans for economic utilization of much of the depleted uranium inventory as an alternative to disposal of it as waste (U.S. Department of Energy 1997a).

Contracting Out

DOE has always relied on the management and technical expertise of the private sector for the operation of its weapon production and scientific and engineering facilities and sites. The objective of the management and operating (M&O) contract concept is to bring management expertise and private market practices to bear in the operation of the government's scientific, engineering, and production facilities. Because the management and operation of the facility or site is in direct fulfillment of the department's mission, M&O contractors operate more as an extension of DOE and less as a true private enterprise. In consideration of national security and other concerns, the M&O contractor has traditionally performed many, if not all, of the functions associated with operating a site or facility. As a result, M&O contractors have not relied heavily on contracting out to improve either operational efficiencies or cost-effectiveness (U.S. General Accounting Office 1998a). Accordingly, activities within the department under the heading of "contracting out" include the transfer of both traditional government enterprise and M&O contractor activities to the private sector.

Contracting out can take many forms, including the relatively straightforward award of a contract for services, long-term arrangements that involve innovative private project financing, lease-back of capital equipment, or long-term per-unit fees for service. In contrast to a functional divestiture, DOE retains a substantial continuing relationship under contracting-out arrangements— often as a primary, and sometimes as the only customer. In some circumstances, however, contracting out can provide a transitional mechanism for eventual divestiture (U.S. Department of Energy 1997a). DOE has recognized that widespread weaknesses exist in its control of contractors' costs and activities and, in 1994, began a departmentwide contract reform effort. The contract reform team report issued in 1994 recommended that DOE decrease its reliance on M&O contracts to accomplish required activities. The report also recommended that DOE improve its "make/buy"[20] decision-making process and explore more cost-effective contracting strategies. The secretary's strategic alignment team reinforced the contract reform team's recommendations by emphasizing downsizing, cost controls, and alternative contract mechanisms. Thus, contracting out represents a privatization strategy that directly flows from and effectively complements reform efforts aimed primarily at the traditional M&O contracting system.

Environmental Management's (EM) privatization approach currently has two key elements. First, privatization uses fixed-price contracts under which the contractor is paid a fixed amount for acceptable goods and services regardless of the costs the contractor incurs. Second, privatization contractors are expected to provide private financing for the construction of facilities, if needed, to produce the final product EM is buying. The privatization program receives a separate appropriation to cover the capital investment portion of these contracts. However, in the event the contract is terminated by the government before completion, the privatization funding will be used to reimburse the contractor for its capital investment. If the contract is continued through completion, the privatization funding will be used to repay the capital investment as acceptable goods or services are provided (U.S. General Accounting Office 1998a). Although this is the current approach to privatization, according to DOE officials, EM's privatization program will continue to evolve over time as DOE learns more through evaluating actual business proposals (U.S. Department of Energy 1997b).

The privatization program was first funded in 1997, when the Congress appropriated $330 million to support five projects. In 1998, the Congress provided an additional $200 million for one existing and four new projects. The 1999 budget request included about $517 million to continue work on ongoing projects at Hanford, Idaho, and Oak Ridge, and one new transportation project administered by the Carlsbad Area Office (U.S. General Accounting Office 1998a). The 2000 budget proposes $228 million to continue the privatization projects at the above mentioned facilities (U.S. Office of Management and Budget 1999). The EM privatization program relies on private financing for the acquisition of needed cleanup facilities and equipment. Under this approach, the contractor will own all facilities required to deliver the desired cleanup services. The contractor is responsible for all construction costs, including the development of technologies, procurement of equipment, and new-facility construction. In addition, the contractor is expected to finance these construction costs until the facilities are completed and operations begin. Financing cost includes the raising of money, paying taxes, and making profit. As the contractor begins to deliver cleanup services, it is paid for its operating costs. In addition, each year the contractor is paid a portion of the construction and financing costs it has incurred until these costs are eventually recouped. These payments for the contractor's construction and financing costs are directly tied to the amount of cleanup services it provides (U.S. General Accounting Office 1998a). Total private financing represents only one end of a continuum of construction financing options. Total government financing, as traditionally used in EM's cost-reimbursement management contracts, represents the opposite end of the continuum. Under total government financing, contractors are paid as costs are incurred, eliminating the need to arrange private financing to carry these costs. The performance risk faced by the contractor is also low because payment is based on costs incurred, not for performance of cleanup services.[21] The government, through EM, bears the bulk of the performance risk (U.S. General Accounting Office 1998a). In between these two extremes, other financing options exist that attempt to strike a balance between financing costs and performance risk. The government could guarantee all or some portion of the total private debt for construction financing (it constitutes about 70 percent of the total financing required) which can lower the interest rate on borrowing, thus significantly lowering the contractor's financing costs. Another option that may be available is a partial-payment plan that is tied to the contractor's performance. Under this option, the government would pay for a portion of the construction costs as they are incurred, while the contractor would be required to finance the balance until it began operations. Then, as in the private financing option, the government would make payments based on the performance of cleanup services—such as the amount of waste processed—that would allow the contractor to recoup its construction costs plus its financing costs. Another alternative is for the government to make progress or partial payments to cover the costs as they are incurred while the contractor would be required to finance the balance of its costs. This option is similar to the performance-based partial-payment plan; however, under the progress payment option, the contractor would recoup its construction costs plus its financing costs as the cleanup facility (asset) is successfully completed. Payment to the contractor for construction would not be based on performance over an initial operations period. Financing costs are expected to be lower because the contractor would not carry its construction costs over a period of operations (U.S. General Accounting Office 1998a).

Assessment

The options that lie between total private financing and total government financing attempt to strike a balance in the trade-off between the cost of financing and the cost of added performance risk. Although the cost of added performance risk to the government is difficult to quantify, it still must be considered in weighing any decision to reduce private sector risk (thereby increasing government risk) by lowering financing costs.

Besides performance risk, the choice of financing options is affected by other factors that should be considered in financing decisions. As government involvement in financing increases, the government assumes more of an ownership role and has to exercise more oversight. As the government provides more financing of construction costs, it becomes more likely that EM will be the owner of the facility instead of the contractor. This ownership is a positive benefit of government financing that addresses monopoly concerns of private ownership. If the private sector owns a facility whose construction costs are paid for after an initial period of operations, it could place the private sector in a monopolistic position for the remainder of the potential operating period. Government ownership, however, requires extensive oversight. According to the U.S. General Accounting Office (1994, 1995a, 1996c, 1998a), DOE has a very poor history of oversight, and in addition to that, the private sector views increased government oversight as meddlesome, inefficient, costly, and something that runs against market mechanisms.

More importantly, the actual terms of performance in the contract will dictate what performance risk is eventually assumed by the contractor and the government. The mix of financing provided by the government and the private sector has no bearing on the actual terms of performance that are agreed to in the contract. Risks must be identified and addressed in the contract so that each party's responsibilities are clearly defined. The government could face more risk and incur more costs from a contract that is totally privately financed if the terms of the contract give the contractor less responsibility for risks compared to another contract that may have government financing.

In 1997 DOE conducted a survey that identified 234 potential privatization opportunities (U.S. Department of Energy 1997a). These proposals were grouped by privatization type (asset transfer, divestiture, and contracting out) and functional areas (e.g., facility operations, personnel support, and alternative financing). Opportunities for contracting out far outnumber other privatization opportunities. This is not unexpected considering the long history that DOE has of purchasing goods and services from the private sector. As the above discussion has shown, however, contracting out has various dimensions.

Next, I will look at one of those dimensions—the Pit 9 privatization pilot effort — and discuss its implications for the DOE privatization direction.

Pit 9: A Study of Privatization Site Background

The Idaho National Engineering and Environmental Laboratory (INEEL) is an 890 square mile federal facility operated by DOE, whose mission was nuclear reactor technology development during the Cold War. Today, INEEL, as many other nuclear weapons complex sites, is primarily engaged in waste management and cleanup activities. INEEL's Radioactive Waste Management Complex (RWMC) is located in the southwestern portion of the site. For 40 years the RWMC has been the primary location at INEEL for disposal and management of low-level and transuranic radioactive waste, including mixed waste (chemically hazardous). The complex includes an area where wastes are stored aboveground (the Transuranic Storage Area). The Subsurface Disposal Area (SDA), however, is the major area of environmental concern at the RWMC and the entire INEEL. SDA is a collection of pits and trenches that have been used for many years for the disposal of radioactive wastes. Prior to 1970, DOE also used SDA to bury solid transuranic wastes containing long-lived radiation with half-lives of thousands of years, such as plutonium. This practice was halted in 1970 but the wastes buried at SDA await environmental cleanup (Smith 1997).

Pit 9, at about 380 feet wide by 125 feet long, represents approximately one acre of the surface area of the 88-acre SDA. The pit contains about 350,000 cubic feet of soil beneath and between the buried waste and approximately 250,000 cubic feet of overburden soil. The average depth of the pit from soil surface to bedrock is approximately 17.5 feet. It was used by DOE for radioactive and hazardous waste disposal from November 1967 through June 1969. Approximately 110,000 cubic feet of transuranic (TRU) contaminated mixed wastes from the Rocky Flats Plant in Colorado and approximately 40,000 cubic feet of low-level and mixed wastes from INEEL were buried in Pit 9 during that period. Most of these wastes were placed in an estimated 4,000 drums, 2,500 boxes, and 80 unspecified containers. Pit 9 is estimated to contain over 30,000 gallons of organics (over 30 percent of the total organic inventory in the SDA) and approximately 66 pounds of TRU radionuclides (between 3 and 4 percent of the total TRU inventory in the SDA) (Schwartz 1995, Smith 1997). Pit 9 lies above Idaho's Snake River Plain Aquifer, a sole source aquifer 580 feet beneath the landfill.

In November 1989, the Environmental Protection Agency (EPA) added the INEEL, including the SDA, to CERCLA's National Priority List (NPL) thus giving it Superfund site notoriety. Starting in 1991, DOE and its regulators— EPA and the state of Idaho— began exploring ways to remediate Pit 9 (U.S. General Accounting Office 1997b). In December 1991, DOE, EPA and the state of Idaho signed a federal facility agreement (FFA) and consent order (CO) to govern the cleanup activities at INEEL. The Pit 9 cleanup was designed to be performed as an interim action under Superfund.[22] Soil and waste were to be retrieved from the pit, those materials that could be returned to the pit without treatment were to be separated, the remaining soil and wastes were to be treated to achieve at least a 90 percent reduction in volume, and the remaining concentrated materials were to be packaged for on-site storage until final disposal.

In its previous cost-reimbursement practices, DOE would tell the M&O contractor how to perform waste-related cleanup activities, and reimburse the contractor for all incurred costs (e.g., labor, materials, overhead, subcontractor costs, legal fees), which were negotiated under the specific contract provisions, regardless of any completed cleanup. In contrast, DOE decided to use a fixed-price approach in contracting out the Pit 9 cleanup activities. Private industry had been marketing capabilities to treat DOE's buried waste, and DOE proposed a demonstration scale project at Pit 9 to evaluate those technologies. A private contractor would finance, design, build, own and operate any required waste cleanup facilities, and DOE would pay the contractor only for a successful cleanup. Under a fixed-price contract, the contractor is paid a specified amount that is not subject to adjustment on the basis of the contractor's actual costs. However, under certain conditions, the contractor can request an adjustment to the contract price for work that is done outside the scope of the original contract. Such an adjustment is subject to review and approval by DOE and results in a contract modification if approved (U.S. General Accounting Office 1997b).

Besides the fixed-price contract option, DOE decided to have its contractor, EG&G Idaho, Inc., conduct the procurement process, select the subcontractor, and oversee the contractor's efforts at Pit 9. The decision was based on the notion that DOE lacked the in-house capabilities to evaluate the technical proposals and oversee their implementation, and considered EG&G to possess the necessary expertise and to be better suited for the task. In addition, DOE considered Pit 9 to fall under EG&G's area of responsibility and wanted the M&O contractor to exercise oversight. Also, DOE believed that subcontracting through EG&G would simplify and streamline the procurement process and would allow for easier implementation of the best private market practices.

In 1991, DOE authorized its M&O contractor to start the procurement process and select a subcontractor. The Pit 9 cleanup was to be conducted in three phases. The first included a technical review of the results of prior projects to verify that the proposed remedial systems were effective. Then a limited production test was to be conducted on a smaller scale to verify that the system worked as designed (phase II). Finally, full scale operations were to be resumed (phase III).

About 50 private companies responded to EG&G's initial call for proposals. The company issued a draft request for proposal (RFP) to qualified firms, held a preproposal conference to discuss the project in detail, conducted a tour of the site and consequently revised the draft RFP to incorporate comments from potential project candidates. The final RFP was

complete on the retrieval facility and approximately 60-65 percent complete on the treatment building. Design was approximately 90 percent complete on all systems except the soil sorter and the chemical leach systems, which are integral to waste treatment, and their completion hovered around the 25 percent mark (Pit 9 Fresh Eyes Team Report 1997). On the basis of its reported actual costs of $197.2 million through December 1996, LMAES estimated its total reimbursable costs to be $257.4 million by June 30, 1997.[28] For any work conducted after April 1, 1997, LMAES asked to convert the existing subcontract to give it a cost-reimbursement basis. LMAES estimated that the total cost of the project could reach $600 million with an 80 percent confidence level, or $517 million with a 50 percent confidence level. In any case, those estimates were well above the original $200 million stated value of the subcontract.

DOE had also incurred additional costs related to Pit 9. For example, it had paid $23.1 million for Phase I testing and preliminary design activities, $12.35 million for project oversight by the M&O contractor, and about $3 million for DOE oversight costs. DOE was also fined $970,000[29] by its regulators—the state of Idaho and EPA—for failure to meet enforceable deadlines as stipulated in the federal facility agreement (FFA) and consent order (CO) for the Idaho Falls site. In addition, DOE was responsible for all legal fees that its M&O contractor had been incurring ever since contract difficulties surfaced.

Subcontractor's Difficulties with Pit 9

On March 28, 1997, LMAES submitted a request for equitable adjustment (REA) to DOE and LMITCO in which it provided its rationale for the delay in the project's completion. The factors that LMAES pointed out for the cost and schedule problems can be grouped into three main categories: (1) misadministration of the fixed-price subcontract; (2) intrusive interference with the fast-track project delivery; and (3) changing estimates of the pit contents.

Privatization Design Misadministration. According to Albert Narath, President, Energy and Environment Sector of the Lockheed Martin Corporation, LMAES bid the Pit 9 project based on the assumptions that Pit 9 would be a well-defined project with stable requirements and specifications, and minimal government involvement, and that "LMAES would have the sufficient authority and discretion to engineer, procure, construct and operate the Pit 9 facilities essentially as a commercial project" (Narath 1997, 153). The company's assumptions for minimal government oversight and administration were based on subcontract specifications which indicated Pit 9 to be an "integrated 'turnkey' pilot" effort, with the "subcontractor assuming maximum responsibility, authority, and liability." Thus, LMAES expected to be able to follow a results-oriented approach by employing the best commercial practices and its own judgments and discretion for cleanup completion.

In contrast, LMAES claims that Pit 9 was not administered as a fixed-price subcontract but rather the company endured "substantial and intrusive control in virtually every aspect of the design and construction of the retrieval and processing equipment and facilities" (Narath 1997, 153). Under the privatization agreement, LMAES was to construct, own, and operate the facilities and accept the financial risk by providing a guarantee that payment for its services would depend on successful remediation of the wastes. However, LMAES officials believe that DOE administered the project as if DOE itself was incurring the risks. As evidence LMAES points out that between January 1995 and July 1996, DOE and its M&O contractor made more than 7,000 detailed review comments on the firm's construction and facilities designs. The excessive oversight and the expectation for LMAES to incorporate every review suggestion into its operational design slowed the process and hindered the ability of the company to exercise flexibility.

Fast Track Project Delivery. DOE's approach also limited the company's ability to respond to the extraordinary pressures of a fast-track project, according to LMAES officials. Fast-track, phased construction requires design and construction to proceed on contemporaneous, parallel tracks. Design and construction are broken into several discrete packages and completed in phases. As soon as the design is completed for part of the project, construction work on that portion of the project begins. For example, LMAES began construction of the treatment building before the design for the chemical treatment system was finalized. LMAES, DOE and the other parties agreed on this approach in order to comply with the construction schedule specified in the December 6, 1993, request for price proposal for phases II and III of the project, which included a required January 1, 1995, date to start "staging and installation." The request for price proposal also specified that the subcontract to remediate Pit 9 would be awarded on June 1, 1994. The subcontract was not effective until August 1994, and LMAES claims the delay risked achieving the mandatory January 1, 1995, date for the start of construction.

The fast-track approach required that the subcontractor be allowed a great deal of discretion in determining the manner, means, and methods of meeting the project's price and scheduling deadlines. LMAES contends, however, that DOE's oversight and involvement were so excessive that they removed all discretion in the project's implementation. For example, LMAES argues that about one-quarter of the 2,500 safety-related review comments were inappropriate for a fast-track project because they were attributable to the fact that design of facilities was progressing simultaneously with construction (U.S. General Accounting Office 1997b). DOE also failed to provide those review comments in a timely manner, claims LMAES. The agreement called for DOE to provide feedback on plans and designs within 30 days, and based on LMAES' analysis the average review response was 53 days.

Contents of the Pit. The subcontractor says that its proposed remediation technology and price were based on the preaward Pit 9 inventories provided by the government. After award of the subcontract, several additional disclosures concerning Pit 9 contents were made. For example, significant pit inventory data were disclosed on February 22, 1995, and again on February 20, 1996. LMAES claims that although those postaward inventories were submitted to the company as "for information only," the new content data were so extensively different from the preaward representations as to materially affect the treatment system's design.

DOE admits that it had limited information on the actual contents of the pit. At the time (the late 1960s) when wastes were buried in Pit 9, DOE did not intend to retrieve them and thus did not create a tracking record. Few actual records were kept and no precise information existed about the actual content of the pit. However, in 1991, the M&O contractor attempted to create an estimate of the waste based on available shipping records, process knowledge, written documentation and other information from DOE. In 1993, the M&O contractor initiated an effort to broaden its information for its baseline risk assessment for all the disposal pits and trenches in the SDA, including Pit 9. The content record for the pit was revised several times, and LMAES cites multiple instances in which the content record changes induced substantial changes in the remediation design. For example, in February 1995, DOE and its M&O contractor provided LMAES with updated information that the level of salts, organics, and radioactive activation and fission products were considerably higher than initially estimated. These materials would slow the speed of the plasma melter, which was a key element of the treatment process. In addition, the new estimates of radioactive materials increased the potential for workers' exposure to radiation. In 1996, LMAES received another updated revision of the radioactive elements in the waste. These estimates indicated higher quantities of cobalt 60 and cesium 137, both of which emit radiation in the form of gamma rays.[30] LMAES claims that its original remediation designs did not include such high levels of radioactive materials and subsequently needed to be changed, which again resulted in scheduling delays and additional costs.

U.S. Department of Energy and Its Management and Operations Contractor's Difficulties with Pit 9

According to DOE and its M&O contractor, their oversight has been related to ensuring adequate consideration of environmental safety and health. Although a fixed-price approach shifts the risk of nonperformance to the subcontractor, DOE still retained some of the risks. For example, the subcontract indemnified LMAES in the case of a catastrophic nuclear accident; it remained DOE's responsibility. DOE, LMITCO and their regulators argue that the LMAES personnel lacked adequate expertise and knowledge about necessary regulatory requirements for dealing with nuclear materials, which resulted in ill-prepared construction and treatment designs and called for stricter than anticipated oversight by DOE and its M&O contractor.

For example, DOE points out that the retrieval building was designed by a company called SONSUB, which had little nuclear experience. LMAES planned for SONSUB to be the operator of the facility as well, but the company had never operated in a nuclear environment. The initial design of double confinement to some systems and structures had been changed in the course of construction thus increasing the likelihood of possible release of contaminates into the atmosphere. In addition, the chemical treatment system was assembled with serious safety-related inadequacies. In effect, it was a standard piping system without consideration of the nuclear environment of Pit 9. The piping was subject to leaks at the joints, and more significantly, susceptible to "criticality" accidents; i.e., it had the potential for radioactive materials to be brought together in sufficient concentrations to sustain a nuclear chain reaction. The piping also lacked a mechanism to track the radioactive materials that were moving in the chemical treatment process.

DOE acknowledges that the large number of comments made it more difficult for LMAES to accomplish the fast-track schedule, but disagrees that they were slow in providing review comments. Most of the LMAES submittals were incomplete to begin with and the review period should not have started until a complete document was received.

Contents of the Pit. DOE and its M&O contractor argue that LMAES overplays the significance of the updated information they received about the pit's inventory. It was not a formal revision of the contractual estimate of the contents, and therefore LMAES had discretion whether to use it or not. In addition, the initial subcontract proposal submitted by LMAES stated that its treatment system was "very robust, in that any chemical, radiological, or physical characteristic of waste in Pit 9 can be successfully processed" (quoted in Rezendes 1997, 12), and that it can handle other buried or stored transuranic and transuranic mixed wastes as well as low-level mixed wastes and hazardous wastes in the DOE complex. LMAES was confident in its treatment approach and agreed to a clause in the subcontract which allowed for future adjustments in the site conditions, such as different than estimated pit contents.

Mismanagement and Lack of Technical Expertise. When awarding the subcontract, DOE and its M&O contractor were operating under the assumption that Lockheed would employ its vast worldwide resources to provide the necessary management and technical expertise to cleanup the pit. This never happened, claim DOE and LMITCO officials. In a 1995 peer review of LMAES' Pit 9 activities, Lockheed reported that the personnel lacked sufficient expertise in the areas of nuclear materials handling and environmental safety and health oversight during construction and operation. Similar findings were reported in a DOE assessment at that time (U.S. General Accounting Office 1997b).The high turnover of LMAES staff was indicated as another reason for the lack of progress on the project — there had been four project managers as of May 1997. LMAES explains that the increased complexity of the requirements in the administrative approach used by DOE and LMITCO created a need for managers with broader experience. The last assigned manager, for example, was one of the most respected within Lockheed Martin. Those frequent changes in leadership DOE asserts, left important decisions unaddressed for lengthy periods of time. For example, it was not until February 1997 that LMAES developed a complete system requirements document, which compiles the system performance and design requirements of the subcontract into one part.

Implications

The Pit 9 project has proven to be a failure. Not a single ounce of waste has been removed from the site since the subcontract was signed. While the courts untangle the legal dispute, privatization still remains a viable and preferred option for DOE in its nuclear waste cleanup efforts.

Although DOE acknowledges the failure of its pilot project, it still insists that valuable lessons can be drawn from that particular experience, and fixed-price contracting is the "direction to go in" (Rezendes 1997, 13).

DOE points out two other fixed-price projects (two laundry facilities at Hanford and Idaho Falls) which were very successful in their implementation. The difference between them and Pit 9, however, is that the work scope was clearly defined in the former example, and there were very few unquantifiable uncertainties. That was not the case with Pit 9. As the brief historical overview has shown, the pit inventory was a major stumbling block in the way of the treatment design and construction. In addition, DOE signed a subcontract without proven test results. Even after spending $8 million on the proof-of-process testing, LMAES still had missing links in the complete treatment design that were left for future configuration. The major problem, however, was the failure of both sides to comprehend the organizational restraints to which each was subjected, and to communicate those cultural differences to the other side.

Although DOE had tried to shift the performance risk to its subcontractor, the ultimate risk of a major catastrophic occurrence remained within the department. The buck stopped at DOE; it was DOE's responsibility to guarantee the final cleanup in accordance with safety and environmental regulations. Pit 9 was subject to various provisions of the following public laws and regulations.[31]

- Hazardous Waste Facility Siting Act.
- Idaho Air Pollution Control Program.
- Resource Conservation and Recovery Act (RCRA).
- Idaho Hazardous Waste Management Act.
- Toxic Substances Control Act (TSCA).
- Superfund Amendments and Reauthorization Act (SARA).
- Emergency Planning and Right to Know Act.
- Clean Water Act — National Pollutant Discharge Elimination System.
- National Emission Standards for Hazardous Air Pollutants Authorization.
- Atomic Energy Act.
- Radiological Safety and Health.
- Occupational Safety and Health.

LMAES understood that its activities at Pit 9 would be scrutinized in terms of state and federal environmental and safety rules, but their extent and complexity was either ignored or underestimated in the subcontract negotiations.

Dealing with this particular set of laws and regulations is an every-day business for DOE; it was not for LMAES. However, it was not only the lack of knowledge that led it to accept the terms of the subcontract. Lockheed Martin had no previous experience with nuclear waste but was eager to expand its activities into what it expected to turn into a profitable market niche in the near future. The company was positioning itself to become a major player in the lucrative, $250-350 billion nuclear waste cleanup business. The fixed-price contract seemed to provide the needed flexibility and LMAES was optimistic that it could get the job done with a profit margin. In addition to that, the site M&O contractor was a sister company and LMAES expected to lower some of its costs by sharing per-sonnel and information. What seemed a straightforward process— dig-ging out waste, reprocessing it, and either packaging it for storage or returning it — turned into a managerial and technical quagmire for the subcontractor.

DOE made LMAES its subcontractor despite the fact that the com-pany did not meet the three selection process technical criteria: it had no remediation experience; its personnel was underqualified in nuclear waste; and the treatment system had never been proven or demonstrated. One explanation is that DOE was under pressure both from private industry and "less-government" political drives. Private industry claimed that it possessed "robust" cleanup technology and the administration expected significant savings from the privatized projects.

Unequivocally, the subcontract contained a certain degree of vague-ness, misunderstanding and dissonance between what DOE assumed was in the subcontract and what LMAES thought it was taking as a subcon-tract responsibility. Both sides failed to convey properly their view and expectations. DOE took at face value assurances from Lockheed that it was capable of remediation with existing technologies. Having a guarantee from such a formidable corporation as Lockheed seemed to clear the way for a successful project completion. After all, as one of the Lockheed pres-idents put it: "We sent a rocket to Mars, we can clean a pit." Lockheed expected a degree of discretion that was never realized. Without prior experience in fixed-price contracting, DOE faced a lose-lose oversight sit-uation. It approached the subcontract with the intention of providing as little oversight as possible. In a November 16, 1994, letter, to its regula-tors, the state of Idaho and EPA, DOE even urged that "direct contact between the agencies [i.e., DOE, EPA and Idaho] and LMAES be kept to an absolute minimum" (Green 1994, 1). Red flags were ignored all along the way (e.g., DOE had a very negative experience with concurrent design and construction projects; it took LMAES two years into the project to submit a systems baseline requirements document[32]). At the same time, it was DOE's responsibility to guarantee that environmental and safety regulations were followed. Thus, DOE's intentions to allow the subcontractor as much flexibility as possible conflicted with its responsibilities under the federal facilities agreement and consent order that the agency had signed with EPA and the state of Idaho. The crucial element here, however, is the subcontractor's knowledge and experience. Probably, the process would have worked well if LMAES had had extensive nuclear waste disposal experience and realized fully what the process implied, not only from a technical point of view, but also regarding government regulations and community relations. Without going into further finger-pointing, what surfaces is a clear picture of poor subcontracting decision making, before and after the subcontract was awarded. Does this mean, however, that DOE should turn away from fixed-price contracting and go back to its old M&O financing practices? Are the differences between DOE and the private sector forever irreconcilable?

Because of its lack of in-house capabilities, DOE does not really have a choice but to rely on the private sector for its on-ground activities. Starting with the Manhattan Project, the nuclear weapons complex was run by private contractors. Pit 9 has not been a complete failure,[33] in that it has actually provided some important lessons for DOE. One of the recent examples is the $1.18 billion contract INEEL negotiated with British Nuclear Fuels, Inc., (BNFL) for the remediation of its Advanced Mixed Waste Treatment Project (AMWTP).[34]

The contract again is a fixed-price one: BNFL will fund the $270 million construction costs with DOE paying a fixed price for successfully treated waste as the facility comes on line in 2003. However, the contract includes a clause for progressive payments to be made by DOE to offset some of the capital investment expenses of the company. The payments, however, are to be made after BNFL has completed phases in the process as indicated in the contract. DOE signed a direct contract with BNFL, rather than a subcontract. The company has an extensive nuclear waste remediation experience[35] in the United Kingdom and all over the world, and possesses a proven technology system to clean up mixed wastes. From the initial construction and design stages, the company has assigned a management team with proven expertise in nuclear waste decommissioning. In addition to that, BNFL has not only signed a corporate guarantee to indemnify the government if it does not meet the expected performance levels but has also accepted responsibility to "develop an environmental safety and health (ES&H) requirements document from existing laws, regulations, court or consent orders, and DOE directives with assistance and input as appropriate by DOE" (Contract No. DE-AC07-97ID13481, J-D-3), and apply directly to regulatory agencies for the applicable permits. In contrast to the Pit 9 subcontract, DOE has not only shifted the responsibility to the contractor to have all ES&H requirements in place, but also clearly communicated what the oversight requirements were.

A similar example of lessons learned and heightened attention paid to contract negotiations and setup is provided by the DOE experience at its Hanford Tank Waste Project. The project, as currently envisioned, is substantially different from DOE's 1996 initial privatization strategy. Although the project award was made on the basis of a fixed-price contract, further competition between contractors and short-term demonstration facilities have been eliminated in favor of more permanent facilities that could operate for 30 years or more. In addition, the design phase as well as the date when DOE and BNFL's (BNFL is the project contractor) are to reach agreement on final contract price, were extended by two years to August 2000. BNFL's specific project financing arrangements, which were to be established in May 1998, were deferred until August 2000. In addition, to ensure that BNFL can obtain affordable private financing, DOE has agreed to repay much of the project debt if BNFL defaults on its loans and DOE terminates the contract. This is an unusual feature of the fixed-price contracting which burdens DOE with substantial financial and performance responsibility. DOE has agreed to assume this risk because it did not think that BNFL would be able to obtain affordable financing unless the government provided some assurance that the loans would be repaid (U.S. General Accounting Office 1998b).

In part, because of the Pit 9 failure, DOE has paid considerable attention to developing an approach to overseeing BNFL's operations. For example, to resolve procedural and other issues that may come up, DOE required BNFL to establish four teams specifically covering project management, contract and finance matters, interfaces and environment, safety, and health-related issues. To help with the complicated interrelationships between DOE and its contractors, it has followed a systems engineering process that involves using "interface control documents" for those areas where it or the site contractor has interrelationships with the BNFL contract. The contract also ensures DOE's access to key information. For example, BNFL will be conducting numerous tests to ensure that its treatment processes will work. In addition, DOE has subjected its entire management process to both internal and external review (U.S. General Accounting Office 1998b).

As these examples show, DOE has made serious attempts to update its privatization approach and learn from its pilot efforts at Pit 9. It tries to identify possible unknowns ahead of time and to deal with surfacing problems in a timely manner. Recent developments also indicate that privatization as a management tool has serious potential when employed while considering the overall conditions under which it is used. However, they also show that privatization is not a panacea for what constitutes one of the most serious problems facing the nation.

Conclusion

The failed effort to remediate Pit 9 exemplifies the complexity of the nuclear waste disposal problem. Begun with great enthusiasm both on the part of DOE and the private subcontractor, the pilot project failed to meet expectations. Although it is up to the courts to decide who was at fault, my analysis indicates that both sides approached the subcontract with a series of unfounded assumptions which were mainly due to a lack of a clear understanding of the institutional constraints that each side was laboring under. Lockheed Martin approached the subcontract as a private venture: achieve performance results with the most efficient means available. Although DOE seconded that approach, defining how exactly to reach that goal is where differences arose. DOE had to ensure the compliance of the project with numerous state and federal environmental and safety laws and regulations although LMAES was the one actually performing work on site. Hindsight would say that it was a poorly drafted subcontract. Not only that, but LMAES should not have been subcontracted in the first place. The company failed to meet all three technical criteria that DOE imposed. The fact that the number of interested companies dropped from 50 to 18, and then only three of them actually submitted proposals should have raised serious concerns. DOE has had a bad experience with fast-track delivery systems before. The fact that same design, was never tested as an assembly, was exacerbated by the proposed company having no nuclear waste disposal expertise. The subcontract should not have been signed at all.

Some recent examples indicate that DOE is incorporating the Pit 9 experience into its privatization strategy. The nuclear waste disposal problem has too many complex facets which require greater public and private ingenuity than the one which created the nuclear weapons complex in the first place.

What emerges is a situation where DOE has to do a balancing act between performance and risk. Presently, it is engaging the full spectrum of alternative financing and contracting options. Clearly, the government has to guarantee the initial capital investments or assume a certain degree of financial responsibility if cleanup is to be accomplished. As the experience with BNFL shows, very few companies would be willing to take such a big capital investment risk. In addition, the number of companies with sufficient nuclear remediation expertise is limited. Most recent DOE contracts have been awarded to only one company, BNFL, which seems to be emerging as DOE's "darling" at this point. If this trend is sustained, serious monopolistic concerns could arise, undermining the theoretical justification for market solutions to the nuclear waste disposal problem.

In addition, the Pit 9 experience reveals that a different approach to the technological uncertainty is required for fixed-price contracts to work. The private sector lacks readily available, off-the-shelf technologies to remediate nuclear waste. Since those technologies are in different stages of development, more elements of R&D contracts need to be incorporated into future contractual arrangements between DOE and the private sector. DOE has a substantial experience in technology development projects. For example, in 1996, it and the private sector were involved in more than 500 cost-shared projects[36] aimed at developing a broad spectrum of cost-effective, energy-efficient technologies in the areas of environmental protection, economic competitiveness and energy resources use. Universities and national laboratories also participate in many of these government-industry collaborations. Most of the projects that involve technology development beyond basic research are funded under cost-shared contracts, cooperative arrangements, and cooperative research and development agreements (CRADAs) (U.S. General Accounting Office 1996b). An analogous experience that could be utilized by DOE exists in the Department of Defense (DOD), which spent about $1.25 billion in 1995 for research, development, engineering, and analytical services from the ten federally funded research and development centers (FFRDCs) it sponsors (U.S. General Accounting Office 1995d).

The new privatization effort at DOE is still too incipient for any definite conclusions about its failure or success to be drawn. What Pit 9 and other examples[37] indicate is that a pure market approach to the nuclear waste disposal problem is not a viable option. Yet, privatization's potentiality, in one form or another, to tackle the environmental legacy of the Cold War is undeniable. Harnessing private energies to public purposes, however, can be a difficult exercise in contractual architecture. It would be reckless to claim that private delivery is any sweeping remedy for the fundamental complexity of what remains essentially an overwhelmingly public challenge. That brings back the old theoretical proposition of finding the appropriate public-private mix to address social problems.

Endnotes

1. BNFL estimates the market to grow to this figure by the early part of the next century. The amount is in 1995 dollars.

2. BNFL estimates the market to grow to this figure by the early part of the next century. The amount is in 1995 dollars.

3. In 1939, Nobel Prize–winning physicist Niels Bohr argued that building an atomic bomb "can never be done unless you turn the United States into one huge factory." Years later, he told his colleague Edward Teller, "I told you it couldn't be done without turning the whole country into a factory. You have done just that" (qtd. in DOE 1996, 2).

4. The main mission of AEC was administration and regulation of the production and uses of all atomic power: from building a stockpile of nuclear weapons to peaceful uses of atomic energy.

5. Mining and milling involve extracting uranium ore from the earth's crust and chemically processing it to prepare uranium concentrate. Uranium concentrates are then refined, or chemically converted to purified forms suitable as feed materials for the next step in the process.

6. Enrichment is the process of separating naturally occurring isotopes of the same element.

7. The process consists of the foundry and machine shop operations required to convert uranium feed material, principally metal, into fuel and target elements used in nuclear materials production reactors.

8. Reactor operations include fuel and target loading and removal, reactor maintenance, and the operation of the reactor itself.

9. Chemical separation is the process of dissolving spent nuclear fuel and targets and isolating and concentrating the plutonium, uranium, and other nuclear materials they contain.

10. Weapons component fabrication includes the manufacturing, assembly, inspection, bench testing, and verification of specialized nuclear and nonnuclear parts and major subassemblies.

11. Includes the assembly, maintenance, and dismantlement of nuclear weapons. Assembly is the final process of joining together separately manufactured components and major parts into complete, functional, and certified nuclear weapon warheads for delivery to the Department of Defense (DOD).

12. RD&T includes the design, development, and testing of nuclear weapons and their effects. It takes place concurrently with the other seven processes. Research and development are mostly complete before component fabrication begins, but testing may continue until a weapon system is retired from the stockpile (DOE 1997b, 117).

13. The term refers to solids and liquids that are radioactive, hazardous or both. That particular waste is only one element in all the "waste streams" generated before 1992 by the nuclear weapons complex. The other three are: contaminated environmental media, which includes soils, groundwater, surface water,

sediments, debris, and other materials; surplus facilities once used for nuclear weapons production that are no longer needed and are slated to be deactivated and decommissioned; and materials in inventory, which includes all materials not used in the past year and not expected to be used in the upcoming year (DOE 1997a).

14. Defined as such under section 11e(2) of the AEA as amended by Title II of the Uranium Mill Tailings Radiation Control Act of 1978.

15. A curie is a unit of radioactivity expressed in terms of nuclear disintegration per second. It provides a measure of the immediate radioactive emission of the radionuclides in the waste, but it does not take into account the type of particles or amount of energy released per disintegration or the shielding effect of the waste's physical matrix (The League of Women Voters Education Fund 1993).

16. According to DOE data, all high-level waste remains in storage — except for about one million gallons that has leaked from storage tanks at Hanford, Washington (1997a, 32)!

17. In Circulars A-120 and A-76, OMB defines governmental function as one that is so intimately related to the public interest that it must be administered by the government. The key principle to adhere to is that the government should not contract out its responsibilities to serve the public interest or to exercise its sovereign powers. A key criterion in determining whether service contracts are appropriate is whether the government maintains sufficient in-house capability to be thoroughly in control of the policy, decision making, and management functions of the agency. In a 1991 study, GAO found the term to be rather nebulous and difficult to define in practical applications.

18. An area greater in size that the District of Columbia and the states of Delaware and Rhode Island combined.

19. Roughly an annual production output of a large chemical manufacturer.

20. The "make/buy" decision-making process analyzes whether it is beneficial for the government to *make* a good or provide a service instead of *buying* it from outside sources.

21. The DOE's traditional cost-reimbursement contracts may include an award fee that is dependent on the performance of the contractor. However, typical award fees in DOE's cost-reimbursement contracts represent a small percentage of the total value of any single contract (GAO 1998a).

22. Interim action is not necessarily a final cleanup action. Interim actions are remedial actions taken at Superfund sites to accelerate the overall cleanup and reduce the risks associated with site contaminations.

23. The teams had to demonstrate that (1) they had substantial experience in treating plutonium and americium contaminated materials, (2) had access to lab facilities capable of analyzing radioactive, hazardous and mixed wastes, and (3) that they had an established environmental, safety, and health program.

24. Those technical criteria are: (1) technical feasibility of the remediation approach (i.e., best technologies availability), (2) personnel's demonstrated experience and qualifications, and (3) ability to meet schedule and budget requirements.

25. When Lockheed merged with Martin Marietta, the entity assumed the name of Lockheed Martin Advanced Environmental Systems (LMAES).

26. EG&G Idaho, Inc. was the M&O contractor when the privatization process was initiated. In 1994, however, when the M&O contract came up for renewal, Lockheed won the competitive bidding. LITCO became the new M&O contractor in October 1994, but later it merged with Martin Marietta and assumed the name of Lockheed Martin Idaho Technologies Company (LMITCO).

27. By this date LMAES was supposed to retrieve and process all wastes from the pit, return untreated soil to the pit, decontaminate and decommission the retrieval and treatment facilities, and remove its retrieval facility from the site.

28. LMAES asked for $158.1 million in payments in addition to the $52.9 million already received through March 1997. LMAES expected an additional $46.4 million to be recovered through future milestone payments or some other method (GAO 1997b).

29. Of the $970,000, $870,000 was set aside in trust for the purposes of Supplemental Environmental Projects. The other $100,000 was specially appropriated by Congress under the terms of the FFA/CO and paid to the EPA Superfund. Of the $100,000 penalty, $40,000 was because INEEL missed an enforceable milestone on Test Area North (TAN); not all of it was attributable to Pit 9.

30. Gamma rays are the strongest of the three forms of radioactivity and thus require special shielding to protect personnel from exposure.

31. They fall under the jurisdiction of three main agencies: Idaho Department of Health and Welfare, Division of Environmental Quality; Environmental Protection Agency Region 10; and Department of Energy.

32. A final paper with the complete design systems and costs associated to help managers better plan tasks and activities.

33. It can also be argued, as Federico Peña did, that if the old M&O financing system had been used, the government would have lost close to $200 million dollars (the amount that LMAES has spent), rather than the $58 million which has been spent so far. DOE is attempting to recoupe the $58 million in the litigation action.

34. Contains 65,000 cubic meters of mixed radioactive contaminated material — transuranic waste mixed with hazardous chemicals.

35. BNFL was established in 1971.

36. These are expected to cost more than $15 billion by the time of their completion; DOE plans to fund about $8 billion and the industry is to cover the balance (GAO 1996b)

37. Recently DOE announced a $373 million privatization initiative for its depleted uranium program. The issue has proven to be thorny; however, as one consultant who has worked on the matter for years put it, "to say it's not clear, is understating it" (qtd. in Wald 1999, A12). The government's role is expected to be significant — although it has not yet been precisely determined — during the different program development and implementation phases (GAO 1995c).

REFERENCES

British Nuclear Fuels. 1998. *A Company Profile: World Winning Nuclear Technology & Environmental Solutions.* Cheshire, UK: BNFL Corporate Communications.

Fehner, Terrence K., and Jack M. Holl. 1994. *Department of Energy, 1977–1994: A Summary History.* Washington, DC: U.S. Government Printing Office, DOE/HR-0098.

Gosling, F. G. 1994. *Closing the Circle: The Department of Energy and Environmental Management, 1942–1994.* Washington, DC: Government Printing Office.

Green, Lisa. Manager, Environmental Restoration Program, DOE-Idaho. 1994. Letter to Wayne Pierre, Chief Federal Facilities Section, EPA-10, and Dean Nygard, Federal Facilities Supervisor, Idaho Department of Health and Welfare, Division of Environmental Quality. *Subject: Agency Partnership for Success (OPE-ER-297–94).*

Hewlett, Richard G., and Francis Duncan. 1969. *Atomic Shield. Vol. 2, A History of United States Atomic Energy Commission.* University Park: Pennsylvania State University Press.

League of Women Voters Education Fund. 1993. *The Nuclear Waste Primer.* Washington, DC: The League of Women Voters.

Narath, Albert. 1997. Prepared Statement Before the Committee on Commerce, House of Representatives, 105th Congress, First Session. Hearings Before the Subcommittee on Oversight and Investigations, July 28 and 29, 1997. *The Department of Energy's Implementation of Contract Reform: Problems with the Fixed-Price Contract to Clean Up Pit 9.* Washington, DC: U.S. Government Printing Office, 151–155.

Pit 9 "Fresh Eyes" Team Report. Attorney Work Product. 1997. Published in *The Department of Energy's Implementation of Contract Reform: Problems with the Fixed-Price Contract to Clean Up Pit 9.* Committee on Commerce, House of Representatives, 105th Congress, First Session. Hearings Before the Subcommittee on Oversight and Investigations, July 28 and 29, 1997. Washington, DC: U.S. Government Printing Office, 85–122.

Peña, Frederico. 1997. Prepared Statement Before the Committee on Commerce, House of Representatives, 105th Congress, First Session. Hearings Before the Subcommittee on Oversight and Investigations, July 28 and 29, 1997. *The Department of Energy's Implementation of Contract Reform: Problems with the Fixed-Price Contract to Clean Up Pit 9.* Washington, DC: U.S. Government Printing Office, 32–35.

Rezendes, Victor S. 1997. Prepared Statement Before the Committee on Commerce, House of Representatives, 105th Congress, First Session. Hearings Before the Subcommittee on Oversight and Investigations, July 28 and 29, 1997. *The Department of Energy's Implementation of Contract Reform: Problems with the Fixed-Price Contract to Clean Up Pit 9.* Washington, DC: U.S. Government Printing Office, 7–13.

Schwartz, Frank G. 1995. *Management of Pit 9: Highlights of Accomplishments and Lessons Learned to Date. Internal publication.* Idaho Falls: US Department of Energy-Idaho National Engineering and Environmental Laboratory-95/00233.

Smith, Randall F. 1997. Prepared Statement Before the Committee on Commerce, House of Representatives, 105th Congress, First Session. Hearings Before the Subcommittee on Oversight and Investigations, July 28 and 29, 1997. *The Department of Energy's Implementation of Contract Reform: Problems with the Fixed-Price Contract to Clean Up Pit 9.* Washington, DC: U.S. Government Printing Office, 45–48.

U.S. Atomic Energy Commission. 1948. *Report of the Safety and Industrial Health Advisory Board.* Washington, DC: U.S. Government Printing Office, Declassified 12/13/88.

U.S. Department of Energy. 1994. *Making Contracting Work Better and Cost Less.* Report of the Contract Reform Team. Washington, DC: U.S. Department of Energy.

U.S. Department of Energy. Office of Environmental Management. 1995. *Private Sector Working Group: Privatization Resource Document.* Washington, DC: U.S. Department of Energy, DOE/ORO/2037, (December).

U.S. Department of Energy. Office of Environmental Management. 1996. *Closing the Circle on the Splitting of the Atom.* Washington, DC: U.S. Government Printing Office, DOE/EM-0266.

U.S. Department of Energy. A Report to the Secretary of Energy. 1997a. Dan W. Reicher, Chair. *Harnessing the Market: The Opportunities and Challenges of Privatization.* Washington, DC: Department of Energy.

U.S. Department of Energy. Office of Environmental Management. 1997b. *Linking Legacies.* Washington, DC: U.S. Government Printing Office, DOE/EM-0319.

U.S. General Accounting Office. 1991. *Government Contractors: Are Service Contractors Performing Inherently Governmental Functions?* Washington, DC: U.S. Government Printing Office, GAO/GGD-92–11.

U.S. General Accounting Office. 1994. *Department of Energy. Challenges to Implementing Contract Reform.* Washington, DC: U.S. Government Printing Office, GAO/RCED-94–150, (March).

U.S. General Accounting Office. 1995a. *Department of Energy. A Framework for Restructuring DOE and Its Missions.* Washington, DC: U.S. Government Printing Office, GAO/RCED-95–197, (August).

U.S. General Accounting Office. 1995b. *Audit of Department of Energy's Administration of Precious Materials.* Washington, DC: U.S. Government Printing Office, DOE/IG-0375.

U.S. General Accounting Office. 1995c. *Uranium Enrichment: Observations on the Privatization of the United States Enrichment Corporation.* Washington, DC: U.S. Government Printing Office, GAO/T-RCED-95–116.

U.S. General Accounting Office. 1995d. *Federally Funded R&D Centers: Use of Fee by the MITRE Corporation.* Washington, DC: U.S. Government Printing Office, GAO/NSIAD-96–26.

U.S. General Accounting Office. 1996a. *Environmental Protection: Issues Facing the Energy and Defense Environmental Management Programs.* Washington, DC: U.S. Government Printing Office, GAO/T-RCED/NSIAD-96–127.

U.S. General Accounting Office. 1996b. *Energy Research: Opportunities Exist to Recover Federal Investment in Technology Development Projects.* Washington, DC: U.S. Government Printing Office, GAO/RCED-96–141.

U.S. General Accounting Office. 1996c. *Department of Energy. Contract Reform Is Progressing, but Full Implementation Will Take Years.* Washington, DC: U.S. Government Printing Office, GAO/RCED-97–18.

U.S. General Accounting Office. 1997a. *Nuclear Waste: DOE's Estimates of Potential Savings from Privatizing Cleanup Projects.* Washington, DC: U.S. Government Printing Office, GAO/RCED-97–49R, (31 January).

U.S. General Accounting Office. 1997b. *Nuclear Waste: Department of Energy's Project to Clean Up Pit 9 at Idaho Falls Is Experiencing Problems.* Washington, DC: U.S. Government Printing Office, GAO/RCED-97–180.

U.S. General Accounting Office. 1998a. *Department of Energy: Alternative Financing and Contracting Strategies for Cleanup Projects.* Washington, DC: U.S. Government Printing Office, GAO/RCED-98–169.

U.S. General Accounting Office. 1998b. *Nuclear Waste. Department of Energy's Hanford Tank Waste Project — Schedule, Cost, and Management Issues.* Washington, DC: U.S. Government Printing Office, GAO/RCED-99–13.

U.S. Office of Management and Budget. 1983. *Circular A-76.*

U.S. Office of Management and Budget. 1993. *Circular A-120.* 1993.

U.S. Office of Management and Budget. 1999. *FY2000 Budget. http://frwebgate2.access.U.S.GovernmentPrintingOffice.gov.*

Wald, Mathew L. 1999. U.S. Seeks to Build Plants to Process Uranium Wastes. *New York Times.* 2 March 1999, A1+.

Chapter Four

Regional EPA Offices and the Regulation of Hazardous Wastes: Top Down or Bottom Up?

Charles Davis

Introduction

Regional offices of federal executive branch agencies were established to achieve greater uniformity in the location of field organizations and to promote cooperation between federal, state and local governments in the development and implementation of national policy objectives (Glendening 1977). While the role of regional officials varies according to policy type and agency customs, the job takes on a decidedly managerial cast within the context of intergovernmental regulatory laws administered by the U.S. Environmental Protection Agency (EPA). Key responsibilities include the oversight of state efforts to implement federal policies under the partial preemption doctrine (Advisory Commission on Intergovernmental Relations 1984).[1] However, a decision to maintain a strong oversight role makes it difficult to nurture a close working relationship with state environmental agencies.

Regional EPA officials are asked to make administrative decisions that not only demonstrate loyalty to higher-ups within the organizational hierarchy but the need to use discretionary judgement to ensure that varying policy contexts and conditions are taken into account. In practice this is difficult if not impossible to achieve. Are regional EPA officials more inclined to assume the control function that is commonly associated with regulatory agencies? Or are they more inclined to display greater sensitivity to site-specific problems encountered within a given state?

Despite the important role played by regional offices in the implementation of environmental policies, relatively little scholarly attention has been devoted to how they operate. The question addressed in this chapter is whether regional EPA officials tend to act more like controllers by upholding the agency goal of uniformity in the application of environmental policies across all states, or whether they are more inclined to evaluate the need for consistent enforcement efforts within the context of regional policy issues and problems. Efforts to shed light on this question are based on the analysis of data from the federal hazardous waste regulatory program, the Resource Conservation and Recovery Act of 1976 (RCRA).

Research Expectations

Existing institutional arrangements for federal regional centers emphasize accountability in administrative decisions to the headquarters office. Thus, regional administrators are expected to act like "principals" to ensure that their "agents" (i.e., state program administrators within their region) carry out regulatory goals (Mitnick 1980). This is achieved by not only offering financial carrots in the form of grants to defray program costs, but regulatory sticks as well. To prevent "shirking" in the form of noncompliance with federal pollution control laws, they can utilize policy tools such as warning letters, administrative orders, or the referral of especially recalcitrant offenders to the Department of Justice (U.S. Environmental Protection Agency, 1990). A study by Patricia Crotty found that regional EPA officials were more likely to obtain state compliance with federal policy objectives with a more authoritative enforcement style than with a more conciliatory approach (Crotty 1988). It is unclear, however, whether a top-down orientation can be sustained over the long run. William Gormley cautions that a coercive approach such as withholding federal funds until state compliance is achieved is only effective for "short term, issue specific" problems (Gorniley 1987).

Other studies suggest that regional directors may be more responsive to organizational factors within the area office or the sociopolitical characteristics of member states than to directives issued from the headquarters unit. The Office of Enforcement within EPA was reorganized several times in the Reagan, Bush and Clinton administrations not only to shift the regulatory emphasis played by regional personnel but to address the issue of regulating single media (such as air and land) versus multimedia enforcement strategies (Mintz 1995). A comparative case study of Superfund implementation across three federal regions by Thomas Church and Robert Nakamura revealed substantial differences in enforcement style.

One region exhibited a tendency to adopt a strict no-nonsense attitude in dealing with pollution-generating firms, while another used a accommodative approach and the third utilized a public works strategy that epitomized the "shovels now, lawyers later" philosophy (Church 1993).

Regional variations in state enforcement actions have also been reported in analyses of programs administered by the federal Office of Surface Mining and Enforcement and EPA. Key constraints to a more active oversight role for regional officials include a lack of budgetary support for enforcement activities (U.S. General Accounting Office 1991), the diversity of the regulatory environment (Hunter 1996) and a growing distaste for strong federal regulation among elected officials at all levels of government (U.S. General Accounting Office 1995). Greater empathy with state-level policy goals was also found in Denise Scheberle's analysis of regional EPA officials with jurisdiction over radon and safe drinking water programs (Scheberle 1997).

Overall, the preponderance of evidence tilts in the direction of adherence to a facilitator role for regional EPA officials. Several studies, including the more recent ones, are consistent in finding that regional factors trump national factors when administrators take enforcement actions. This research expectation comes with an important caveat, however. While Crotty's study is somewhat dated, she did analyze several policy areas over a longer period of time than subsequent authors.

Hazardous Waste as an Intergovernmental Policy Problem

Congress enacted the Resource Conservation and Recovery Act (RCRA) in 1976. Subtitle C of RCRA provided a management framework for the regulation of toxic chemicals currently generated by industry or other entities. EPA has defined hazardous waste in generic terms (as ignitable, corrosive, reactive or toxic) and by listing specific wastes and industrial waste streams. A "cradle to grave" tracking system designed to keep tabs on the whereabouts of wastes from the production phase to the disposal or recovery phase was established. A key ingredient in the monitoring process is the requirement that any individual or organization involved in the generation, treatment, transport, storage or disposal of these wastes prepare a manifest for recordkeeping and reporting purposes. Organizations performing any or all of these functions must also obtain a permit from EPA or a state agency which has received EPA authorization to administer hazardous waste programs.

While EPA was initially tapped by Congress to assume overall responsibility for the management of RCRA, federal policymakers assumed that most regulatory decisions would eventually be shouldered by state officials. However, one important dimension of policy control is reflected in the manner in which program management authority or primacy was delegated. States could receive program management authority by adopting legislation that was "equivalent to" and "consistent with" RCRA and promulgating guidelines, standards and regulations that were at least as stringent as those used by EPA.

Even though states were given an opportunity to tailor programs to address jurisdiction specific problems, the available options were restricted somewhat by the "equivalency" and "consistency" criteria. In addition, the federal government retained the authority to step in and reestablish control over the hazardous waste program if state officials were unable or unwilling to do the job.

RCRA was reauthorized with significant changes in 1984. Under the Hazardous and Solid Waste Amendments Act (HSWA), Congress not only retained or extended environmental quality standards for industry compliance with hazardous waste laws but added a number of political and economic incentives as well. Perhaps the most significant modification was the expression of a clear preference for the use of waste disposal methods other than land-based containment. Wastes identified as hazardous within California's management program were banned from disposal in landfills along with bulk or noncontainerized liquid hazardous wastes (Davis 1993). Congress also removed the statutory exemption originally granted to small quantity generators of hazardous waste (i.e., firms producing between 100 and 1,000 kilograms of waste per month). Third, owners of underground storage tanks containing petroleum or other hazardous substances were required to meet new regulatory guidelines. Finally, corrective action requirements were added which strengthened the hand of regulators to induce or coerce waste handling firms or governments to manage existing wastes in an environmentally responsible fashion.

From a policy implementation perspective, the political burdens added to the shoulders of EPA and state administrators through the enactment of HSWA were significant. Increased scrutiny from Washington quickly became apparent through EPA's decision to more closely evaluate whether states possessed the necessary fiscal and organizational commitment before granting them authorization to carry out the new regulatory responsibilities. States were already expected to fulfill a number of delicate tasks; that is, finding acceptable sites for the construction of hazardous waste treatment, storage and disposal (TSD) facilities, and issuing the necessary permits to ensure that facility managers would conduct operations in a safe and responsible manner (U.S. Environmental Protection Agency 1990).

Under HSWA, the universe of regulated parties was expanded dramatically by eliminating the small quantity generator exemption while the number of permitted facilities equipped to store or dispose of these wastes shrank by nearly two thirds because of increasingly stringent land disposal requirements. Another development contributing to a tense political mood in some states was the decision by policymakers in some jurisdictions traditionally regarded as "waste havens" to consider waste import bans using a public health rationale to counter legal arguments pertaining to the restraint of interstate commerce. This suggests that enforcement decisions are likely to be dealt with in an even more contentious and politically charged atmosphere than is the case for less complicated regulatory programs. Finally, a study by the U.S. General Accounting Office of both state and regional EPA administrators concluded that more cooperative approaches to hazardous waste regulation such as state–EPA working agreements were difficult to put into place because of severe funding constraints (U.S. General Accounting Office 1995).

Findings

Variations in the enforcement of RCRA across regional EPA offices in 1990 and 1994 are shown in Table 1. The data indicate that there are sizeable differences in the absolute number of enforcement actions. Region 5 stands out as the most vigorous regional office in 1990 while Regions 2, 4, 5 and 6 were all more active in exercising regulatory oversight in 1994. On the other hand, Regions 8 and 10 exhibit relatively low levels of enforcement activity, which reflects a corresponding lack of industrial activity in the western states other than California.

Table 1: Distribution of Enforcement Actions for the Federal Hazardous Waste Program Across Regional EPA Offices

	Number of Enforcement Actions*	
Regional EPA Offices	1990	1994
Region 1	75	77
Region 2	200	125
Region 3	110	14
Region 4	87	94
Region 5	369	95

Region 6	116	97
Region 7	40	74
Region 8	24	31
Region 9	156	80
Region 10	53	43
Total	1230	730

* Enforcement actions include warning letters, administrative orders, and case referrals to federal and state courts.

Source: U.S. Environmental Protection Agency, Freedom of Information Act Request, 1996.

If the midterm enforcement records of the Bush Administration in 1990 and the Clinton Administration in 1994 are compared, it is somewhat surprising to report the higher incidence of actions taken under the Republican EPA Administrator Reilly than under his Democratic successor, Carol Browner. In part, this is a product of organizational changes within the Bush administration that resulted in a renewed emphasis on enforcement of hazardous waste programs in the regional offices. Regional administrators and deputy administrators became subject to performance evaluations from headquarters staff on their handling of enforcement responsibilities.

Conversely, the interregional differences were less pronounced in 1994. To some extent, this represents a growing maturation of the RCRA program as EPA administrators gained experience in working with elected policymakers, state hazardous waste managers, environmentalists and industry officials, which resulted in less uncertainty about thresholds of acceptable regulatory behavior. Both Administrators Reilly and Browner sought to convey the message that pollution control laws would be enforced. Consequently, greater consistency of effort has been achieved; e.g., the overall level of state enforcement activity stayed the same.

We now turn to a more explicit comparison of enforcement behavior across federal regions. This requires that state and regional variations in the generation of chemicals and toxic by-products be taken into account to ensure that absolute differences in enforcement activity are not masking an understandable tendency for administrators to respond according to the magnitude of the threat to public health or environmental quality. The adjusted measure is based on the number of regional EPA enforcement actions divided by the overall number of hazardous waste generators within the affected states.

The data are summarized in Table 2. Analyses of variance were calculated comparing each region to the others for both 1990 and 1994. Very few differences were found in regional enforcement activity in either year. Only Region 5 stood out as a particularly vigorous regional office in the

1990 implementation of RCRA, a finding that is reinforced in other studies of EPA and environmental policy issues. A contributing factor may also be the presence of Valdas Adamkus, the long-serving Administrator of Region 5 with a legendary zeal for the enforcement of pollution control laws. Since he left the EPA in the early 1990s, the number of enforcement actions in Region 5 declined from 369 in 1990 to 95 in 1994, a more representative level of regional activity.

Table 2: Comparing the Enforcement Vigor* of Regional EPA Offices, 1990 and 1994

	Sum of Squares		Mean Square		F Ratio		Stat. Signif.	
	1990	1994	1990	1994	1990	1994	1990	1994
Region 1	9.2	4.3	9.2	4.3	0.79	0.14	ns**	ns
Region 2	9.2	0.0	9.2	0.0	0.79	0.00	ns	ns
Region 3	12.0	30.8	12.0	30.8	1.06	1.11	ns	ns
Region 4	7.5	2.3	7.5	2.3	0.63	0.08	ns	ns
Region 5	42.1	6.5	42.1	6.5	5.55	0.21	.05	ns
Region 6	8.2	7.0	8.2	7.0	0.69	0.23	ns	ns
Region 7	16.4	201.0	16.4	201.0	1.51	30.9	ns	.001
Region 8	0.4	13.4	0.4	13.4	0.03	0.45	ns	ns
Region 9	8.6	15.7	8.6	15.7	0.73	0.53	ns	ns
Region 10	8.6	0.1	8.6	0.1	0.03	0.00	ns	ns

* The enforcement vigor measure (derived from analysis of variance) is based on the overall number of warning letters, administrative orders and court referral decisions divided by the number of hazardous waste generating firms.
** Not statistically significant.

In 1994, only Region 7 consisting of Iowa, Kansas, Missouri and Nebraska generated a statistically higher than average number of enforcement actions. While a closer inspection of the data indicates that much of the regional increase occurring in 1994 was attributable to the issuance of more than three times the earlier number of warning letters and administrative orders within the state of Nebraska, there is no clear explanation for this finding. Overall, then the predominant conclusion to be drawn from these analyses is that regional differences in the implementation of the federal hazardous waste program are not as pronounced as we might expect from prior studies after measures of enforcement activity are adjusted to consider disparate numbers of hazardous waste generators within each region.

Conclusions

The objective of this chapter was to consider the role played by EPA regional offices in the implementation of the federal hazardous waste program. Did regional officials consistently apply the law in issuing warning letters and administrative orders to recalcitrant regulatees or in referring difficult cases to state or federal attorneys general for further action? Or did patterns of enforcement reflect political, economic and demographic differences between the regions? We found that the regional offices displayed a consistent level of enforcement activity in both 1990 and 1994, and that expected differences in regulatory vigor between Republican and Democratic administrations in overseeing state RCRA programs did not materialize. While our data were limited to the analysis of regulatory activities for a single program at two time points, they do suggest a need to reexamine the behavior of regional EPA offices to determine whether administrators are paying closer attention to the programmatic priorities of Washington-based officials than earlier studies have indicated.

In a more theoretical vein, these results call into question the idea that regional officials are more receptive to regional or state constituencies than hierarchical superiors within EPA. In actual fact, there are probably incentives for administrators to toe the line, especially in more high-visibility programs like clean air or hazardous waste. This may not be quite the case, however, in low profile programs such as radon control. To more accurately assess the administrative role of regional administrators in terms of their role within the intergovernmental implementation of environmental policies will require additional studies that combine documentary evidence with survey data and related information.

Endnotes

1. Partial preemption is the regulatory design which guides the implementation of intergovernmental regulatory statutes. Federal agencies are assigned the responsibility of developing minimum performance standards for regulated parties to meet in the process of ameliorating given policy problems such as pollution or hazards to worker safety. By establishing a floor of statutory protection for U.S. residents, Congress has filled a policy void. States either lacked programs oriented toward these policy problems or had laws or regulations in place which were found to be incompatible with federal statutes.

Following the promulgation by federal agencies of standards to implement the policy, state officials are given an opportunity to assume program management authority. A state implementation plan (SIP) is prepared and submitted to the appropriate federal agency for review. A decision is then made to either reject the plan or to grant a state full or conditional approval to administer the program (sometimes referred to as primacy). After receiving authorization, state officials become eligible to obtain grants to cover some of the program operation costs.

The federal role is subsequently restricted to oversight activities. Federal pre-emption of state administrative authority can be invoked if states choose to opt out of the process or if they renege on the actual enforcement requirements. Under these circumstances, the federal agency would directly carry out the law in the non-participating state using staff from the regional office. See Advisory Commission on Intergovernmental Relations. 1984. *Regulatory Federalism: Policy, Process, Impact and Reform*. Washington, D.C.: Advisory Commission on Intergovernmental Relations.

References

Advisory Commission on Intergovernmental Relations. 1984. *Regulatory Federalism: Policy, Process, Impact and Reform*. Washington, D.C.: Advisory Commission on Intergovernmental Relations.

Church, Thomas W., and Robert T. Nakamura. 1993. *Cleaning Up the Mess: Implementation Strategies in Superfund*. Washington, D.C.: Brookings.

Crotty, Patricia McGee. 1988. Assessing the Role of Federal Administrative Regions: An Exploratory Analysis. *Public Administration Review*. 48 (March/April): 642–48.

Davis, Charles. 1993. *The Politics of Hazardous Waste*. Englewood Cliffs, NJ: Prentice-Hall.

Glendening, Parris, and Mavis Mann Reeves. 1977. *Pragmatic Federalism*. 2nd ed. Pacific Palisades, CA: Palisades Publishers.

Gormley, William T., Jr. 1987. Intergovernmental Conflict on Environmental Policy: The Attitudinal Connection. *Western Political Quarterly*. June: 301.

Hunter, Susan, and Richard Waterman. 1996. *Enforcing the Law: The Case of the Clean Water Acts*. Armonk, NY: M.E. Sharpe.

Mintz, Joel A. 1995. *Enforcement at the EPA*. Austin, TX: University of Texas Press.

Mitnick, Barry M. 1980. *The Political Economy of Regulation*. New York, NY: Columbia University Press.

Scheberle, Denise. 1997. *Federalism and Environmental Policy*. Washington, D.C.: Georgetown University Press.

U.S. Environmental Protection Agency. 1990. *The Nation's Hazardous Waste Management Program at a Crossroads: The RCRA Implementation Study*. Washington DC: U.S. Government Printing Office (September).

U.S. General Accounting Office. 1991. *Environmental Enforcement: Penalties May Not Recover Economic Benefits Gained by Violators*. U.S. General Accounting Office/RCED-91-166.

US. General Accounting Office. 1995. *EPA and the States: Environmental Challenges Require a Better Working Relationship*. U.S. Government Accounting Office/RCED-95-64.

Chapter Five

Brownfield Voluntary Cleanup Programs: Superfund's Orphaned Stepchild, or Innovation from the Ground Up?

ROBERT A. SIMONS AND KIMBERLY WINSON

Introduction

State brownfield programs have been around for about five years. Brownfields are sites that formerly had industrial or commercial uses and are currently prevented from attaining their highest and best use as a result of real or perceived contamination (Simons, 1998b). Commonly known as voluntary cleanup programs (VCPs), brownfield programs represent a major departure from the Superfund model for cleaning contaminated sites. Many regard Superfund as a failure in its ability to get sites cleaned up, noting the excessive expense for legal fees, and small output of cleaned sites. However, the strongest criticism of Superfund is that it served to freeze redevelopment of contaminated sites because of liability fears of potential investors. The "Fleet Factors" court case was an important indicator of this problem and led to a change in paradigm for the development of brownfields.

Lately, the United States federal Environmental Protection Agency (US EPA) has taken a hands-off attitude to brownfield sites, delegating the bulk of the tasks to the individual state EPAs. The state EPAs and mandatory programs, delisting sites, US EPA brownfield pilot grants, and federal delegation of authority to state VCPs are examples of this delegation process. However, Superfund is a very strong "stick" without which the more flexible state voluntary cleanup program "carrots" would not be very effective. VCPs focus on limiting liability, financial support and other inducements designed to make contaminated sites attractive to investors.

So, how is the brownfield stepchild doing? Does the hands-off approach taken by US EPA, featuring the brownfield pilot grants and delegated agreements with state VCPs, appear to be working? Are innovations, output (cleaned and redeveloped sites), and local developer-EPA relationships working?

Our conclusion, based in part on a nationwide study of mandatory and voluntary cleanup programs undertaken by us in collaboration with the Washington, DC–based Environmental Law Institute, is that brownfield programs are indeed flourishing. Brownfields are truly a decentralized "grassroots" success with a promising future, rather than an orphaned stepchild.

Before Superfund: Substantial Economic Growth, Little Environmental Regulation

At the turn of the 20th century, manufacturing in America was flourishing. Industry created jobs, and the land surrounding factories was quickly converted into residential neighborhoods that supported industrial businesses. The population of the cities, especially those in the northeast and midwest, experienced tremendous growth. Neighborhoods gave way to steel mills, and farmland became housing plots, as cities became the epicenter of their respective regions. Economic changes saw the rise of the middle class, the creation of suburbs and the proliferation of the automobile. Through the success of industrialization, America was thrust into the role of the greatest economic power in the world.

Decentralization of the cities started in earnest with the inception of the national highway system in the decade following the second world war. Since that time, hundreds of thousands of the same factories, warehouses, rail yards, and other industrial facilities that stimulated the growth of America have closed due to economic restructuring. In some cases the business closed, in others they relocated abroad or to the southern and western parts of the US. Many of these former sites have been financially and physically abandoned. Despite following environmental laws in effect at the time, many of these abandoned industrial facilities were in use before there was significant regulation of hazardous substances and now have some type of contamination that prevents their redevelopment without site remediation. Quite often the type and extent of contamination is unknown, as is the financial cost of cleanup. Many times the party responsible for the contamination is no longer in existence (Rusk 1995).

Although a few of these sites have been reused, most continue to sit idle. There are large concentrations of inactive formerly industrial and commercial properties in cities like New York, Chicago, Detroit, Cleveland, Newark and Philadelphia. The challenges imposed by abandonment of industrial properties are not limited to these areas. Almost all regions of the country and some suburbs and rural areas also face the problem of viable reuse of brownfields. Depending on which estimate is set forth, there are in excess of 650,000 sites in the USA (Simons 1998a).

Major Federal Environmental Laws: CERCLA AND RCRA

In the mid–1970s, the now infamous "Love Canal" situation sparked the revolution in US environmental law. Until that time, there was relatively little regulation of hazardous substances. When chemicals began seeping into the basements of Niagara Falls residents, the New York Commissioner of Health ordered an evacuation of the area. In the 1940s and 1950s, the Hooker Chemical Company had disposed of 21,800 tons of industrial waste in the Love Canal. The company covered waste-filled drums with clay and then sold the land to the Niagara Falls Board of Education for one dollar. Housing and a school were built over the site. By 1980 the federal government had subsidized the relocation of all but a few of the residents, closed the school and begun instituting federal law for the regulation and disposal of hazardous substances. National attention was drawn to Love Canal and the impact of hazardous waste on human health and well-being (Rahm 1998).

Although the regulation of the disposal of hazardous waste was nonexistent for almost a century, when it came, it came with a vengeance. The federal program centered around two main pieces of legislation, signed into law by 1980. They are the Resource Conservation and Recovery Act of 1976 (RCRA)[1] and the Comprehensive Environmental Response, Compensation, and Liability Act of 1980 (CERCLA).[2] These were eventually supplemented by legislation reauthorizing the EPA's Superfund, the Superfund Amendments & Reauthorization Act of 1986 (SARA).[3]

RCRA's primary purpose is to regulate the generation, transportation, treatment and disposal of hazardous wastes. RCRA mandates that persons or organizations which generate hazardous waste are required to track the disposal of these substances through state and federal environmental protection agencies. The waste must end up in a licensed recycling, incineration, or disposal facility whose operators must obtain a permit and meet hundreds of pages of onerous requirements for bonding, safety, recordkeeping, training, and design. These controlled substances must have a manifest (equivalent to a passport for people) as they move about. Despite sometimes onerous paperwork requirements, RCRA has been quite successful in stopping illegal dumping and helping control the safe handling and disposal of dangerous materials (Simons 1998b).

Under CERCLA an elaborate liability scheme was established for the remediation of virtually all contaminated properties. The Superfund National Priorities List (NPL) was established to determine which sites were to be cleaned up. The focus was on public health problems, not on economic development.

To ensure that private parties incur the cost of cleanup, a strict level of responsibility was established. Not only were responsible parties liable for cleanup, they were liable even if they were in compliance with laws prior to the passage of CERCLA. This legislation extended to all sites that were contaminated with a hazardous substance, regardless of the level of contamination. This is contrary to RCRA that limits liability to those sites that present an "imminent hazard." The liability imposed by CERCLA is imposed on all covered parties regardless of fault and intent. Its effects could be felt by anyone in the chain of title, as well as generators and transporters of regulated materials (Davis 1997).

The introduction of Superfund legislation provided little stimulus for the cleanup and redevelopment of these sites. Beginning in the early 1980s, and going through the mid–1990's, any party involved in a brownfield could typically be held liable for cleanup, regardless of who actually contaminated the land or whether or not the party knew of the contamination. This is the so called "strict, joint, and several liability" clause under CERCLA and its reauthorization act, SARA. Lenders who foreclosed on a loan and took possession of a property were included in this liability. There was also uncertainty about cleanup and the value of contaminated real estate as collateral for a potential loan. Financing was nonexistent for the majority of these sites (Simons 1998b).

In 1996, Congress assuaged the fears of the lenders by passing an amendment to CERCLA that provided a "safe harbor" from federal liability. This amendment effectively codified a prior EPA rule covering lender's liability that was overturned on procedural grounds by a federal court.

Success of Superfund: No Carrots Without Sticks

Superfund was well-intentioned. Beginning in 1980 and through the early 1990s, sites were selected or nominated to be on the Superfund NPL.

The first list was published in the National Register in 1983, and potentially, any site could be put on it. At its largest, the potential list of Superfund sites was about 42,000. Later, after evaluation of each site using the 28.5 hazardous ranking score cutoff, the list was broken down into those sites that had indeed been found to be a Superfund site (about 1,500 nationwide), those that had been evaluated but fell short of Superfund status (no further remedial action planned, NFRAP), and those still waiting to be evaluated (CERCLIS).

Because of the strict joint and several liability issue, much of the effort concerning Superfund sites focused on who was responsible for cleanup, rather than on actual site cleanup and remediation. Initially it was widely assumed that legal costs consumed about half of Superfund expenditures over the life of the program. Presently, $1 of every $7 goes toward legal costs.

Of the 1,510 NPL sites, only 217 have been processed and made ready for redevelopment although 76 percent of the sites have remedial "construction" under way. In 1993 only 42 percent of the sites had achieved this status. An average of about ten sites have been cleaned per year since the program's inception. So overall, Superfund has been a pretty dismal failure in respect to getting sites cleaned up and back into productive use (US EPA interview 2000).

Superfund is a valuable stick without which brownfield programs may not have originated. The threat of litigation motivates participation by potentially responsible parties in other plans. Superfund's "failure" encouraged the development of brownfield programs.

Delegation to the States Patterned After Superfund

State mandatory cleanup programs (MCPs) have evolved over the past two decades. State EPAs were created to implement state mandated provisions (under the federal Clean Air Act amendments in the 1970s) for meeting air quality requirements. Beginning in the late 1980s, the state EPAs began carrying out land-based cleanups. Many states created a list of sites, and began with the most offensive or those deemed to be a threat to public health. The state EPA program administrators would try to find a responsible party, then get them to agree to site cleanup using court action.[4]

Regulatory authority for sites not on the National Priorities List (NPL) can and has been delegated from the federal EPA to state agencies. Registry on the NPL indicates those sites that have the worst contamination, and pose an immediate public health hazard. Numerous other contaminated sites exist that do not pose an immediate public health hazard. Many states have developed their own "mini–CERCLAs" or MCPs, to regulate these other sites. The programs typically provide the state with authority to force potentially responsible parties to clean up contaminated sites. In many cases the state law also establishes a fund to finance state-led cleanup initiatives. The states generally adopted CERCLA verbatim, but have been known to impose more stringent requirements on liable parties.

As the federal and state cleanup programs matured and effectively cleaned property, they had limited success in the redevelopment of contaminated sites into viable economic uses with private sector financing. Although they were able to enforce cleanup, comprehensive liability provisions, broad jurisdictional reach and typically costly cleanup standards of RCRA, CERCLA and the MCPs impaired successful redevelopment. The quantification of cleanup costs was difficult due to the unwillingness or inability of governing agencies to determine what constitutes an acceptable cleanup. Prospective purchasers were wary of developing a site due to the inability to assess the cost of remediation, the cost of development, and the liability associated with redevelopment.

These state programs have adopted an extremely broad definition of contamination. Even sites with mild contamination can create nightmares for potential developers. Liability pursuant to federal and state regulations applies to the following:

1. Any place where a hazardous substance that does not occur naturally has come to be located, if the hazardous substance is entering or threatens to enter the environment.

2. Any site where petroleum has been disposed of if the petroleum presents an imminent and substantial endangerment to health or the environment.

3. Any underground storage tank (UST) that is leaking a hazardous substance or petroleum product.

4. A building containing asbestos that will be subject to renovation or demolition or that contains friable asbestos posing a health hazard to workers in the building or violating state or local regulations (Simons 1998b).

The courts have reinforced the broad definition of contamination provided above. If a site has any detectable level of a hazardous substance or concentrations of hazardous substances exceed background levels, it may be the subject of a cleanup action.

Another deterrent to the potential redevelopment of these sites is the large number of possible plaintiffs who can insist that the site be cleaned up. Both RCRA and CERCLA have provisions for federal, state and local governments to file suit for cleanup, as well as for private citizens to do so. This multitiered enforcement authority makes it almost impossible to secure liability waivers from all potential plaintiffs. The risk and uncertainties associated with redeveloping these properties often outweighs the benefits or profits that may be gained.

The MCPs have resulted in a substantial number of recycled sites. Using a combination of persuasion and legal tactics such as consent decrees and court orders, state EPAs were directly and indirectly responsible for about 24,000 cleanups, an average of about 2,000 per year, although that number is declining. Very few of these cleanups were voluntary, especially after the Fleet Factors case, discussed below. However, the cleanup of most of these sites was not driven by redevelopment potential, but by health hazards.

Lender Liability: The Fleet Factors Case

The importance of liability issues, especially to lenders who provide development financing, is underscored in *United States v. Fleet Factors Corp.* (1990). Prior to the Fleet decision, the courts fairly consistently held that a secured creditor would not be liable as a potentially responsible party unless and until: (i) the secured creditor foreclosed on contaminated real property or personal property; or (ii) the secured creditor became active in the day-to-day management of the borrower's facility. In the Fleet decision, it was perceived throughout the lending community that the rules of the game had been drastically changed and that liability was as real for them as it was for those who had contributed to contamination. In its opinion, the court stated:

> ...a secured creditor may incur § 9607(a)(2) liability, without being an operator, by participating in the financial management of a facility to a degree indicating a capacity to influence the corporation's treatment of hazardous wastes. It is not necessary for the secured creditor actually to involve itself in the day-to-day operations of the facility in order to be liable ... Nor is it necessary for the secured creditor to participate in management decisions related to hazardous wastes. Rather, a secured creditor will be liable if its involvement with the management of the facility is sufficiently broad to support the inference that it could effect hazardous waste disposal decisions.

After Fleet, the fear was that merely the presence of environmental covenants in loan documents, monitoring a borrower's financial condition or collateral, or conducting workout discussions with a borrower would trigger CERCLA liability. Redevelopment and financing of contaminated sites came to a standstill. No more voluntary cleanups were able to be financed. For a brief period of time in the early 1990s, lenders were so averse to the potential liability that they were returning contaminated properties to their borrowers or owners in the event of technical default, instead of pursuing the loan workout route, thus sidestepping potential liability while sacrificing lending capital.

In 1992, the EPA published its rule on lender liability. This was an effort to restore some sense of certainty to lenders in the wake of Fleet's controversial decision. The rule specified the range of permissible activities that may be undertaken by lenders and other secured creditors while still qualifying for CERCLA's "secured creditor" exemption. Although it doesn't alleviate all financing fears, the EPA's rule provides secured creditors with certain objective tests to assist in minimizing their potential liability under CERCLA for cleanup costs in the case of environmental contamination. In 1996, Congress passed a law that effectively codified the EPA's position on lender liability.

Decentralization and More Delegation: NFRAP and Pilots

Several years after the Fleet case was in play, the US EPA was accumulating sites on its Superfund castoff list. These were sites that had been considered for the NPL, but did not qualify because they did not meet the 28.5 hazardous ranking cut-off point. Around 1995, the US EPA started a policy of not reviewing the cleanup status of any sites not on its list. Further, they "delisted" the NFRAP sites, delegating them to the states for any necessary cleanup action. However, the US EPA was still being asked to review sites that were cleaned up, and to issue statements of completion, or "comfort letters" stating that even though it had not regulated the site's remediation, it did not foresee any other cleanup action as being required. This trend eventually led to the State Memorandum of Agreement (SMOA) letter.

By 1993 the US EPA was looking for ways to get out of the business of reviewing contaminated sites that were not severe health problems. The brownfield pilot program came into being about this time, and the agency made the grants under it available to cities and county local governments. Cuyahoga County, Ohio was among the first such pilots, and received a

$200,000 grant in the mid–1990s. The brownfield pilot program was an experiment, an innovation. To date over 300 grants have been offered, and the relating projects have covered such diverse tasks as setting up a site inventory, establishing a GIS data base, conducting site assessment, planning for area-wide groundwater cleanup, site remediation, and so on. These pilots have had tremendous popular support and many items learned during their development have been incorporated into the state voluntary cleanup programs.

Evolution of State Voluntary Cleanup Programs

The evolution of voluntary cleanup programs in the United States was predicated on the inability of the federal government to significantly decrease the number of contaminated properties. Demand for brownfields is far lower than supply, due in part to the regulatory quagmire and liability requirements resulting from CERCLA, RCRA and the state mini–CERCLAs, and also due to slow demand for industrial, commercial and housing sites in many cities in the US. It is estimated that in several major midwestern cities, a large enough number of available brownfields exists to meet demand for an estimated 30 to 50 years (Simons and Iannone, 1997). This oversupply may become even greater in some markets because the number of former industrial sites being abandoned exceeds those that are being developed. In 1993, Chicago lost 334 plants to closures, relocations, or mergers but only attracted 243 new plants (Fischer 1997).

The oversupply of brownfields is less extreme in other regions of the country and outside the city centers. Even in the largest Rust Belt cities, such premium properties as high-quality industrial sites and land near central business districts are in great demand. In most areas, though, there will be more brownfields than can be used in the short term.

To combat the disuse of former industrial sites, most states have enacted legislation, generically referred to as voluntary cleanup programs. The reforms inherent in VCPs help to counteract the liability concerns of potential developers, lenders and purchasers and promote the redevelopment of these sites. VCPs have typically been designed to address development obstacles while recognizing that public health and economic development must coexist. The goals of these programs involve integrating legal liability, technical cleanup requirements, and economic incentives. Often, technical and financial assistance is provided, and liability is minimized through legal commitments on the part of the state with respect to the completion of cleanups. These legal agreements are known as covenants not to sue (CNTS). They are typically not available through other state regulatory programs.

As of July 2000, 46 states had instituted VCPs, the first being created in 1993. In a working study of the frequency and depth of voluntary programs conducted by these authors and the Environmental Law Institute in 2000, all but three states had programs created by legal statute, and two were administrative only. Four states plus DC had no program, and one state (Louisiana) had a pending program. Most states had only one program, but several (New York, Texas, and Connecticut) had multiple programs, as they had tailored VCPs to submarkets in the pollution spectrum (Simons and Pendergrass 2000).

These state led initiatives are usually developed independently of each other, but are comparable based on a number of elements critical to the redevelopment of brownfields:

1. The use of risk-based corrective action to form the basis for remediation, including specific standards for the presence of certain substances and an allowance for characteristics of the site and its users. This enables cost savings as some contamination may be safely left on site under caps. "Capping" a site involves the partial encapsulation of contaminated soil. The undesirable contamination (sometimes intact, other times partially removed) is covered with a barrier of clay or uncontaminated soil, building structures, parking lots or a plastic barrier.

2. The availability of closure letters or no further action (NFA) letters and governmental releases from liability in the form of CNTS.

3. The presence of a state memorandum of agreement (SMOA) between the state EPA and US EPA.

4. The establishment of financial inducements to encourage development of brownfields, including loans, grants, tax credits, property tax abatement and other local initiatives. This often requires close coordination with state or local economic development agencies.

5. The presence of codified liability exemptions for lenders.

6. The overall depth and comprehensiveness of a state's VCP, which is an indication of market acceptance (Simons 1998).

Risk-based corrective action (RBCA) standards form the core of most VCPs. Successful RBCA compares the risk associated with a type of land use with the level of contaminants, and strictly specifies what levels of contamination are acceptable for a particular use. RBCA considers specific site conditions such as type of soil, groundwater, and background contamination levels and also specifies investigation procedures. Progressively cleaner standards are stated for land uses such as industrial (highest allowable level of contamination), commercial, and residential (lowest allowable level of contamination).

Closure letters serve to notify developers and lenders that site remediation is complete. There are three types of closures letters: no further action (NFA), CNTS and SMOA. NFA is the weaker of the two letters; it signifies that the remedial work on the site that just occurred is complete. A CNTS is generally issued by the state attorney general or lead environmental agency and is indicative of a release of liability from the state and sometimes local jurisdictions within the state. The quality of closure letters also varies. There are essentially four levels. The first is an administrative letter from the state EPA stating NFA, but without statutory backing. The second is an NFA, certificate of completion, or comparable letter, with statutory backing. This is good, but only for the environmental event described in the action. The third level is the covenant not to sue (CNTS) issued by the state attorney general, and protecting the developer and future site owners from actions by all state and county agencies. The final level is where the federal EPA has joined in a state memorandum of agreement (SMOA) with the state VCP, not to reopen cases.

A SMOA is important because it addresses the applicability of the liability release of a CNTS or other closure letter to the federal EPA. SMOAs are negotiated with the regional EPA offices. Rather than issue a SMOA for each individual site, the EPA enters into an agreement with the state, and conveys its intention not to take further action unless an "imminent and substantial threat" to human health or the environment occurs or under "emergency or exceptional circumstances." At least 14 states had entered into a SMOA with US EPA through November 2000. The federal EPA virtually never evaluates or reviews voluntary actions, confining itself to properties on the NPL and candidate NPL lists.

Liability exemptions are key to VCPs. In almost all programs, lenders are specifically exempt from liability as are new owners who did not contribute to the contamination, and in rare instances, responsible parties. However, responsible parties are usually not released from liability, and neither are potentially responsible parties and known polluters.

Financial incentives are the featured attraction to the redevelopment of brownfields, from the private redeveloper's standpoint. Often the cost of remediation prohibits a market rate transaction and requires combining several sources of financing. Some states have funding available to pay for site assessments and site remediation, while others offer tax incentives and abatements (Council of Great Lakes Governors 1998).

Michigan has a very extensive financing program that involves the creation of municipal brownfield redevelopment authorities that develop and implement redevelopment financing plans. The redevelopment authority is made up of individuals from public, private and nonprofit groups, and specifically identifies sites that are eligible for cleanup and the recapture of taxes. Authorities may issue revenue and TIF (tax increment financing) bonds and notes, borrow from the Michigan Department of Environmental Quality Revitalization Revolving Loan Program, or use other resources to finance initial response activities (Council of Great Lakes Governors 1998).

Many other forms of monetary assistance exist. Tax credits are unique financial incentives because they do not deplete appropriations, as grants or other expenses do. However, tax credits do require municipal or state-level approval to be effective. In Ohio, for example, developers can receive a tax credit equal to 10 percent of the total eligible costs, up to a maximum of $500,000. The Quebec government created a brownfields trust that is responsible for all liability for environmental contamination and manages funding for remediation of contaminated sites where the responsible party is no longer in existence. Grant and below market loan programs are also available (Council of Great Lakes Governors 1998).

These state voluntary cleanup programs have borne substantial fruit—cumulative output is substantial. Since program inception around 1993, there have been over 9,000 sites cleaned through voluntary action in the USA (almost 7,000 through the end of 1999). There are an average of 1,500 sites being cleaned per year, but recently the total has exceeded 2,000 and is accelerating. Some of the most active states are New Jersey, Minnesota, and Illinois.

To summarize the intergovernmental relationships between the various parties, the schematic diagram (Figure 1) shows the interrelationship between US EPA, the state EPAs, environmental behavior, health issues, economic development, and federal, state and voluntary cleanups over time.

Success of the Three Cleanup Programs

An analysis of the three programs over time reveals their cycles and longevity. Superfund was officially inaugurated in 1980. As has been previously mentioned, its initiation was predicated on the realization that contamination problems posed an immediate danger to human health. When Superfund regulations came, they came quickly but tapered off as the EPA recognized the magnitude of the situation and focused its efforts on the worst sites.

Figure 1. Event History
Environmental Cleanup Legislation

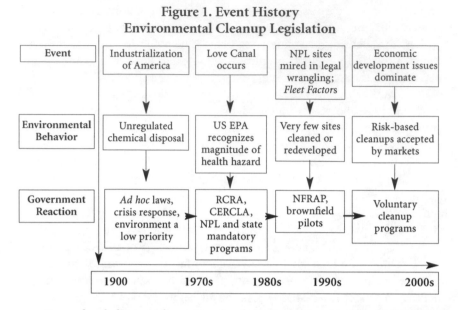

Superfund cleanups have remained steady in the past few years, as has the growth of the NPL. EPA promulgated an original NPL of 406 sites on September 8, 1983. The NPL has been expanded since then, most recently on July 27, 2000. NPL sites are the worst of the worst environmental health problem sites, warranting federal oversight. The total number of sites currently on the NPL is 1,238. Of these, 217 sites have been deleted because the required remediation was completed (204 through the end of 1999). A total of 226 sites have been deleted, the remaining nine being delegated to a different governing authority. An average of ten sites have completed cleanup annually, but it must be understood that the contamination is so deep it often requires many years to remediate. Conversely, VCP cleanups typically take a year or less and generally do not require as extensive remediation as Superfund or MCPs.

State mandatory programs picked up Superfund's slack, and had a decade-long run of productive site cleanup activity. Overall, state MCPs supervised the cleanup of over 24,000 sites, exclusive of Leaking Underground Storage Tanks (LUSTs). The average number cleaned each year peaked at about 3,000 annually, in the mid–1990s, and decreased to under 2,000 per year at the end of the century. Sites remediated under MCPs generally take less time to remediate than Superfund sites, but as with Superfund, the sites are steeped in a regulatory quagmire with the threat of court action.

The eventual rise of VCPs in the mid–1990s appealed to the private sector distressed with the stringent regulations of both Superfund and the state mini–CERCLAs. The number of sites entering voluntary programs has increased steadily since inception as have the number of closure letters. If VCPs continue to gain market share and maintain the level of popularity they have experienced, it is possible for the number of remediated sites to more than double in the next five to ten years. VCP participation is increasing, and the number of successfully completed sites exceeded 2,000 per year for the first time in 1999.

While Superfund and the state mandatory programs are slowing, VCPs are picking up steam and beginning to dominate the cleanup of contaminated sites. VCPs reached 1,000 cleaned sites several years faster than did MCPs, and after their first decade of existence the nation's VCP output was double that of MCPs. Table 1 and Figure 2 show the redevelopment of sites by year and program type.

Table 1: Annual Environmental Cleanup Closures by Type of Program, USA

Year	Superfund	Mandatory	Voluntary
1981	0	16	—
1982	4	18	—
1983	1	20	—
1984	0	28	—
1985	0	44	—
1986	8	63	—
1987	0	394	—
1988	6	565	—
1989	9	859	—
1990	1	1,153	6
1991	9	1,409	14
1992	9	1,779	67
1993	11	1,926	133
1994	9	2,362	203
1995	25	3,023	330
1996	45	3,629	835
1997	25	2,846	1,353
1998	19	2,127	1,870
1999	24	1,740	2,160
Total	205	24,001	6,971

Source: Robert Simons and Environmental Law Institute, 2000.

Conclusions and Future Vision

VCPs are innovation from the ground up, not an orphaned stepchild. The US EPA still acts in a nurturing role, yet trusts the private sector to choose sites while indirectly controlling the quality of site cleanups and

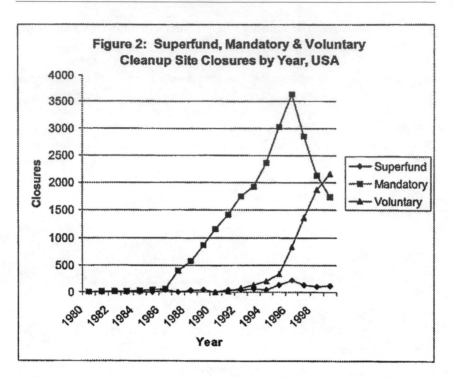

Figure 2: Superfund, Mandatory & Voluntary Cleanup Site Closures by Year, USA

redevelopment through the states. The federal-state SMOAs are playing a large role as they diminish the risk associated with the redevelopment of contaminated sites. Fourteen states currently have SMOAs, and several more states are currently in the negotiation process with the US EPA.

Limiting risk is the key to the success of VCPs. The use of CNTS and SMOAs has curbed the fear of potential lenders and developers, "paving" the way for the redevelopment of these sites. However, VCPs are not without their limitations. It is possible that a site may lose its NFA status, in what is commonly known as a "reopener." Sites may be reopened temporarily or permanently due to the failure of the owner or developer to abide by one or more restrictions in the site closure agreement or CNTS. The closure letter may be reissued when the site becomes compliant or it may be permanently revoked. Reasons for reopeners include failure to file deed restrictions, fraud, new contamination found, change in government standards, and acts of God. As of July, 2000, only about a dozen reopeners had been recorded out of over 8,000 voluntary cleanup program NFAs issued nationwide (Simons and Pendergrass 2000).

The next generation of environmental cleanups may be guided by the local governments. These governments are posed with a daunting task as brownfields consume much of the available land in the inner city. It is important that this land be redeveloped for several reasons. Not redeveloping vacant land has a substantial opportunity cost to the community, and these empty blighted brownfield sites represent a wasted resource. Jobs and tax revenue losses mean lost votes and continued decline if nothing is done. These brownfield sites tend to be located in areas with a disproportionate share of poverty and social problems. Often the neighborhoods surrounding an industrial site were traditionally stable and working class but deteriorated as local industries declined, the housing stock aged, and suburbs flourished. Finding a way to reuse former industrial sites is an indispensable part of any strategy to revitalize urban neighborhoods. The issue of redevelopment has refocused from primarily the preservation of public health to economic development.

Finally, old industrial sites present an opportunity to address the deterioration of the central city that afflicts every metropolitan area in America. As residents and industries have left, they have consumed open space in rural areas and created unnecessarily high infrastructure and transportation costs. Reusing old sites and existing infrastructure can make metropolitan areas more efficient and sustainable, and reduce urban sprawl by providing a place to accommodate efficient infill development, also sometimes called "Smart Growth" (English 1999).

With the advances made at both the federal and state level in cleanup programs, local governments now have the chance to reverse the trends that have led to the abundance of brownfields in urban areas. Programs should be designed that encourage developers to maximize the potential of VCPs. Local officials must understand the nuances of the programs and provide a cooperative framework within which developers can work. Financial incentives such as tax abatements should be made available to make these sites competitive with suburban greenfields, and local governments should not be shy when applying for project-specific federal monies. With the advent of SMOAs and CNTS, neither lenders nor developers carry the risk once associated with this type of development and should feel as free to lend on a brownfield as a greenfield.

As the 21st century begins, the opportunity to correct past environmental indiscretions lies before us. It is the responsibility of local governments, developers and lenders to take advantage of VCPs and use them to benefit the public. Inherent to these programs is the flexibility necessary to make them work for all the important players. So: to US EPA—delegate; to State EPAs—close those remediations; to the banks—lend; to the developers—develop; and to the local governments—support those entrepreneurs who are willing to take a risk on you and your constituency with local economic development funds. With this kind of broad based and decentralized support, brownfields are truly innovation from the ground up.

Endnotes

1. Resource Conservation and Recovery Act of 1976, 42 U.S.C. 6901.
2. Comprehensive Environmental Response, Compensation, and Liability Act of 1980, 42 U.S.C. 9601.
3. Superfund Amendments and Reauthorization Act of 1986, 42 U.S.C. 9601.
4. Leaking underground storage tanks were handled under separate legislation set forth under RCRA. The enforcement period began in 1988 and ran through 1998. LUST cleanups are typically also run by state EPAs, but in some cases other agencies are in charge (e.g., Ohio, from department of commerce) other agencies are in charge. Coordination is often an important issue.

References

Council of Great Lakes Governors. 1998. *Innovative Strategies. Practical Solutions*, Chicago, Illinois: Council of Great Lakes Governors.

Davis, Todd S., and Kevin D. Margolis. 1997. *A Comprehensive Guide to Redeveloping Contaminated Properties*. American Bar Association.

English, Mary R. 1999. A Guide for Smart Growth. *Forum for Applied Research and Public Policy* 14(3): 35–39.

Fisher, William. 1997. Rust Busters: Putting Idle Industrial Sites Back to Work. *Public Management* 79: 18–21.

Meyers, Peter B., and Thomas S. Lyones. 2000. Lessons from Private Sector Brownfield Redevelopers: Planning Public Support for Urban Regeneration. *Journal of American Planning Association*, 66(1): 46–57.

Rahm, Dianne. 1998. Controversial Cleanup: Superfund and the Implementation of U.S. Hazardous Waste Policy. *Policy Studies Journal* 26(4): 719–734.

Rusk, David. 1995. *Cities Without Suburbs*. Washington, D.C., Woodrow Wilson Center Press.

Simons, Robert A. 1998. How Many Brownfield Sites Are There? *Journal of Public Works Management and Policy* 2(3): 267–273.

Simons, Robert A. 1998. *Turning Brownfields Into Greenbacks*. Urban Land Institute.

Simons, Robert A., and Donald Iannone. 1997. Supply and Demand for Brownfields in Great Lakes Cities. *Urban Land* 36–38, 78–79.

Simons, Robert A., and John Pendergrass. 2000. The State Voluntary Cleanup Programs: Are Reopeners Really an Issue? A National Study. Presented at Brownfields 2000 in Atlantic City, NJ. Washington DC, Environmental Law Institute.

US EPA Interview. 2000. ECRA Information Specialist, Personal Interview. November 7, 2000.

United States v. Fleet Factors Corp., 901 F.2d 1550 (11th Cir. 1990).

http://www.epa.gov/superfund/, Superfund Website, November 11, 2000.

Chapter Six

Over *Your* Meadow and Through *Your* Woods: The Transport of Nuclear and Hazardous Waste[1]

SANTA FALCONE

Introduction

Current figures indicate that hazardous waste transporters ship approximately 16 million tons of hazardous waste annually in the US (U.S. Environmental Protection Agency 1995). While some state and local governments have enacted hazardous waste transport regulations for the protection of their citizens, the federal government has had primacy in initiating and setting the course of such regulations. As a result, the predominant perspective on hazardous waste transport has been technical in orientation. This chapter identifies and discusses how the technical perspective and the social perspective differ and what the consequences are for government policies and actions regarding hazardous waste transport.

Iron triangles, issue networks, and policy networks, policy subsystems and policy communities are terms that have been used to describe the complex interplay of power and influence in the public sector arena (Heclo 1978; Milward and Walmsley 1982; Rainey and Milward 1983; and Kingdon 1984). The essence of networks and subsystems is that, for any issue, there is always more than one vantage point and each vantage point will yield differing conclusions concerning the identification of issue components and issue resolution strategies. Vantage points can be categorized according to many dimensions. Two perspectives, one emphasizing technology and the other emphasizing societal concerns,[2] are used to structure this discussion. After identifying the basic premises of these two vantage points and the stakeholders for hazardous waste transport, the consequences for stakeholders of these divergent perspectives will be analyzed for intergovernmental relations, organizational or institutional interests, and the locus of authority for decision making.

The basic technical premise is that societal problems are solvable through the application of sufficient technical expertise as directed by government. Since "safe" transport is the desired public good to be produced, the technical perspective would advocate that the public sector should apply mechanical, organizational, and legal technologies to provide acceptably small risk of harm to transport workers and the public as hazardous waste is moved from one geographic location to another. Transport is thus seen both as inevitable and as a technical problem distinct from other hazardous waste issues.

The basic social premise is that government exists to foster the optimal use of society's resources when markets fail and, specifically, in solving societal problems. Since optimal stewardship of societal resources is the desired public good to be produced, all avenues to eliminate the generation of hazardous waste should be pursued since transport contributes 50 percent of the cost of hazardous waste disposal (Testa 1993). The other factors that are inextricably linked to the transport of hazardous waste in addition to generation, from this perspective, are hazardous waste treatment and storage. This is so because if the waste is either not *created* at all or less of it is created through using alternative nontoxic substances or processes, there is either a decreased need or no need for transport. If the waste is *treated* in situ (in the place where it is created) and the toxicity is removed or decreased, the hazard involved in transport has been removed or diminished. Whether treated or not, if the waste is *stored* in situ the need for transport has been eliminated.

The stakeholders or constituencies of hazardous waste transport can be classified into five general categories to help place hazardous waste transport in context and to highlight how very diverse the participants in this arena are. Ideology, professional and organizational affiliation and economic self interest probably exert strong influence on whether members of the five categories hold either a technical or social perspective on hazardous waste transport.

Category one includes the industries that generate, transport, treat, and store hazardous waste. Generators include all commercial, industrial, utility, medical, defense, government, and educational organizations using hazardous material. Transporters include generator organizations that have their own transport divisions and commercial interests that provide air, land or sea hazardous waste transport services. The treatment, storage, and disposal facility (TSDF) industry includes generators that store or treat waste as well as commercial organizations that either provide mobile treatment or provide treatment, storage, or disposal services at a site.

The second category comprises all organized interest groups, and encompasses environmental and community organizations as well as industry trade associations, professional associations, political parties, and economic development organizations. The third category includes taxpayers and the general public, including communities where hazardous waste currently is, pass-through communities, and disposal site communities. The fourth category embraces the government. This consists of all elected and appointed government officials with executive, legislative, or judicial jurisdictional authority. It also includes the executive organizations with delegated authority to create and implement policies. It extends further to include all civil servants, such as law enforcement and emergency response workers, who will be directly involved in monitoring and resolving problems with hazardous waste transport. The fifth category contains scientists, engineers, lawyers, and all those who contribute to the design of processes, creating of policies, and resolving of conflicts involving hazardous waste transport.

Intergovernmental Relations

Transport does not, by the nature of the activity, create a vested interest on the part of transporters to protect the health and safety of pass-through communities. From a technical perspective, intergovernmental relations are the interactions between local, state, regional, and national government organizations to structure and coordinate their legal and organizational technologies. The examples that follow illustrate the complexity of these relations.

Since a universally accepted authority having worldwide jurisdiction does not exist, the transport of hazardous waste is subject to each nation's laws as it enters each respective jurisdiction. Multinational collaboration has consisted primarily of gathering and reporting information and setting safety standards and guidelines. For example, national studies within the European Community found that 11 nations had some and one nation had no form of required training for workers involved in the road transport of hazardous waste. There was no required training for rail or sea transport of hazardous waste (Haines and Bardsley 1992).

At the national level in the US, federal legislation regulating hazardous waste has created a markedly intertwined system of intergovernmental relations since its inception in 1965 (with the passage of the Solid Waste

Disposal Act, SWDA). This act provided federal assistance to local, regional, and state governments to develop their own solid waste management plans. Amendments to the SWDA (Resource Recovery Act, 1970; Resource Conservation and Recovery Act (RCRA), 1976; Hazardous Waste and Solid Waste Act (HSWA), 1980,1984) had specific provisions for the management of hazardous wastes (Subtitle C).

The legislation that delegates oversight and regulatory authority to federal agencies specifically regarding hazardous waste transport includes:

Year	Act of Congress	Agency
1972	Marine Protection, Research, and Sanctuaries Act (MPRSA)	Environmental Protection Agency (EPA)
1975	Hazardous Materials Transportation Act (HMTA)	Department of Transportation (DOT)
1976	Resource Conservation and Recovery Act (RCRA)	Environmental Protection Agency (EPA)
1980	Comprehensive Environmental Response, Compensation, and Liability Act (CERCLA)	Environmental Protection Agency (EPA)
1982	Nuclear Waste Policy Act (NWPA)	Department of Energy (DOE)
1982	Nuclear Waste Policy Act (NWPA)	Nuclear Regulatory Commission (NRC)

These executive agencies then developed regulations to implement the acts. For example, DOT's 49 CFR 171-180 is intended to: track hazardous materials from their point of origin to final destination, to prevent midnight dumping, to promote uniform safety standards in the states, to minimize the barriers to interstate commerce, and to minimize the dangers posed by hazardous material and waste transport. The initial agency regulations are published in the Code of Federal Regulations (CFR). Changes to the regulations have been and continue to be published in the Federal Register. In addition to the regulations, guidance documents and policy statements are also issued by federal agencies to direct implementation and enforcement.

Two of the acts of Congress, RCRA and HMTA, govern the majority of issues regarding the shipment of hazardous waste from origin to endpoint. It is important to note, in regard to these two acts, that the purposes of the DOT regulations are somewhat different from those of EPA regulations. As a result of this difference and DOT's consideration of hazardous wastes as a subset of hazardous materials, the terminology and classification systems to identify hazardous substances are different in the EPA and DOT regulations (Lindgren 1989). The two agencies' respective regulations are interconnected through the manifest system as follows.

Specific responsibilities are assigned to the generator of the waste, the transporter of the waste, and the treatment, storage, or disposal facility (TSDF). Primary responsibility from origin to endpoint is placed on the

waste generator. The basic eight EPA and DOT-designated responsibilities of the *generator* for shipping hazardous waste are the following. The
generator must determine 1) *if* and 2) *where* the waste will undergo treatment, storage, or disposal. The generator must ascertain 3) if the transporter and TSDF have the appropriate EPA ID numbers and permits to
accept the generator's specific waste.

The generator must correctly 4) prepare the EPA shipping manifest,
5) describing the waste using DOT shipping descriptions. Prior to transport, the generator must 6) ensure the containers holding the waste meet
the DOT regulatory requirements for the generator's specific type of waste,
are in the required condition for transport, and are correctly marked and
labeled; and 7) ensure that the vehicle transporting the waste is correctly
placarded. Finally, the generator must 8) verify that the waste is received
by the TSDF. Fines and other regulatory action can be incurred if these
requirements are not correctly fulfilled (Lindgren 1989). However, identifying violations is not straightforward. This manifest system in operation has problems with waste code definitions, errors, and data
interpretation that make enforcement difficult (Pekelney 1990).

Vehicles used to transport hazardous materials are regulated by DOT
through the Motor Carrier Safety Act (49 USC 1803). This act includes
rigid safety standards for vehicles, safety training, and driver training for
hazardous materials transporters. In addition, transporters (along with
generators and TSDF owners and operators) can be held financially liable
for costs from the remediation of a Superfund site under CERCLA. Transporters are also regulated under MPRSA (as amended in 1988) in regard
to offshore dumping of industrial waste and sewage sludge.

As noted earlier, formal intergovernmental connectedness was instituted by Congress with SWDA and continued with RCRA. Congress designated that the authority and responsibility to administer RCRA would
be transferred to each state as it established a state program that received
approval from the EPA. To obtain EPA approval, state programs are
required to be equivalent to and consistent with RCRA. New federal regulations either require incorporation into state programs or must take
effect simultaneously at the state and federal level as specified by Congress
(Soesilo and Wilson 1995).

State programs delegate authority and responsibility, in turn, to state
agencies. In the State of California, for example, the Hazardous Waste
Control Act of 1987 delegates specific authority to the Department of
Health Services and, in regard to the transport of hazardous materials, to
the California Highway Patrol. The California Vehicle Code also desig-
nates the California Highway Patrol as the lead agency in additional aspects

of hazardous waste transport such as transportation, spills, and licenses. California's State Office of Emergency Services has delegated authority for hazardous waste emergency response, releases, and business plans through California Administrative Code Title 19 (Griffin 1988). Also, state building codes may involve additional state agencies in the regulation of the construction or removal of facilities generating or storing hazardous wastes.

At the local level, county agencies are frequently given the authority to issue licenses necessary to transport hazardous wastes. In addition, local fire codes, building codes, and zoning laws may require the involvement of the local offices charged with their administration in some aspects of hazardous waste transport (Robinson, Thompson, Conn, and Geyer 1993). Thus, from a technical perspective, functions such as rule making, standard setting, enforcement, coordination, education, training, and information gathering are the juncture of intergovernmental relations.

The following studies were conducted to assist governments in tracking hazardous waste in transport and are characteristic of the technical approach. They each recommend coordination of governmental efforts in information gathering or the use of advanced technology that will be used to make decisions concerning the transport of hazardous materials or waste. While each acknowledges that alternative choices should be assessed and the outcomes evaluated, the assessment is done through mathematical and statistical models without mention of public participation and involvement in the decision process.

Lindell and Perry (1997) note that data do not exist to systematically estimate the probability and consequences of earthquake-initiated hazardous material releases both from fixed facilities and from hazardous material in transport. These authors recommend that assessments should be made across seismic zones rather than within jurisdictional boundaries of state or local governments because variation in seismic risk precludes generalization from one zone to another. Lovett, Parfitt, and Brainard (1997) used geographic information systems (GISs) to simulate hazardous waste transport using archived records of the London Waste Regulatory Authority. The authors noted that GIS use could potentially lead to risk tradeoffs (between, for example, routing hazardous waste near population centers or near water supplies) rather than hazard mitigation. Finally, "GIS can also be integrated with sophisticated mathematical models and search procedures to analyze different management options and policies" (Baaj, Ashur, Chaparrofarina, and Pijawka 1995, 144).

Intergovernmental relations, from a social perspective, refers less to complexity than to a seemingly closed system of government entities that the public would like to interface with and influence. The following two examples contrast the ease and the difficulty of transporting a special type of hazardous waste (nuclear) when factors such as sensitivity to public opinion and density of population vary.

In both Europe and Japan, the majority of the land available for storage is not tectonically stable due to the frequency of earthquakes and volcanic activity (Carter 1988). As a result, since the 1960s, Japan and Europe have been shipping nuclear waste to the United Kingdom and France for reprocessing. In 1995, shipments began from Europe back to Japan of its now older, vitrified nuclear waste for permanent disposal (Nakajima 1995). The ships that carry the waste are built in accordance with the Japanese Ministry of Transportation safety standards and standards established by the International Maritime Organization. The ships use containers for the waste that conform with International Atomic Energy Agency (IAEA) regulations for irradiated fuel flasks. Approximately 150 shipments with 7,000 tons of irradiated nuclear fuel have been transported on this sea corridor (Miller 1995).

While these shipments of nuclear waste travel many miles between continents with relatively little incident, in Germany, the 300-mile government transport of six nuclear waste canisters from the south to the north in March 1997 incited thousands of protestors to try to block the shipment by putting logs on rail lines and digging holes in roads. It required , the deployment of 30,000 troops and an estimated $60 million of expense to complete the move (Kris 1997).

Consequences of Divergent Organizational or Institutional Interests

The following discussion uses the example of nuclear waste transport to illustrate the consequences for the public of the divergent interests of the technical and social perspectives. First, several brief statements are made to identify the context of the discussion and then the divergence in the technical and social perspectives are delineated and the consequences projected. There are several types of nuclear waste existing in the US: spent fuel from nuclear power reactors; high-level, transuranic, and related wastes from weapons production; and low level from medical and other uses.[3] The problem with this nuclear waste is the long-term risk it poses to hazardous waste workers and to the public. In this discussion, risk refers to the probability that hazardous substances will find a pathway to cause harm.

From the technical perspective, the goal of nuclear waste cleanup efforts is to remove nuclear waste from the sites where it is currently stored, treat it, and store it in remotely located sites that, through the use of probabilistic models to site and construct, are predicted to minimize post-treatment risks to as close to zero as possible. Technical adherents who are scientists and engineers consider this minimization of risk to be a technical question. They are inclined to think that people that oppose this technical approach do not have enough knowledge (Sjöberg and Drotz-Sjöberg 1991; Cohen 1983). In sum, technical adherents support remote siting as the solution to nuclear waste disposal, a solution emanating from credentialed technical experts.

The consequences or outcomes of remote siting include the following. In category one (nuclear waste industries), in the case of high level and transuranic waste, federal funds would be used to clean up the land where waste is currently stored. For spent fuel, land that is currently used to store the fuel rods could be put to other use. In category two (organized interest groups), environmental and other associations that have opposed remote siting would probably intensify their efforts to oppose the transport of the waste.

In category three (public), current storage sites would receive economic benefit from the dollars spent in removal and the removal of the stigma of nuclear waste from the community. In the past, federal siting efforts have galvanized local and regional opposition (Kriz 1996). The economic benefit that disposal sites would receive from the construction of the repository and the actual storage of the waste has been insufficient for nonvolunteered sites because disposal site communities also receive potential increased risk and the stigma of being a disposal site (Easterling 1997).

For example, there was vigorous and successful opposition to the siting of a TSDF in Ward Valley, CA (Weisman 1996), and the State of Nevada has circled the wagons to fight the federal government concerning the siting of a TSDF at Yucca Mountain, Nevada (Whipple 1996; Swazo 1996; and Flynn and Slovic 1995). Rail and highway routes that would be used to transport radioactive waste to Yucca Mountain have been identified through studies sponsored by Nevada's Agency for Nuclear Projects to assess the transportation impacts and risks. The agency has posted the routing maps on the internet, cataloging approximately 43 states that could be affected and vigorously disputing the safety and efficacy of the DOE-designated routes (NWPO 1997).

Attempting to ameliorate the legacy — NIMBY (not in my backyard) — of past federal siting efforts, current federal and industry efforts have shifted to emphasizing and providing economic benefits to localities volunteering to site TSDFs (Richardson 1995). Volunteered sites do address the earlier errors of not prioritizing land use and of environmental conflicts on proposed sites. They do not address, however, the increase in potential risk to human health and the environment as hazardous wastes are transported to volunteered TSDFs through or close to nonvolunteered pass-through communities. Pass-through communities would receive no economic benefit and increased risk.

For example, the Waste Isolation Pilot Plant (WIPP), the United States' first final disposal site for radioactive waste, has been enthusiastically and aggressively supported by the community that welcomed it, Carlsbad, New Mexico (Rempe 1995). Although the WIPP site was welcomed by Carlsbad, opposition to the transport of nuclear waste through New Mexico and other states has delayed the opening and use of the facility for approximately ten years (Rempe 1995). In the search for communities to volunteer their land, David Leroy, as the first appointed executive of the US Office of the Nuclear Waste Negotiator, targeted Native American Indian nations' land in the United States and Canada for TSDFs (Hanson 1995). Initial financial incentives of $1 million in grants to the National Congress of American Indians and 20 $100,000 grants to individual communities proffered by the Department of Energy to encourage consideration of siting TSDFs, have resulted in ongoing negotiations with three tribes: Mescalero Apache in New Mexico, Paiute-Shone in Oregon and Nevada, and Goshutes in Utah (Hanson 1995). Should these or other communities volunteer to house a TSDF, currently the federal government has not recognized that the pass-through communities en route to the volunteered sites need to be a part of the negotiations.

In category four (government), elected officials might be expected to distance themselves from responsibility to ameliorate the concerns of constituents who oppose remote siting. At all levels of government, officials would continue to expend resources to endeavor to prevent and train for accidents or other unplanned events involving the transport of nuclear waste. In category five (experts), additional research would endeavor to monitor and evaluate the research that has been used to support remote siting.

From the social perspective, due to the cost and the uncertainty (Schrader-Frechette 1996) that surrounds the remote siting models promulgated by the technical coalition, the concept of rolling stewardship is supported as it would enable the optimal use of societal resources (Russell 1997). Rolling stewardship is a management approach to risk whereby the stewardship over nuclear waste would roll over from generation to generation. The waste, in this approach, is not moved, buried or totally isolated, but instead is closely monitored at the site of generation and additional treatment is instituted only if something other than expected outcomes occurs. In situ storage is considerably less expensive than remote or deep burial siting. This reduces the burden of disposal and storage costs, reduces the likelihood of harmful exposure to future generations due to unanticipated risks at remote sites since continual monitoring is occurring, and reduces the costs for and exposure to risk of pass-through communities.

The consequences or outcomes of rolling stewardship include the following. In category one (nuclear waste industries), in the case of high level and transuranic waste, federal funds would be used to contain the waste where it was generated. For spent fuel, the waste would be contained and monitored where it is currently generated. In category two (organized interest groups), industry associations that successfully lobbied for legislation passing responsibility for nuclear waste to the federal government may attempt to profit from their earlier success by suing the federal government for damages (Maloney 1997). Environmental and other associations that have opposed remote siting would probably give increased attention to the monitoring of in situ storage.

In category three (public), current storage sites would contain and monitor the waste. Volunteered disposal site communities would need to explore other types of economic development. Pass-through communities would incur neither the increased risk nor the costs associated with transport. Taxpayers would be required to shoulder considerably lower costs for rolling stewardship. In category four (government), elected officials would endeavor to appease the members of category one and join with all levels of government to support monitoring systems for in situ storage. In category five (experts), research efforts would intensify in the areas of in situ storage and monitoring.

Locus of Authority for Decision Making

The two examples in this section illustrate the impact of locus of authority for decision making on hazardous waste transport, first in regard to enforcement of regulations and second in regard to nuclear waste siting. In terms of hazardous waste generation, the regulations that the EPA promulgated to implement the RCRA (EPA 1995) distinguish between:

Large quantity generators (LQGs) 2,200 pounds (1,000 kilograms) or more per month or 2.2 pounds of acutely hazardous waste in any calendar month.

Small quantity generators (SQGs) more than 220 pounds (100 kg) but less than 2,200 pounds (1000 kg) per month or less than 2.2 pounds of acutely hazardous waste in any calendar month.

Conditionally exempt small quantity generators (CESQGs) 220 pounds (100kg) or less per month.

With the exception of sources of a specific classification of hazardous waste (acute), enforcement authority over generators is delegated by the EPA to states whose programs have been approved, and retained by the EPA for states without approval. In the past, EPA estimated that 90 percent of hazardous waste was generated by LQGs and 10 percent by both SQGs and CESQGs. Schwartz and Pratt (1990) persuasively argued that the EPA estimates of the number of SQGs and of CESQGs and the volume of waste they generate are probably not reflective of (are less than) the actual numbers. In addition, Schwartz and Pratt (1990) noted that the toxicity of the waste generated by SQGs and CESQGs, their proximity to densely populated urban centers, and very low voluntary compliance rates necessitate more comprehensive oversight.

For example, a metal-plating shop in Los Angeles was illegally dumping 1,500 gallons of cyanide waste in concentrations 1,000 times the allowable limit into the city sewer system every day for more than six months. Schwartz and Pratt's (1990) compilation of studies across the nation indicated that as much as 50 to 90 percent of SQGs' hazardous waste is disposed of illegally. This illegal dumping exposes collection and disposal workers at nonhazardous waste landfills and water treatment plants to very toxic substances and contaminates the soil and drinking water in urban areas.

States generally follow the EPA size classification of generators, but some do not. While 21 of the 50 states have additional regulations and seven states have city or county regulations that are more stringent than those of the EPA, enforcement for SQGs is very weak, making the cost of noncompliance quite low. Hazardous waste transport regulations that create disincentives to compliance for SQGs make transport an important issue at the state and local level (Schwartz and Pratt 1990).

For example, as with all other types of shipping, economies of scale encourage lower rates for larger volume and higher rates for smaller volume. Large-and-small volume generators must use licensed transporters and licensed disposal facilities. With a predictable flow of waste and noncompliance costs high, large-volume generators can more easily schedule pickup and TSDF delivery. Compliance with RCRA accumulation and storage limitations and the needed one to two week appointment advance for TSDF delivery make scheduling transporters much more difficult for small-volume generators. In addition, CERCLA liability creates a disincentive for small-volume generator compliance. Under CERCLA regulations "a generator that disposed of a few drums of waste at a TSDF could be held liable for the entire cleanup costs if there is a release of hazardous waste from that facility"(Schwartz and Pratt 1990, 45). Generators are encouraged to actually monitor transporter performance of waste disposal to ensure that compliance is fulfilled because generator liability for transporter errors or negligence is so high (Sharp, Novack, and Anderson 1991).

At all three levels of government (federal, state, and local) resources for enforcement are very limited. As a result, enforcement focus is on large-volume generators, making the regulation of SQGs and CESQGs a lower priority. With noncompliance costs low, transporters not as oriented to service them, CERCLA liability high, and compliance with accumulation and storage regulations difficult, SQGs and CESQGs are less likely to *properly* dispose of and, therefore, transport hazardous waste. Hazardous waste that may more imminently threaten urban populations may not be receiving the oversight it should although technically, according to the established standards, practices, and regulations, it is. While the policy of giving larger generators higher enforcement priority is rational from the technical perspective, from the social perspective, it creates a high risk of long-term and costly toxic exposure for urban populations.

Since the federal government has preeminence over issues related to interstate commerce, it is the formal locus of decision-making authority regarding the transportation of hazardous materials. Although that authority may in actuality reside at the national, state, or province level, the potential real and perceived risks to human health and the environment are acutely sensed by locals proximate to disposal routes. In the past, government and industry tended to employ the decide-announce-defend approach to hazardous waste transport and management decisions. However, RCRA did empower citizens' suits, which provided a check on centralized authority.

Legal challenges have subsequently been mounted to delay or block announced activities. The legal approach is costly, however, and often of uncertain final result. As part of the legal approach, scientific studies have been funded to provide the "best" scientific evidence which has then been disputed by the opposition. Informally, therefore, the power to control outcomes in the transportation of hazardous waste has, like most areas of hazardous waste management, shifted between opposing interests.

Currently, the philosophy, world-view, perceptions of reality, vested interests, and goals of the technical or social adherents across the categories are more different than they are similar. As noted earlier in the example of nuclear waste, historically, the best interests of the federal government and industry, *as perceived by those in positions of authority*, structured the thinking, approach, beliefs, and process for dealing with nuclear waste. "The federal government sees itself as trustee of the nation's energy future, and, peering through that lens, is inclined to see local people and local governments opposing them as parochial, ill-informed, and insensitive to the nation's welfare"(Erikson, Colglazier, and White 1994).

At the state and local level, confusion can be created because more than one voice may claim to speak for and represent these interests. The best interests of local communities, *as perceived by either duly elected representatives, true grass roots spokespersons or by self-appointed authorities*, also structured the thinking, approach, beliefs, and process for dealing with nuclear waste. "Locals, meanwhile, see themselves as trustees of poorly understood and lightly defended territories or ways of life. Viewing the world from that vantage point, they are inclined to see the acts of the federal government as indifferent, unjust, and insensitive to local needs" (Erikson, Colglazier, and White 1994).

Analyzing the fiascoes and blunders that groups of intellectual powerhouses have made in modern-day defense and war efforts, Irving Janis (1971) coined the term "groupthink" to describe several key characteristics that these groups shared (such as unswerving loyalty to policies to which the group has committed itself regardless of the policies' efficacy). As is common in groupthink, those who do not share the belief system established by the group are perceived as adversaries. True openness and careful consideration of opposing views and conflicting needs are jettisoned by the barricading necessary to defend the group's position, which is usually accomplished by attributing high moral purpose to the group.

> The debate then shifts into the realm of high principle. It no longer focuses on the suitability of a particular site for a particular use but upon such matters as justice, democracy, environmental rights, local versus national prerogatives, aesthetic versus economic values, and even religion.... Matters of principle are always more difficult to resolve than matters of fact.... Failure of a powerful authority to take seriously or to consider respectfully a local community's understanding of the world may be perceived by citizens of that community as a challenge to their fundamental understanding of reality. For a community to have its basic conception of the nature of things disregarded may be so alienating that it leaves no common ground on which the authority and community can stand and no common language by which they can converse [Erikson, Colglazier, and White 1994].

The apparent groupthink commitment to deep underground burial, has kept the federal government focused on TSDF siting. The overreliance on "science" to persevere in justifying the deep burial policy is drawing serious criticism.

> Given the potential for human error, the technology's novelty, and the extraordinary time horizon — twice the length of recorded human history — it is inevitable that the actual impacts (physical, biological, social, psychological, and economic) will differ from the best projections. Thus, the surest finding likely to emerge from current research is that the most important questions about the repository's impacts cannot be answered with even minimal assurance [Erikson, Colglazier, and White 1994].

The shift from forced to volunteer siting demonstrates an awareness of public sentiment without a real acknowledgment of the priority it should have. The method used to create volunteers pits communities against their neighbors, escalating rather than diffusing conflict. For example, three communities, Carlsbad, New Mexico for WIPP, the Mescalero Apache Tribal Council (MATC) for a monitored retrieval storage (MTS), and the Meadow Lake Cree Native American Nation in Saskatchewan, Canada for a permanent deep-geologic repository, that have negotiated or are negotiating agreements for TSDFs, are economically disadvantaged or depressed areas (Rempe 1995 and Hanson 1995). The immediate economic benefit of jobs, revenue from disposal fees, and community improvements appear to be the primary motivation for these communities.

There appears to be a presumption that the act of commerce creates a right of way, regardless of consequences to others. However, "transportation has emerged as the most contentious issue in the intensifying federal debate over how to handle the nation's nuclear waste" (Kriz 1997). While anticipated economic development is traded for potential risk by the three communities negotiating to site a TSDF, the siting agreements do not require the participation or approval of the communities through which the waste will travel. These communities do not anticipate receiving economic benefit worthy of exposure to the risk caused by the routing of radioactive waste through their communities (Kris 1997).

Perhaps because nuclear power plant sites and government facilities where the waste is currently stored did not want to use their land for storage or sustain the long-term responsibility for monitoring the waste, early legislation was structured to mandate the removal by the federal government of nuclear waste from these sites. The initiation of this and like imperatives that force unwanted nuclear waste on others, endeavor to shift the true costs of using nuclear material. The long time period of risk posed by nuclear material is unique and the associated cost should be incorporated into decisions concerning its use.

Public opposition to the forced transport of nuclear waste and government deafness to it is not just an American phenomenon, however. Kemp (1991) noted that there is little popular support for a deep burial policy in the United Kingdom. Yet, "the voice of local authorities, communities, and environmentalists is not being heard or heeded "(Kemp 1991, 144).

Exploring alternatives to deep underground burial or perhaps even to centralized storage of any form would appear to avoid: inciting widespread protest and confrontation, increasing exposure risk through the transport of nuclear waste to a centralized facility, providing opportunity for terrorist activity, trusting the accuracy of unverifiable computer modeled projections, and, for underground storage, extremely difficult access to the waste should unanticipated problems or technical advances make access desirable. The exploring of alternatives to the transport for all types of hazardous waste should be pursued.

Cost is a factor in considering alternatives to transport, however. Current rates for the remediation of hazardous waste are dependent on many variables including capital costs, insurance, the characteristics of the waste (e.g., toxicity), the quantity of waste to be treated, and duration of the remediation. Examples of the variation in operating rates for different remediation technologies are shown below.

technology	waste	$ operating cost (only) / unit water or soil[4]
UV radiation	ground water	
	w/ cholorinated solvents	$0.20–.45/ 1000 gallons
	w/ TCE and toluene	$1.57 / 1000 gallons
	industrial waste water	
	highly contaminated	$30.00–40.00/ 1000 gallons
reductive chlorination	soil w/ waste oil & PCBs	$815/yd³
transport & storage at TSDF	soil w/ waste oil & PCBs	$300–500/ton
solvent extraction	soil, sludge, sediment w/PCBs	$150–400/ton
surfactant washing	soil contaminated	$ 73–155/ton (1988 dollars)
extract w/ critical fluids	soil, sludge, sediment w/PCBs	$150–400/ton
rotary kiln	soil contaminated	$200/yd³
infrared conveyor furnace	soil contaminated	$150–550/ton
plasma arc furnace	sludge contaminated	$600–1,400/ton
land farming & bioventing	soil contaminated	$20–100/yd³
engineered slurry reactor	soil contaminated	$100–200/yd³.

Least-cost comparisons for alternative technologies at existing contaminated sites begin with order-of-magnitude estimates that compare the alternative to conventional technologies. For current generators, accurate data concerning the amount and types of hazardous waste being generated are necessary to develop valid estimates.

In general terms, there were 1,187 hazardous waste sites on EPA's National Priority List in October 1990 (Testa 1993). In 1987, 228 million tons of hazardous waste were generated; the amount estimated for 1995 was 235 million tons, and for 2005, 260 million tons (Soesilo and Wilson 1995). Under the combined designations of congressional legislation and federal agency rule promulgation, there are 724 hazardous substances and 1,500 radionuclides regulated (Testa 1993). Since there are approximately 50,000 chemical products in use with approximately 1,000 added each year (Testa 1993), the regulated list can be expected to continue to increase in length.

Due to the absence of resources allocated to regulatory agencies and consequent dearth of manpower in enforcement, there may be a lack of awareness of the requirement to collect and report data and, even with awareness, an economic disincentive for generators to comply and self-report. (EPA estimates that there are 750,000 sources of hazardous waste, with 90 percent of the waste produced being disposed of improperly [Testa 1993].) Once submitted, these self-reports must be aggregated and accurately maintained by state and federal government environment agencies to enable analysis that can improve the assessment of alternative technologies. In the early 1990s, the US General Accounting Office reiterated its late 1980s finding that federal and state hazardous waste data management needed improvement (U.S. General Accounting Office 1991; U.S. General Accounting Office 1990).

There is increasing controversy regarding the shipments of hazardous waste into and across states. In a 1989 study, 15 states were reported to be net importers of hazardous waste and 37 states were net exporters (Environmental Information, Ltd 1993). While on the average, states export to approximately 20 states and import from approximately 20 states (Environmental Information, Ltd 1993), some have enacted legislation to restrict the importation of waste from other states and to make the transport of waste through their states less likely (Soesilo and Wilson 1995). In 1988, two routes— one from New York to California, and the other from Maine to Florida — each required payment of approximately $2,500 in-state imposed hazardous waste tolls or permits to pass through the intervening states with a truckload of hazardous waste (Hilton 1989).

Discussion

Hazardous waste transport is a public policy issue of very high complexity. The four root causes that underlie the complexity are: the existence of already contaminated land and water; the increasing volume of hazardous waste generated; no currently known low-cost methods to remediate hazardous waste once created; and no worldwide enforced standard of hazardous waste remediation. Public response in the United States, both through government and local efforts, includes the NIMBY syndrome regarding TSDF sittings and the increasing quantity and strictness of legislation and regulation designed to reduce or eliminate the potential hazard of this waste. This response has resulted in soaring costs of hazardous waste remediation, increased difficulty in exporting hazardous waste to other states, and geographic variation in the regulatory environment regarding the costs of the negative externalities of production.

Consensus appears to be building that even though it is a complex issue, there are steps that can be taken to move toward the goal of clean air, water and land, and to reduce the risk posed by the transport of hazardous waste. These include: the continuing promotion of waste minimization and pollution prevention with multimedia enforcement; determination of cleanup standards; and state and local partnership (O'Brien and Gere Engineers, Inc. 1995; Soesilo and Wilson 1995; Testa 1993).

Regarding the continuing promotion of waste minimization and pollution prevention, the federal government and large corporations have endeavored to make source reduction (the effort to prevent initial generation of hazardous waste) instead of end-of-pipe treatment the higher priority (Soesilo and Wilson 1995). For example, the EPA's hazardous waste management hierarchy prioritizes source reduction, recycling, waste treatment, and land disposal, first, second, third and fourth in importance (Soesilo and Wilson 1995).

While the decision to adopt or implement any alternative treatment of waste requires an in-depth analysis of its efficacy, the list of alternatives for the current spectrum of hazardous waste includes: transportable treatment units (Schwartz and Pratt 1990); constructing TSFDs near to or at generating sites; oxidation; extraction; thermal technologies; physical or chemical treatment (air sparging, air stripping, carbon absorption, evaporation, distillation, filtration, flocculation, freeze crystallization, oil-water separation, resin adsorption, reverse osmosis, sedimentation, soil flushing, soil washing, soil-vapor extraction, stabilization, steam stripping, supercritical extraction, vitrification); bioremediation (Bellandi 1995; Glass, Raphael, Valo and Eyk 1995); and hybrid systems (Kowalski 1997).

Multimedia enforcement is an important feature of waste minimization and pollution prevention. Media here refers to land, water or air that pollutants are released into. The concern is to ensure that remediation does not transfer pollutants from one medium to another. Anderson and Herb (1992) give the example of the transfer first of air pollutants in stack emissions to water with a wet air scrubber and then back to the air as the water from the scrubber is treated with an air stripper.

O'Brien and Gere Engineers, Inc. (1995, 11) note the divergence in the top priorities of the parties interested in the remediation of a site. "To government representatives, compliance with government standards may be paramount: to the owner of the site, an economical operation and limit to future liability may be foremost. To the community, a minimal risk may be the goal." However, economic considerations have motivated the leadership of some communities to forego concern about risk and permit relaxation of responsible industrial behavior. As a result, the issue of environmental justice has arisen as economically depressed nations or areas in a nation are "... disproportionately burdened by environmental threats such as hazardous waste." (Soesilo and Wilson 1995, 250). Developing, adopting, and enforcing realistic and technically justifiable cleanup standards nationwide or, more preferably, worldwide that include risk estimates that more accurately reflect reality and that balance sustaining the environment and economic development, may diminish current incentives to relocate and continue releasing hazardous wastes into the environment.

Finally, regarding state and local partnership, Soesilo and Wilson (1995) suggest that the existing federally controlled system of hazardous waste management in the US is more productively viewed as a partnership than a mandated program. Although it is a program mandated by the federal government to the states, the authors persuasively argue that to reverse the current lack of compliance, a change in approach to enforcement must occur. Soesilo and Wilson (1995) recommend that states should first establish the legality of formally delegating responsibility to local or regional organizations and then clearly and uniformly delineate specific responsibilities to specific local or regional organizations. EPA (1993) has identified the following important tasks to be delegated:

1. Promote compliance through additional outreach to the regulated community.

2. Provide referrals on suspected hazardous waste violations to the state environmental agency.

3. Perform inspections, and furnish written inspection reports.

4. Secure facility compliance with hazardous waste laws and regulations (as cited by Soesilo and Wilson 1995, 245).

True partnership will require sharing of power. In regard to nuclear waste, recently two trends have emerged. The first is a convergence of voices calling for a reconsideration of the process of decision making (Krannich and Albrecht 1995; Hunter and Leyden 1995; Robertson 1996).

> No matter which agency is assigned the job, however, a radical new management approach is needed — one committed to implementing the recommendations listed above and doing so in an open, consultative, and cooperative manner that does not seek to deny or avoid the serious social and economic dimensions of the HLNW disposal problem (Flynn, Chalmers, Easterling, Kasperson, Kunreuther, Mertz, Mushkatel, Pijawka, and Slovic, with Dotto 1995).

The second is a new willingness to involve and share decision-making authority with the public (Gallagher 1995; Kerr and Ozaki 1995; Gray 1995).

When these steps to promote waste minimization and pollution prevention with multimedia enforcement, to determine cleanup standards, and to establish state and local partnership, reduce the amount of hazardous waste produced, the desired decrease in the transport of hazardous waste will be realized.

Conclusion

Current figures (compiled in 1995) indicate that hazardous waste transporters (19,567 in number) ship approximately 16 million tons of hazardous waste annually in the US (U.S. Environmental Protection Agency 1995). While some state and local governments have enacted hazardous waste transport regulations for the protection of their citizens, the federal government has had primacy in initiating and setting the course of such regulations. As a result, the predominant perspective on hazardous waste transport has been technical in orientation.

The technical perspective predominates particularly in the federal government, possibly as a long term by-product of the professionalization of the public service. The shift in focus from the *position* in the civil service system to the *person* in the career system began in the mid–1950s and has been accelerating (Henry 1995). Professions refer to those occupations that require at least a college degree at the entry level and, increasingly, advancement is predicated on the acquisition of advanced degrees. Emphasis and value is placed on expertise in professionalization and may well be a natural outgrowth of federal civil service examinations that sought to place individuals in government jobs according to their ability to do jobs rather than according to their contribution to the successful election of the currently flourishing political machine.

This emphasis on and importance of expertise in government has paralleled the increase in technological complexity in society. In fact, one theory of government growth argues that government is required by society to be isomorphic to its environment (Gordon and Milakovich 1995). To do so as technologic advances occur, government must grow to obtain the specialized expertise to effectively communicate with and serve the public.

The permeation of technical expertise in the government service is so pervasive that the terms "technocrat" and "technocracy" have been substituted for bureaucrat and bureaucracy. It is not surprising that with a higher percentage of professional and technical workers than the private sector (Henry 1995), the government's first response to problems would be to apply technical expertise, in accordance with the saying credited to Abraham Maslow: "If the only tool you have is a hammer, you tend to see every problem as a nail."

Interestingly, within what might be regarded as the technical community, a study was conducted that ostensibly compared male and female scientists' perceptions of risk. Barke, Jenkins-Smith, and Slovic (1995, 7) concluded that, among the scientists studied, "men tend to see substantially less risk from nuclear technologies and materials than do women." The study surveyed members of the American Association for the Advancement of Science in Colorado and New Mexico. Respondents were categorized as either physical or life scientists. The number of females was very small in both categories, but particularly small in the physical sciences.

As might be expected, given the presence of two national defense laboratories in New Mexico, the authors found a heavy concentration of physical scientists there (48 percent of the sample). For the physical sciences— 94 percent were male and 6 percent were female. For life sciences— 78 percent were male and 22 percent female. Since physical scientists were more different from life scientists, regardless of gender, the conclusion that gender differences were not a function of training may be premature. It may be that a specific type of scientific training, such as coursework in radiation, is the correlate that would explain differences more accurately than gender, if a sample without potential bias due to affiliation with nuclear research were drawn.

More interesting, perhaps, is the list of reasons for the greater risk perceived by women that the authors cite from past studies of the general public and propose in their own. Female heightened perceptions of risk are hypothesized to be due to female's social role, status differentiation, and biological differences. While not stated overtly, the implication appears to be that a deficit, such as a limited social experience of women or an aspect of female physiology, causes a perception of risk above the actual risk that exists. This appears to preclude the possibility that women are, in fact, perceiving risk accurately and some factor in male physiology or socialization leads to the denial of actual risk and, therefore, lower than reasonable perceptions of risk.

While this may seem to be an arcane point, in fact, it is an example of the subtle marginalization of the opinions of the loyal opposition in which advocates of both the technical and social perspectives engage. This tendency enables each side to fortify its belief that the opposition is not perceiving the issue "correctly" and therefore does not need to be acknowledged.

For example, in 1987 a text dealing with radioactive wastes began with a chapter that would discuss "real and imaginary problems." The author cited two prominent individuals who indicated that "radioactive waste disposal was, in a technical sense, comparatively easy" and nuclear waste disposal was "last among the major problems of nuclear power"(Clark 1987, 9–10).

While yet in a position of power and authority, the Director of Oak Ridge National Laboratories was quoted as saying that the above text "was the best book by far on radioactive wastes" in 1987. By this, the director appeared to agree with the book's characterization of disposal as an "imaginary" problem and, by implication, that those who expressed concern about disposal misperceived reality. By 1994, however, the now former director stated that "If he could do it over, he would elevate waste disposal to the very top of ORNL's agenda" (Flynn et al. 1997, 8).

Another example of this marginalization is the technical response to the perceived risk entailed in hazardous waste transport in the case of high level nuclear waste (HLNW). The as-needed routine transport on highways of hazardous *materials* (whose transport provides benefit to society) is offered as justification for the HLNW deep burial policy that will entail the massive (approximated at 79,300 truck-case shipments and 12,600 rail-cask shipments traveling an average distance of 2,300 miles across 43 states [Flynn, Kasperson, Kunreuther, and Slovic 1997]) transport of hazardous *waste* (whose transport provides no benefit to society).

Conflict being the consequent companion of human endeavor, it is not surprising that an issue with economic, health, and environment factors would be fraught with it. Resolution can be attempted through suppression, avoidance, and confrontation but, this author would argue, will only be achieved through negotiation among all five categories of stakeholders. Open participation will buttress the process against group-think and the decide-announce-defend approach. Also key to the mediation of differences will be the trust established with all stakeholders regarding the fairness of the process (Lober 1995). Government can exert true leadership in identifying principles that need to be a part of the process. For example, acknowledging the need for equity in geographic (Rabe 1994) and economic (Schwartz and Pratt, 1990) burden sharing will help to establish trust. Another would be revoking legislation and policies that create incentives for litigious blaming that, to date, have absorbed time and finances that could and should have been spent on actual remediation of hazardous waste. In sum, concentration on identifying mutually desired outcomes and directing all efforts to their accomplishment, rather than the victory of any group of interests, ultimately is more likely to bring satisfactory results.

Endnotes

1. Gratitude is here expressed for the anonymous reviewers and Vern Hershberger for their comments and suggestions on an early draft of this chapter.
2. Special thanks to David Bjornstadt for his insightful comments concerning this construct.
3. Low level waste is frequently mixed with hazardous waste and other toxic materials.
4. The source of all examples is O'Brien and Gere Engineers, Inc.

References

Anderson, S., and J. Herb. 1992. Building Pollution Prevention into Facilitywide Permitting. *Pollution Prevention Review* 2 (4): 479–490.

Baaj, Hadi, Suleiman Ashur, Miguel Chaparrofarina, and David Pijawka. 1995. Design of Routing Networks Using Geographic Information Systems: Applications to Solid and Hazardous Waste Transportation Planning. *Transportation Research Record* 1497: 140–144.

Barke, Richard, Hank Jenkins-Smith, and Paul Slovic. 1995. *Risk Perceptions of Men and Women Scientists.* University of New Mexico Institute for Public Policy.

Carter, Luther. 1987. *Nuclear Imperatives and Public Trust.* Washington DC: Resources for the Future.

Cohen, Bernard. 1983. *Before It's Too Late: A Scientist's Case for Nuclear Energy.* New York: Plenum Press.

Easterling, Doug. 1997. The Vulnerability of the Nevada Visitor Economy to a Repository at Yucca Mountain. *Risk Analysis* 17(5): 635–647.

Environmental Information, Ltd. 1993. *Interdependence in the Management of Hazardous Waste.* Minneapolis, MN: EI, Ltd.

Erikson, Kai, William Colglazier, and Gilbert White. 1994. Nuclear Waste's Human Dimension. *Forum for Applied Research and Public Policy.* Fall.

Flynn, James, James Chalmers, Doug Easterling, Roger Kasperson, Howard Kunreuther, C.K. Mertz, Alvin Mushkatel, David Pijawka, and Paul Slovic, with Lydia Dotto, Science Writer. 1995. *One Hundred Centuries of Solitude: Redirecting America's High-Level Nuclear Waste Policy.* Westview Press as excerpted with permission on internet web site http://www.state.nv.us/nucwaste/yucca/100cent.htm.

Flynn, James, and Paul Slovic. 1995. Yucca Mountain: A Crisis for Policy: Prospects for America's High-Level Nuclear Waste Program. *Annual Review Energy Environment* 20: 83–118.

Flynn, James, Roger Kasperson, Howard Kunreuther, and Paul Slovic. 1997. Redirecting the U.S. High-Level Nuclear Waste Program. *Environment* 39(3): 7–30.

Gallagher, J. 1995. Sharing Power: Building Public Consensus for Environmental Cleanup Programs. Paper published in conference proceedings: Fifth International Conference on Radioactive Waste Management and Environmental Remediation, 125–127.

Glass, David, Thomas Raphael, Risto Valo, and Jack Van Eyk. 1995. Worldwide Markets for Bioremediation. *HazMat Management* October, 141–149.

Gordon, George, and Michael Milakovich. 1995. *Public Administration in America*, fifth edition. NY: St. Martin's Press.

Gray, R. 1995. Public Involvement in Environmental Activities: Initiatives and Lessons Learned. Paper published in conference proceedings: Fifth International Conference on Radioactive Waste Management and Environmental Remediation, 137–141.

Griffin, Roger. 1988. *Principles of Hazardous Materials Management.* Chelsea, Michigan: Lewis Publishers.

Haines, R., and D. Bardsley. 1992. *The Education and Training of Personnel Involved in the Handling and Monitoring of Hazardous Wastes.* Luxembourg: Office for Official Publications of the European Communities.

Hanson, Randel. 1995. Indian Burial Grounds for Nuclear Waste. *Multinational Monitor.* 21–26 September.

Heclo, Hugh. 1978. Issue Networks and the Executive Establishment. In the *New American Political System.* Edited by Anthony King. Washington, DC: American Enterprise Institute.

Henry, Nicholas. 1995. *Public Administration and Public Affairs*, sixth edition. Englewood Cliffs, NJ: Prentice Hall.

Hilton, Cynthia. 1989. States Slap Fees on HazWaste Transport. *Waste Age* May, 69–71.

Hunter, Susan, and Kevin Leyden. 1995. Beyond NIMBY: Explaining Opposition to Hazardous Waste Facilities. *Policy Studies Journal* 23(4): 601–617.

Janis, Irving. 1971. Groupthink: the Desperate Drive for Consensus at Any Cost. Reprinted in Jay Shafritz and Stephen Ott. 1992. *Classics of Organization Theory.* Pacific Grove, CA: Brooks/Cole Publishing Company.

Kemp, S. 1991. Radioactive Waste Disposal: Is There an Acceptable Solution? In *Managing Radioactive Waste* edited by S. Kemp. London, England: Thomas Telford, 140–163.

Kerr, T., and C. Osaki. 1995. What Makes an Effective Citizens Advisory Group? Paper published in conference proceedings: Fifth International Conference on Radioactive Waste Management and Environmental Remediation, 129–132.

Kingdon, John. 1984. *Agendas, Alternatives, and Public Policies.* New York: Little, Brown.

Kowalski, Ludwik. 1997. Will New Technology Solve the Nuclear Problem? *The Physics Teacher* 35(February):126–127.

Krannich, Richard, and Stan Albrecht. 1995. Opportunity/Threat Responses to Nuclear Waste Disposal Facilities. *Rural Sociology* 60(3): 435–452.

Kris, Margaret. 1996. What a Waste. *National Journal.* 4/6/96, 763–766.

Kris, Margaret. 1997. No Place to Go. *National Journal.* 5/10/97, 919–922.

Lindell, Michael, and Ronald Perry. 1997. Hazardous Materials Releases in the Northridge Earthquake: Implications for Seismic Risk Assessment. *Risk Analysis* 17(2):147–156.

Lindgren, Gary. 1989. *Managing Industrial Hazardous Waste.* Chelsea, Michigan: Lewis Publishers.

Lober, Douglas. 1995. Why Protest?: Public Behavioral and Attitudinal Response to Siting a Waste Disposal Facility. *Policy Studies Journal* 23(3): 499–518.

Lovett, Andrew, Julian Parfitt, and Julii Brainard. 1997. Using GIS in Risk Analysis: A Case Study of Hazardous Waste Transport. *Risk Analysis* 17(5): 625–633.

Maloney, Stephen. 1997. The Winstar Precedent and Nuclear Fund Claims. *Public Utilities Fortnightly* May 15, 1997, 34–45.

Miller, M. 1995. The Sea Transport of Irradiated Nuclear Fuel. Paper published in conference proceedings: Fifth International Conference on Radioactive Waste Management and Environmental Remediation, 309–312.

Milward, H. Britton, and Gary Walmsley. 1982. Interorganizational Policy Subsystems and Research on Public Organizations. *Administration and Society* 13:457–478.

Nakajima, M. 1995. Transport of HLW and Spent Fuel in Japan. Paper published in conference proceedings: Fifth International Conference on Radioactive Waste Management and Environmental Remediation, 289–294.

NWPO. 1997. Will Nuclear Waste Travel Through Your State? Article posted on website (http://www.state.nv.us/nucwaste/yucca/travel.htm) on 12/15/97. Email: nwpo@govmail.state.nv.us

O'Brien, and Gere Engineers, Inc. 1995. *Innovative Engineering Technologies for Hazardous Waste Remediation* edited by Robert Bellandi. NY: Van Nostrand Reinhold.

Pekelney, David. 1990. Hazardous Waste Generation, Transportation, Reclamation, and Disposal: California's Manifest System and the Case of Halogenated Solvents. *Journal of Hazardous Materials* 23: 293–315.

Rabe, Barry. 1994. *Beyond NIMBY.* Washington D.C.: Brookings Institution.

Rainey, Hal, and H. Britton Milward. 1983. Public Organizations: Policy Networks and Environments. In *Organizational Theory and Public Policy* edited by Richard Hall and Robert Quinn. Thousand Oaks, CA: Sage.

Rempe, N. 1995. Champion for Radioactive Waste Disposal Host of the WIPP: Carlsbad, New Mexico. Paper published in conference proceedings: Fifth International Conference on Radioactive Waste Management and Environmental Remediation, 149–151.

Richardson, P. 1995. Classification of Methodologies in Use for National Repository Siting Programs. Paper published in conference proceedings: Fifth International Conference on Radioactive Waste Management and Environmental Remediation, 115–119.

Robertson, John. 1996. Why Have Earth Scientists Failed to Find Suitable Nuclear Waste Disposal Sites? *Geotimes* August, 16–21.

Robinson, Janet, Paul Thompson, David Conn, and Leon Geyer. 1993. *Issues in Underground Storage Tank Management.* Boca Raton, FL: Lewis Publishers.

Russell, Milton. 1997. Towards a Productive Divorce: Separating DOE Cleanups from Transition Assistance. July, 1997. JIEE Occasional Papers, 97–3.

Schwartz, Seymour, and Wendy Pratt. 1990. *Hazardous Waste from Small Quantity Generators.* Washington DC: Island Press.

Sharp, Jeffrey, Robert Novack, and Michael Anderson. 1991. Purchasing Hazardous Waste Transportation Service: Federal Legal Considerations. *Transportation Journal.* Winter, 4–13.

Shrader-Frechette, Kristin. 1996. Nuclear Waste: The Academy and Million-Year Estimates. *The Quarterly Review of Biology* 71(3): 381–385.

Sjöberg, Lennart, and Britt-Marie Drotz-Sjöberg. 1991. Knowledge and Risk Perception Among Nuclear Power Plant Employees. *Risk Analysis*, 11.

Soesilo, Andy, and Stephanie Wilson. 1995. *Hazardous Waste Planning.* Boca Raton, FL: CRC Publishers.

Swazo, Sonny. 1996. The Future Of High-Level Nuclear Waste Disposal, State Sovereignty And The Tenth Amendment. *Natural Resources Journal* 36: 127–144.

Testa, Bernard. 1993. *Geological Aspects of Hazardous Waste Management.* Boca Raton, FL: Lewis Publishers.

U.S. General Accounting Office. 1990. *EPA's Generation and Management Data Need Further Improvement.* Washington, DC: U.S. General Accounting Office.

U.S. General Accounting Office. 1991. *SARA Capacity Assurance: Data Problems Underlying the 1989 State Assessments.* Washington, DC: U.S. General Accounting Office.

U.S. Environmental Protection Agency. 1993. *Enforcement Accomplishments FY 1992.* Washington, DC: U.S. Environmental Protection Agency.

U.S. Environmental Protection Agency. 1995. *Preliminary 1995 National Biennial RCRA Hazardous Waste Report.* http://www.epa.gov/epaoswer/osw/generate.htm#regway.

Weisman, Jonathan. 1996. Study Inflames Ward Valley Controversy. *Science* 271(15): 1488–1489.

Whipple, C. 1996. Can Nuclear Waste Be Stored Safely at Yucca Mountain? *Scientific American*, June, 72–79.

Chapter Seven

Community-Based Watershed Remediation: Connecting Organizational Resources to Social and Substantive Outcomes

TODDI A. STEELMAN AND JOANN CARMIN

Introduction

Acid mine drainage (AMD) from hardrock mining pollutes approximately 12,000 miles of streams and waterways in the American West (Mineral Policy Center 1999), and from coal mining, 9,700 miles (U.S. Environmental Protection Agency 2000). Often flowing from existing and abandoned mining sources, AMD can result in heavy metal contamination of water, posing threats to infrastructure (U.S. Geographic Survey 1997), aquatic plant and animal life (U.S. Geographic Survey 1997), and human health (U.S. Environmental Protection Agency 1995). The sheer scope of the AMD problem, combined with the disbursed constituencies affected, creates challenges for remediating existing damage and preventing further damage from occurring.

Beginning in the 1980s, community-based environmental management (CBEM) emerged as a new institutional form for dealing with difficult environmental problems. CBEM refers to local groups working in partnership with agencies, local governments, or other organizations to address and manage environmental problems. After reviewing the evolution of environmental management institutions and the resources that can influence the CBEM process, this chapter presents two case studies of CBEM initiatives that have been used to remediate watersheds polluted by AMD. The cases suggest that there are variations in the way that CBEM projects can be structured, and that the initial organization and objectives of an endeavor are tied to the resources that are available, utilized, and leveraged by a group. Further, these resources, and the way in which they are managed, are associated with the degree of success a project has in achieving substantive as well as social outcomes. It is therefore important that government agencies, community organizations, and other groups initiating CBEM activities consider project structure and resource availability relative to the specific focus and desired goals of the effort.

The Evolution of New Institutions for Environmental Management

Over the past five decades, institutions for environmental management have been transformed. In the post–World War II era, bureaucratic structure was touted as a means to achieve efficient outcomes. Placing faith in science to provide a reliable and stable basis for making decisions and fortified by a belief in linear, deterministic models of causality, many natural resource and environmental agencies institutionalized bureaucratic procedures to meet preset objectives (Shannon and Antypas 1997; Kaufman 1969; Hays 1959). To foster norms that supported and reinforced rational scientific values and bureaucratic ideals, many agencies adopted formal structures including hierarchical chains of command, defined and compartmentalized jurisdictions, detailed rules, and clear boundaries demarcating the agency from its surrounding environment (Meidinger 1997, 1987).

Challenges to traditional scientific management models and bureaucratic structures began to emerge in the 1960s. In contrast to rational perspectives, scientists began to view environmental and natural resource processes as being defined better as nonlinear, stochastic relationships with unpredictable outcomes (Shannon and Antypas 1997; Pickett and Ostfeld 1995). Accompanying this shift in the scientific paradigm was a growing lack of trust and confidence in traditional environmental and natural resource management institutions by the public (Meidinger 1997; DeBonis 1995), greater societal expectations for environmental quality (Kempton et al. 1995; Dunlap and Mertig 1992), an expanded interest in participation (Cutler 1995; Parker 1995; Bosso 1994), and greater policy commitments that made it possible for the public to participate in decision making (Yosie and Hebst 1998). Influenced by these changing views of science, recognizing the need for alternatives to technical bureaucratic structures, and realizing the importance of integrating community values into decision making, environmental and natural resource agencies have come to regard collaboration as an increasingly popular management option (Wondolleck and Yaffee 2000; John and Mlay 1998; Kenney 1997; Yaffee and Wondolleck 1997; John 1996; Yaffee et al. 1996; Selin and Chavez 1995). The growing emphasis on collaboration has produced a need for new interorganizational structures and institutional norms to accommodate the ambiguity and uncertainty that are present in the new era of environmental management (Shannon and Antypas 1997).

An interorganizational structure that has evolved in response to these institutional challenges is CBEM. CBEM has been described as "ad hoc, voluntary and regionally-oriented partnerships that have organized in hopes of addressing and resolving resource and management problems that established institutions and organizations have failed to solve" (Kenney and Lord 1999, 3). CBEM occurs, for example, when a community organization works with the Forest Service to develop community mapping for natural resource management (Poffenberg 1998), or with the Office of Surface Mining to remediate acid mine drainage in a watershed, or with the Environmental Protection Agency to mitigate nonpoint source pollution from agricultural runoff (U.S. Environmental Protection Agency 1997). CBEM is not restricted to community groups working with federal agencies. It can also occur when any combination or number of national environmental organizations, local governments, private firms, or other local nonprofit organizations form partnerships.

CBEM Resources and Outcomes

The resources a community organization has available or is able to generate provide a foundation for executing CBEM projects and for organizations to develop partnerships. Resources contribute to the capacity for collaboration, facilitate action and sustain initiatives over time (Gray 1985; Wood and Gray 1991; Yaffee and Wondolleck 1997; Nelson and Weschler 1998). Seven categories of resources are relevant to community organizations participating in CBEM, as outlined in Table 1. *Human* resources refer to leadership and staffing. CBEM initiatives frequently are championed by those individuals who recognize a problem and are committed to taking action. While these leaders are essential to the mobilization and implementation of a project, volunteer and paid staff members are also important in reinforcing these efforts. *Technical* resources consist of knowledge about the natural resource and its management while *financial* resources refer to the availability of funds. Technical consultations and expertise frequently can be obtained from entities external to the community organization such as government agencies, nonprofits and academic research institutions. Financial resources can be provided through membership, activities the organization sponsors, or from government agencies, foundations, and other nonprofit organizations.

The degree of *experience* that an organization has had with similar types of projects influences its knowledge base and expertise. Experience can occur in two forms. An organization can have previous experience in a CBEM effort or it can cultivate experience as an initial CBEM effort evolves over time. *Structural* resources are the type of organizational arrangements that have been established and the degree to which these arrangements facilitate or impede relationships with other organizations and actors. The *legitimacy* that an organization has achieved within the community determines the extent that it is perceived as being an appropriate actor on behalf of the issue and of the broader population (Gray 1985). Finally, *networks* contribute to organizational strength and the ability to elicit further support within the community (Press 1998) and from partners. Networks may exist at the outset of a project as the result of previous experience and contacts, or they may be developed as groups make efforts to work with the local community and to obtain technical and financial resources from national organizations, foundations and governmental agencies. The concepts of bridging and bonding social capital (Gittell and Vidal 1998) are helpful for discerning different types and functions of network resources. Networks that form strong connections among internal constituents have good bonding capital. That is, members form strong relationships with each other and thus benefit from the trust, reciprocity, and shared norms of behavior that emerge. Bridging capital occurs when the core group reaches out to other organized groups, agencies, or entities in order to create a dense peripheral network of relationships. In essence, the core group builds bridges to other groups. In building these bridges, they benefit from an enhanced sense of obligation, expectation, and trust, an increased potential for reciprocity, and a shared understanding of norms that facilitate interaction with external groups.

Table 1: Summary of CBEM Resources

Human Resources	Leadership and staffing, including full-time, part-time, and volunteer staff.
Technical Resources	Knowledge about the natural resource and its management.
Financial Resources	Grants, membership dues and solicitations, and other monetary contributions.
Experiential Resources	Knowledge base and expertise with similar problems or management efforts.

Structural Resources	Organizational arrangements that facilitate or impede collaborative relationships.
Legitimacy Resources	Degree that CBEM effort is perceived as representative of the community at large.
Network Resources	Relationships formed within as well as external to the core group, including bonding and bridging relationships.

The resources that are available to a community organization participating in a CBEM project influence its capacity to achieve goals and realize outcomes. There are two general categories of outcomes that can be derived from CBEM activities: substantive outcomes and social outcomes. Substantive outcomes are the environmental or resource issues that an organization would like to address or resolve. These may be formulated at the outset or they may develop and be refined as the project evolves. Substantive goals in watershed management typically focus on objective criteria pertaining to terrestrial and aquatic restoration and preservation. For example, CBEM efforts can include activities such as research on water quality or watershed usage, community education, the development of protocols to reduce heavy metal contaminant loads or other pollutants in a waterway to specified target levels, or the overall management of the restoration of a watershed to a precise level of ecological health as determined by the presence of explicit aquatic and terrestrial species of plants and animals.

In addition to substantive outcomes, there are numerous social outcomes that can develop from CBEM projects. One social benefit that can be derived from partnerships that are formed in the CBEM process is that all groups develop deeper *understanding* of the issues and of the implications of different strategic alternatives (Beierle 1999; Koontz and Moore 2000). Partnerships that occur in the CBEM process also may foster *trust* (Slovic 1993; Gray 1985) and help cultivate interaction (Korfmacher 2000) among groups. This is particularly significant when groups have experienced conflict or have not been able to trust each other in the past. Finally, deliberative processes like CBEM can help *elicit the values and preferences* of various stakeholders (Steelman 2001; Webler and Tuler 1999) and, as a result, provide a basis for incorporating these perspectives into the decision-making process (Beierle 1999).

The resources available to a community organization are important because they allow groups to initiate and sustain activities. They also influence a group's capacity to achieve social and substantive outcomes. The relationship between resources and outcomes is more complex than a simple "if-then" clause. Often it is the interaction of different types of resources that shapes the outcomes that emerge. For instance, financial and structural resources can contribute to the internal stability of an organization while human, technical, experiential, structural, legitimacy, and network resources facilitate both concrete environmental actions as well as interactions among groups.

The Problem of Acid Mine Drainage

Throughout America, numerous CBEM initiatives have emerged to address issues of water quality and watershed preservation and restoration (McGinnis 1999). One problem that has surfaced in a significant portion of the country's waterways is acid mine drainage. AMD occurs when sulfur-rich rocks are exposed to air and water in the mining process causing oxidation. For instance, iron pyrites (FeS_2), which is common in the overburden in mining, breaks down into its constituent parts of ferrous iron and sulfur when it is exposed to air, rain, or snow. The sulfate ions react with the water to produce sulfuric acid (H_2SO_4). The composition of the drainage varies from mine to mine and location to location, but typically is made up of acid, sulfate ions, precipitated iron compounds and dissolved metals. The impacts of AMD are varied and depend on the surrounding geophysical conditions. As the amount of acid increases in the streams, the pH level[1] is depressed. A low pH allows metals to dissolve into solution. As the pH in a stream drops, the metal concentrations increase and become toxic to fish and other water-dwelling plants and animals. The metals can include iron, lead, zinc, copper, manganese, aluminum, silver, mercury, nickel, cadmium and arsenic, known collectively as heavy metals. If the pH is buffered through exposure to an alkaline source, such as limestone further downstream, then the metals will precipitate out of the solution. This results in rocks and stream bottoms becoming covered in bright-orange or white sludge depending on the metal. When AMD enters a stream, fish and other organisms usually are killed. Streamside vegetation is radically changed and groundwater can become contaminated with metal ions.

Two federal agencies have played significant roles in addressing the problem of AMD. When AMD results from coal mining, the Office of Surface Mining Reclamation and Enforcement (OSM) is the dominant regulatory agency. In contrast, if hard rock mining results in AMD, often the Environmental Protection Agency (EPA) is the main regulatory body. To address the environmental problems affiliated with strip-mining of coal, including AMD, the Surface Mining and Control Reclamation Act (SMCRA) was passed in 1977. This act requires that mine owners and operators reclaim mined lands and ensure that the water discharged from their property does not exceed specified pH, metals, and suspended solids limits. The SMCRA also created the OSM to oversee the regulations of coal mining and reclamation operations. Additionally, the EPA, through Sections 319(h)[2] and 104(b)3 of the Clean Water Act, can bestow grants to local watershed groups to support the reduction and prevention of non-point source pollution (Office of Surface Mining /U.S. Environmental Protection Agency 1995a). These funds can be applied to either coal or hardrock AMD. The U.S Environmental Protection Agency established in 1994 its Mine Drainage Initiative (MDI) as a model for establishing partnerships to restore streams impacted by AMD (Office of Surface Mining/U.S. Environmental Protection Agency 1995a). The EPA also can make grants through its Regional Geographic Initiative Program.[3]

AMD is a complex problem that has been ineffectively addressed through traditional agency structures and regulatory measures. Partnerships and broader ad hoc collaborations that are the hallmark of CBEM activity bring public, private, and nonprofit organizations together to overcome some of the obstacles that historically have plagued traditional regulatory approaches. In some cases, CBEM activities initiated by local organizations and agencies have been targeted at a specific AMD problem. In these instances, the focus tends to be on substantive goals. In other instances, partnerships have been developed in the absence of an explicit environmental goal. While a substantive goal may emerge at some point, the emphasis in these types of processes is to foster the exchange of knowledge and information about AMD and to generate social outcomes such as trust, commitment, and the understanding of values and preferences so that a basis for collaborative environmental action is developed.

Remediation in the Cheat River Watershed

In 1995, a CBEM initiative was started on the Cheat River to remediate AMD. The Cheat originates from five tributaries located in the heart of the Monongahela National Forest in north central West Virginia. Flowing a total of 157 miles, the river runs north through the Appalachian Mountains and channels into the Cheat Canyon before emptying into Cheat Lake. The river then joins the Monongahela River a few miles downstream of Morgantown, West Virginia near the Pennsylvania state line. Whitewater enthusiasts have flocked to the Cheat River for decades to run its challenging Class III-V rapids in the Canyon section. Spring is the height of the whitewater season with mean average flows around 2,600 cubic feet per second (cfs). The entire Cheat watershed drains 1,425 square miles and is nestled in the heart of northern West Virginia's coal mining country.

In its upper regions, the Cheat is unpolluted and supports a thriving fishery. However, by the time the river enters Preston County and winds its way 20 miles into the Cheat Canyon, the rocks along the river take on the distinctive brownish-orange hue associated with AMD and, as a result, this portion of the river has been rendered virtually ecologically sterile. The Preston County section of the Cheat reflects the devastating impacts that AMD can have within a watershed. The EPA estimated that there were 457 mines on various tributaries of the Cheat (Bryant 1996) and that approximately 188 contribute AMD to the river. The OSM (1996) estimates that in West Virginia a total of 1,900 stream miles are polluted by AMD, making it the major source of pollution to the state's waterways.[4] Over 90 percent of AMD in these streams is from mines that were abandoned before SMCRA was passed, while approximately 10 percent results from mines suffering bond forfeitures and bankruptcy since 1977 (U.S. Environmental Protection Agency, undated brochure). In Preston County there are 147 mines that were abandoned after 1977 and 57 of these are on the Cheat River (Davis 1996b).

Development of the CBEM Initiative on the Cheat River

Following a spring rain in 1994 water pressure inside an illegally sealed off coal mine blew out the side of a mountain, pouring millions of gallons of AMD into a tributary of the Cheat River (Bassage 1995a; Wiles 1999). The resulting discharge not only impacted the Cheat Canyon section, but killed fish 16 miles downstream (Snyder 1995). Since the blowout, the whitewater industry on the Cheat has suffered more than a 50 percent drop in business while whitewater sports nationally have seen a 33 percent increase (Chottiner 1995). A second blowout in 1995 further accentuated the problem and caused American Rivers, Inc, a national river conservation organization, to put the Cheat on its top ten list of the nation's most endangered rivers (Chottiner 1995).[5]

For years, whitewater paddlers, as well as other community members, witnessed the AMD-induced degradation of the Cheat River. When the second blowout occurred, the whitewater community no longer was willing to sit back and watch the river continue to decline. A group of paddlers formed an organization called Friends of the Cheat (FOC) that was founded on two principles. The first was to "restore, protect and promote the outstanding natural qualities of the Cheat watershed" (FOC, 1999a). The second was to "foster a cooperative effort by state and federal agencies, private industry, academics, grassroots organizations and local landowners to address the severe AMD in the Cheat Canyon" (Bassage 1995b).

The federal agency most active in the effort to improve the Cheat River has been the OSM. The Office of Surface Mining established the Appalachian Clean Streams Initiative (ACSI) in 1994, which funds cooperative agreements between OSM and nonprofit groups for local acid mine drainage programs (Office of Surface Mining Reclamation and Enforcement, undated brochure). The OSM can provide funding for mine reclamation and mine drainage cleanup through Abandoned Mine Land (AML) funds.[6] A number of other groups and agencies have been involved in remediation of the Cheat River. One example of the partnerships FOC has developed with these organizations is embodied in the River of Promise Task Force and the "River of Promise" pledge — a document that articulates a shared commitment to clean up the Cheat watershed. The River of Promise Task Force coordinates the massive effort to reclaim eight major tributaries and the lower main stem of the Cheat River and is comprised of over 40 federal, state, local, public, private, nonprofit, and research entities that have committed specific resources to the remediation of the Cheat River watershed.

Friends of the Cheat Resources

Human resources refer to the presence of leadership as well as the presence of voluntary and paid staff. As Friends of the Cheat has evolved, so have its human resources. Dave Bassage served as the executive director of FOC for its initial five years, first as a volunteer for two years then as a paid employee. Bassage was integral to the formation of the group and in keeping it focused on its mission. "Our mission has been our north star since we came up with it," says Bassage, and while temptation has been great to move into issues outside of their main focus, "everything we do has to relate to our mission" (Bassage 1999b). In 1998, FOC was able to hire a second staff member to help with the group's many activities. While Bassage and the second staff member represent hired positions, the organization also has dues-paying members, some of whom volunteer their time, and a board of directors. The board members represent diverse concerns and interests including the coal industry, local landowners, the whitewater industry, environmental activists, teachers, and other local businesses.

FOC has been able to take advantage of *technical resources* across sectors and from all levels of government. During his five years at the helm of FOC, Bassage has educated himself about the various aspects of AMD, mitigation technologies, hydrology, geology and the numerous agencies that work to remedy the problems of AMD in the Cheat watershed. In many ways, Bassage can be considered a first-rate generalist on the topic who knows where to go when he is stumped on a more technical point. Through its many partnerships, FOC has been able to tap many technical advisors. FOC has built a strong relationship with academics and researchers at West Virginia University (WVU), WVU's National Mine Land Reclamation Center, and the Federal Energy Technology Center.

Agencies also have served as technical advisors with the OSM and various state agencies actively providing technical assistance to the group. Both OSM and EPA have signed a "Statement of Mutual Intent" to work together to restore the water quality in AMD-polluted streams in Maryland, Pennsylvania, Virginia, and West Virginia (Office of Surface Mining/ U.S. Environmental Protection Agency 1995a). Signed in 1995, the statement indicates that the federal agencies will share information and data and work with other groups and agencies to remedy AMD problems. Various state technical sources include the West Virginia Department of Environmental Protection, especially the Abandoned Mine Lands Division. A nonprofit group called the Canaan Valley Institute and the West Virginia Watershed Network are also sources of information and advice that have been useful to FOC.

Over the past five years, FOC has begun to generate *financial resources* with the budget for the organization growing from $28 to over $200,000 (Bassage, 1999a). While the group has been successful in finding resources to fund specific remediation projects on the Cheat River, it has been less successful in finding funds to support its day-to-day operations. Nonetheless, the group has been successful in leveraging funds from numerous federal, state, foundation and private sources— OSM and EPA being two main federal sources of funding. Over the past several years, FOC has been successful in garnering approximately $600,000 from OSM's Appalachian Clean Streams Initiative (ACSI) for projects in the watershed.[7] Additionally, EPA has provided FOC with $250,000 for projects to remediate AMD (Haywood 2000). At the state level, the West Virginia Stream Partners program, which makes grants of up to $5,000 to existing and emerging watershed groups throughout the state (West Virginia Rivers Coalition 1997) has been an annual source of support for the group.

With a membership of approximately 600, dues provide a significant financial base for the group. FOC holds an annual festival, which generated

$6,000 its first year and $40,000 in 2000 (Bassage 1999b; Bassage 2000). Most of the money raised by FOC is restricted to funding reclamation projects in the watershed; consequently, FOC has had trouble recently finding money to cover its operating expenses. While several agencies and foundations are eager to fund results-oriented projects, they are less enthusiastic about funding the administrative and day-to-day costs that keep organizations like FOC running.

Since FOC was formed to address the problems of AMD on the Cheat River, it did not possess any previous *experience* with environmental or organizational management. However, Dave Bassage, as well as others within FOC, had a strong commitment to AMD remediation and gained experience by working on the issues. Limited experience may have helped FOC since the organization was not constrained by pre-existing relationships or expectations. The organizational *structure* established by FOC has facilitated management initiatives and the development of partnerships with agencies. FOC is organized so that the board makes strategic decisions, the two core staff members manage programs and day-to-day operations, and the volunteers help the staff implement these larger programs as well as smaller initiatives. The River of Promise Task Force and the River of Promise Pledge are additional structural resources that facilitate relationships with other organizations and actors. Signatories to the pledge have acknowledged publicly a shared commitment to the restoration and remediation of the Cheat River. The River of Promise Task Force is a subset of these some 40 signatories who are charged with coordinating and prioritizing the many reclamation activities within the watershed.

FOC has cultivated strong *network* ties within the group, as well as ties with academics, nonprofits, and private and public entities at the local, state and national levels outside the group. These bridging and bonding networks have helped FOC bring representatives with varied interests and stakeholder groups together. At the state level, FOC works regularly with the West Virginia Department of Environmental Protection, which includes the Office of Abandoned Mine Lands, the Office of Mining and Reclamation, and the Division of Natural Resources. FOC also works with a variety of nonprofit groups throughout the state, including the West Virginia Rivers Coalition, the Canaan Valley Institute, and the West Virginia Watershed Network. At the federal level, the FOC has working partnerships with the federal Office of Surface Mining, Reclamation and Enforcement (OSM), the Environmental Protection Agency (EPA), the Army Corps of Engineers (ACOE), and the Natural Resource Conservation Service (NRCS). American Rivers and River Network are two national nonprofits with which FOC has been active.

FOC has a high level of local *legitimacy*. Being well-networked within the community and making strides to represent the watershed's residents in its activities as well as to inform residents of its many efforts, have enhanced visibility and acceptance of the group. As the organization's legitimacy has grown, it has become an identifiable focal point for people both within and outside the watershed as an entity that can assist with watershed concerns.

Outcomes of CBEM in the Cheat Watershed

The purpose of FOC is to restore the Cheat River to ecological and economic health. The function it serves is to coordinate this effort throughout the watershed. The broad range of activities adopted by FOC reflects the breadth of this enormous mission. Its staff and volunteers carry out remediation efforts, they coordinate technical workshops and meetings, and they educate and involve the community. FOC could not be effective if it were not well connected to the various communities in the watershed. The broadness of its mission "to restore, protect and promote the outstanding qualities of the Cheat watershed" has encouraged the group to build a diverse base of support for its activities. With a mission this broad, the only way the group can accomplish its goals is by casting its net as widely as possible and harnessing the resources within its grasp. This network is the group's greatest strength and is connected directly to the legitimacy of FOC as a community organization.

Substantive Outcomes

Friends of the Cheat has engaged in numerous projects since its inception. Through its partnerships with many state, federal and other nonprofit groups, FOC has been able to channel $12 million into studies of and reclamation projects in the watershed (Friends of the Cheat 1999b). One of the first projects initiated under the River of Promise agreement was by Anker Energy Corporation, a local coal mining company, on a tributary to the Cheat known as Green's Run. On September 18, 1995, Anker Energy committed $250,000 and began construction of an anoxic-limestone drain designed to neutralize the acidity from an abandoned mine on Green's Run.

In May 1995, a project was undertaken by FOC on Sovern Run, also a tributary of the Cheat. The primary emphasis of this project was to enhance metal precipitation from AMD and reclaim abandoned mine lands. Additional funds were added to the Sovern Run project in April 1997 with $80,000 from EPA. This was the first time that EPA Region III provided funds directly to a citizen's group to conduct reclamation projects. In 1998, FOC initiated a project on Beaver Creek, another tributary of the Cheat. This $100,000 project to add alkalinity to the stream also was funded by EPA. This effort works in concert with two other projects in the area that are funded by WVDEP and the Army Corps of Engineers. In 1999, FOC received nearly $240,000 from the ACSI (Appalachian Clean Streams Initiative) program to construct a passive mine drainage treatment system on Beaver Creek (Office of Surface Mining Reclamation and Enforcement 1999) and other tributaries of the Cheat (Haywood 2000).

These reclamation projects have experienced ups and downs. Many of the technologies employed to treat the AMD are experimental passive systems of treatment. In some instances, the projects have been very successful at first and then, for any number of reasons, have become less effective in their treatment of AMD. In other cases, projects have met or exceeded design expectations. Different stream segments have seen improvements, but there have been no quick and easy fixes to the problem of AMD. Commenting on this, Bassage says "tackling a task as immense as restoring a severely ill watershed can be more than daunting at times. Sometimes I get downright depressed.... Muddy Creek is still bright orange, as is Greens, Pringle, Lick, Heather, Morgan and Bull Run," (Bassage 1999c). Adding that it is not all bad news, he stated "A fish kill may not seem like good news, but when 150 red horse suckers turned belly up [in 1999] we were surprised to learn that we had that many fish living [there]," (Bassage 1999c). Bassage also commented that he, and others, have begun to see schools of minnows, larger fish and turtles further down in the Canyon section of the Cheat. Insect life has been spotted on sections of the Muddy Creek that were thought dead (Bassage 1999c). In short, something is happening out there.

Social Outcomes

The activities, structure, and approach adopted by FOC has promoted *understanding* of AMD issues and river restoration within the organization, within the immediate geographical community, within more specialized technical communities throughout the region, and within the state. FOC has a membership of over 600 with individuals in 28 states, one Canadian province, France and the District of Columbia (Friends of the Cheat

1999d). Within their own organization, FOC promotes understanding by sending out a quarterly newsletter to its 600 dues-paying members. The newsletter keeps members informed of the group's many activities as well as the thoughts and ideas that are being tossed around by the staff and board of directors, who often write articles for the newsletter. Within the immediate physical community, FOC sponsors an annual Cheat River Festival, which was started in 1995. The Cheat Fest allows the community to share in a collective understanding of the group's victories and defeats for the year against the backdrop of folk music, local food, information booths and silent auction. Within the regional technical community concerned about watershed and AMD issues, FOC helped promote understanding by helping fund the most comprehensive countywide study into the state of stream health. This study helped the group produce a map that detailed water quality in different stream segments throughout the county. The group has hosted an acclaimed gathering of watershed interests and cosponsored a stream assessment workshop. FOC also helped convince the U.S. Army Corps of Engineers to focus their vast resources on the acid mine drainage problem within the Cheat watershed, instead of trying to dam the river. Working with the Preston County's Commissioners, FOC was involved in establishing an Americorps watershed project, called Mountain's Promise, that attracted six full-time and 14 part-time Americorps members. FOC enlarged the network of organizations that address watershed issues in the region by facilitating the development of other organizations in the watershed, such as the Cheat River Watershed Association, Friends of Laurel Mountain, and Shavers Fork Coalition. Finally, FOC is encouraging understanding of its issues at the state and intrastate level through its work on a documentary of its work in the watershed. The purpose of the project is to produce three half-hour video segments outlining the past, present, and future of the Cheat River watershed from reclamation, recreation, and cultural perspectives. To date, the video has been showing on regional public television stations and illustrates FOC's concern for promoting understanding at the broadest level possible.

These efforts at promoting widespread understanding of AMD issues and FOC activities has helped generate *trust* both from within and outside the organization. FOC activities have fostered interaction and cultivated trust among what would otherwise be considered rival interests. Within the organization, FOC promotes the building of trust at its board meetings, where environmentalists sit by coal industry operators who sit by whitewater kayakers who sit by teachers who sit by local landowners. While they are an eclectic group with varied interests, the common goal of cleaning up the Cheat has helped them bridge their differences. Outside the group, trust is fostered through structures that bring together different entities and allow them to focus on common objectives. The River of Promise Task Force is a good example of how different groups have learned to work with each other.

Implicit in these attempts to promote understanding of AMD and watershed issues and trust among various members and partners are efforts to elicit and understand the *values* that are important to FOC's many constituent communities. Through its newsletter and membership, FOC invites comments and ideas. Staff, the board of directors and volunteers come into contact with the broader community during the annual Cheat Fest and each gains a better understanding of the others' concerns. Workshops, conferences and regular River of Promise Task Force meetings allow for more focused elicitation of values and preferences. All in all, FOC encourages involvement from its various communities to shape its continued efforts to restore the Cheat River watershed.

Watershed Remediation in the Upper Animas

The Animas River is formed by the confluence of three drainages— Mineral Creek, Cement Creek, and the upper Animas. These headwaters are born in the spectacular San Juan Mountains in southwest Colorado. The Animas is significant in that it is the largest remaining free-flowing river in the West (American Rivers 1996). It is not a large river — roughly 100 feet wide on average with winter flows of approximately 500 cubic feet per second and spring flows, fed by snowmelt, at 7,000 cfs (Frodeman 1999). Cascading through stunning 14,000 feet mountains, canyons and cliffs near the old mining town of Silverton, the upper Animas River is part and parcel of the highly mineralized geological zone for which this area is famous (Blair 1996).

Mining is an integral part of the history of the region, and the mountains cannot be separated from the mining that that has taken place in and around them. Millions of tons of metals, including gold, silver, lead, zinc and copper, have been excavated in the last 120 years from the mines that pepper the mountains in the region (Blair 1996). Not surprisingly, the headwaters of the Animas are impacted by heavy-metal loading. Past mining practices as well as natural geological processes account for the copper, iron, aluminum, manganese, lead and cadmium loads that render the waters of the upper Animas, for the most part, ecologically lifeless. An estimated 1,500-2,000 abandoned and inactive mines leak acid mine drainage into the Animas River watershed (McAllister 1999, 8; Kenney 1999, 33)

Development of the CBEM Initiative on the Animas

Until the early 1990s, water quality on the Animas had not been an overt concern. The Colorado Water Quality Control Commission (WQCC) first set water quality standards and use classifications on the upper Animas in 1979 and reassessed these every three years (McAllister 1999).[8] As a result of the low pH and heavy-metals contamination, the Water Quality Control Division (WQCD), the state agency tasked with conducting studies and making recommendations for action to the Colorado Water Quality Control Commission, determined that there was very little aquatic life in the river. Since the river was not being used as source of drinking water, the agency did not attempt to classify use standards for the upper reaches of the Animas and set standards as ambient, which in essence means that there were no standards. However, in the late 1980s, some local residents backpacked trout into one of the streams on a hunch that parts of the watershed could support aquatic life. Following the introduction of trout in the late 1980s, the WQCC needed to reassess the use classification of the river.

From the period 1991–1993, the WQCC tasked the WQCD to perform studies in the upper Animas to determine "the potential for water quality improvement sufficient to allow natural reproducing trout populations" (McAllister 1999, 21). In 1993, the WQCC found reproducing populations of mixed species and determined that water quality in the Animas watershed could be improved (Broetzman 1996). The challenge that remained was how to establish these new standards. Abandoned mines are considered to be nonpoint sources of pollution and thus fall under total maximum daily load (TMDL) programs. Determining TMDLs is a complicated task and EPA in Region VIII has been reluctant to impose TMDL standards on financially vulnerable interests, such as those in the Animas watershed (McAllister 1999, 18). The degree of complexity involved in determining TMDLs led EPA to suggest a community-based watershed approach in the upper Animas. EPA's hope was that through a community-based process, locally determined standards might be set, managed and enforced.

In response to EPA's request, the WQCD retained the services of the Colorado Center for Environmental Management (CCEM) to facilitate the creation of a community-based watershed group (Broetzman 1996). In January 1994, CCEM began discussions with various people in the Animas watershed to understand the different perspectives about water quality. Defining "community" and "stakeholders" for this process was a challenge. Eighty-three percent of San Juan County is on publicly owned land (Animas River Stakeholder Group 1999a). The involvement of federal land agencies was imperative since they own most of the land. San Juan County had a total of 500 residents at the time, so the community as a whole was and is quite small (Animas River Stakeholder Group 1999b). Of all the mines in the region, nearly all are privately owned, but many of the mine owners are absentee landlords. Many of the local people contacted were suspicious of the CCEM's intent and also harbored concerns about EPA, the WQCD and the Colorado Department of Public Health and Environment (Broetzman 1996). Some of the initial participants agreed reluctantly to take part in the process out of "fears that 1) the State would proceed with or without their involvement in initiating cleanup of the area or that 2) EPA would use the information and designate the area for cleanup under CERCLA" (the Superfund law) (Broetzman 1996, 5).

A list of stakeholders was assembled by the CCEM and the first meeting of the Animas River Stakeholder's Group (ASRG) was called in February 1994. According to the CCEM status report on the ARSG, "an acrimonious mood prevailed during [the] early sessions due to general distrust that permeated the setting" (Broetzman 1996, 5). Overcoming some of the initial levels of suspicion, a core group was interested in pursuing the WQCC challenge to set standards in the watershed and began to work in December 1994. The ARSG received its first challenge in February 1995 when the WQCC decided to impose strict numerical water quality standards for the upper Animas without consulting the group. The new standards would require significant improvements in water quality for aquatic life (McAllister 1999). ARSG opposed the imposition of these standards and requested that the WQCC delay the effective date for their establishment and empower ARSG to "locate and evaluate sources of metals contamination, determine potential improvement and prioritize sites for remediation in order to recommend achievable water quality standards and use classifications" (Animas River Stakeholder Group 1999a). The WQCC gave ARSG three years to accomplish its goal, and the group set out a three-phase plan to do so: 1) conduct extensive studies of the water quality in the upper Animas; 2) determine the most serious sources of contamination and prioritize areas for cleanup; and 3) initiate some remediation projects (McAllister 1999).

Animas River Stakeholder Group Resources

Human resources within ARSG have included a part-time watershed coordinator, part-time staff, and various committee members who have taken on the job of determining water quality standards. In the summer of 1994, the WQCD helped the nascent ARSG write a grant application to the EPA to begin some investigations in the watershed. With the EPA monies that were obtained, ARSG hired Bill Simon as the watershed coordinator (Broetzman 1996). Simon is a long-time resident of the basin with a mining and environmental background (McAllister 1999). He oversees many of the administrative tasks that keep ARSG together and acts as spokesperson for the group. He also coordinates ARSG fundraising, and participated in research and data collection for the use attainability analysis and the TMDL framework that had to be submitted to the state in 2000 (McAllister 1999). To help him handle his many activities, ARSG expanded its human resources by hiring a staff assistant in 1998. Several members of the group take on tasks and work as heads of the various committees.

In addition to Simon's own training in mining remediation and environmental issues, *technical resources* were present through the various state and federal agencies that are part of the stakeholder group. Many of these membership agencies have conducted, funded or advised on research in the upper Animas. Stakeholder members such as the Colorado Division of Mining and Geology, the Geological Survey, and the Department of Wildlife have been active technical advisors, as have the US EPA, US Forest Service (USFS) and Bureau of Land Management (BLM).

For *financial resources*, the group has relied most heavily on funding from EPA's Rocky Mountain Headwaters Mining Waste Initiative. EPA also has funneled money to ARSG though the 319 program. For 1999, ARSG received nearly $450,000 — a full 35 percent of EPA's 319 grant money for the state of Colorado (McAllister 1999, 59). All of the 319 monies go directly to remediation projects. Other agencies also contribute funding, but do not play as dominant a role as EPA. For instance, USFS, BLM, and the Colorado Department of Wildlife provide financial resources to the ARSG effort. San Juan County donates office space to the group. Local mining corporations and the Southwest Water Conservation District underwrite a small portion of the group's administrative costs.

ARSG was designed to address a very specific issue. As a result, the group had no collective *experience* prior to being formed. It is organized as "a collaborative effort of public and private interests," (ARSG 1999a) and as such is *structured* to promote working partnerships. To facilitate smoothly working relationships the group meets on the third Thursday of every month in Silverton, Colorado. To take advantage of the comparative advantages offered by the different stakeholders, three working groups were formed: 1) a feasibility studies workgroup to investigate and design remedial actions; 2) a monitoring workgroup to monitor and expand water quality activities; and 3) a funding workgroup to find financial resources for ARSG. Working group meetings, which are devoted to handling specific issues to put before the full group, normally take place immediately prior to the monthly meeting. Action items from these working group meetings are then taken to the group at large. A consensus-based decision-making process was adopted in place of a more formal voting procedure to ensure inclusion of all stakeholder interests and avoid the marginalization of minority interests.

The main ARSG *network* is with its stakeholder members, a mix of mostly public agency representatives with a smattering of local public and private interests. Thus, ARSG is best typified as having built bonding capital among its members. Not all of the original stakeholders identified by the Colorado Center for Environmental Management have remained part of the process. Notably, the federal and state government agencies have been the most persistent members, along with some individual community members who serve as representatives from local government, nonprofits and industry.

The limited connections to the local community have resulted in ARSG facing some challenges to its *legitimacy* over the years, and this can be seen as a consequence of the group's inability to build bridging capital to other entities. In 1995, the group was criticized by locals who felt overwhelmed by the many government agencies that were part of the stakeholder process (Broetzman 1996, 10; McAllister 1999, 50). Bill Simon, in response to these concerns, attempted to make the meetings more attractive to members of the immediate community. He altered the meeting format by leaving highly technical data off the agenda and focused on broader policy concerns. He began meeting individually with local citizens to explain the ARSG process and started a series of topical discussions at the Silverton Library to reach more people (Broetzman 1996). Additional outreach efforts included newspaper articles, holding an open house, and conducting a field trip (Broetzman 1996). A 1996 report on the group encouraged ARSG to "maintain continuous contacts with the local population at large and to seek expanded local participation and/or acceptance in the process" (Boetzman 1996, 12).

Local confusion about the intent of ARSG activities and concern about the involvement of locals persist. At the July 1999 meeting, one participant noted that there was a local perception that ARSG wanted to go beyond mine site remediation and clean up the natural background levels of contaminants (Animas River Stakeholder Group 1999c). At the previous meeting in June 1999, there had been a discussion concerning the lack of large numbers of locals regularly present at stakeholders meetings.

Nonetheless, many felt that the ARSG format was an inclusive and accessible outlet for those that chose to participate. While some residents and landowners regularly attend meetings, it has been noted that attendance increases when issues become more threatening or controversial (Animas River Stakeholder Group 1999c). Simon feels that ARSG "includes all levels of government, corporations, land owners and citizens who feel a need to express their position on matters that affect water quality in the Animas River." He adds, "I think all would agree that community is taken in the larger sense" (Simon 1999).

While ARSG has faced repeated questions about its legitimacy as a community group, it is unclear that this effort at CBEM could be anything else but legitimate. Community concern about the determination of water quality standards is thin. San Juan County as a whole has a total of 500 residents, 83 percent of the land is owned by public agencies, and many of the remaining landowners are absentee landlords. ARSG has operated in a context that is indeed unique in terms of determining who "community" is and how the group might do a better job building a "bridge" to them. Responding to this challenge, ARSG has brought together the public, private and nonprofit stakeholders that are most important to the issue at hand. It has not ignored its immediate community and has made repeated attempts to involve local publics. In the absence of a more palpable catalyzing threat to the community, locals may not be interested in determining water quality standards or may feel they have more pressing concerns to address as a community. However, the stakeholder process is certainly more participatory and community-based than having the WQCC determine use standards without any input from those who would be most affected by them.

Outcomes of CBEM in the Animas

In response to a request from the WQCD, the ARSG was formed with the purpose of developing water quality use standards for the Animas River. While the group also has coordinated some remediation efforts, its dominant purpose has been to provide standards that are derived from studies of the communities most affected by them. The mission of ARSG does not resonate with the local community at large, but it has appealed to those with the greatest stake in the determination of water quality standards on the Animas—notably the state and federal agencies concerned with water quality, the public land agencies that are the dominant land owners in the region, and the mining companies that stand to benefit or lose from the imposition of water quality standards. As ARSG moves toward the end of its data collection efforts, the group will be tested to see if it has built a sufficient base among its members to make the tough judgment calls needed to determine the water quality standards for the river. The monthly meetings have brought together many of the most important decision makers who have a stake in the determination of water quality standards in the watershed. At the same time, ARSG has become familiar in the local community and its reputation has grown over time. Even if the group is not representative of the immediate community at large, it has become known in the community as a forum for addressing water quality issues.

Substantive Outcomes

To date, ARSG estimates that $20 million has been spent on research and remediation projects within the watershed (McAllister 1999). Site characterization and some remediation have comprised most of the group's effort. In 1995, the Colorado Division of Mining and Geology began a study on one of the tributaries to the upper Animas— Mineral Creek. EPA, using Section 319 monies, funded this effort and the USFS and the Colorado Geological Survey provided technical assistance. In 1996, ARSG initiated a similar study on another tributary— Cement Creek, and in that same year, began an evaluation of the Animas River Canyon to determine aquatic habitat limitations (McAllister 1999). USFS, which manages most of the federal lands in the watershed, provided technical help and contracted with the Colorado Geological Survey to conduct an inventory of mines on USFS lands. USFS has conducted biological studies in the area, as has BLM and the Colorado Department of Wildlife. At present, ARSG has nearly fifty individual site characterization studies in progress (McAllister 1999).

ARSG has received support for a Department of Interior-BLM pilot project to compare multiple remediation technologies. Remediation projects have been undertaken in Placer Gulch and at the Silver Wing Mining Company site with funding and support coming from EPA,[9] the Department of Interior, BLM and USGS (Broetzman 1996; McAllister 1999). Three more remediation projects are planned — Animas Mine Waste Control Project, the Cement Creek Mine Waste Control Project, and the Mine Infiltration Identification and Control Project.[10] USFS, BLM and the Colorado Department of Wildlife have contributed money for biological studies (McAllister 1999).

In 1998, the ARSG process came up for review before WQCC. At that time, ARSG had not made any determinations about setting use-designation standards, and asked for an additional three years to continue to collect data in order make the standards. WQCC agreed unanimously to give the group until March 2001 to complete its recommendations for water quality standards in the upper Animas River (McAllister, 1999). At present, existing narrative standards remain. In the meantime, ARSG has undertaken a use attainability analysis (UAA) which is a composite of all the studies conducted in the basin and will provide a basis for determining the standards for use in the watershed. The group formulated a UAA work plan and timeline in order to create a draft UAA by March 2001. If the standards provided by ARSG in 2001 were not adequate, then WQCC will impose the numerical standards suggested in 1995.

Social Outcomes

Given the "acrimonious mood [which] prevailed during [the] early sessions [the] general distrust towards the state's intention, anxiety about CCEM's role, and a lack of harmony among local interests," (Broetzman 1995, 2) perhaps the biggest social outcome accomplished by ARSG is the building of *trust* among this disparate group of individuals within it. According to one ARSG participant, "There was a lot of animosity toward the process at first. It took a while before people started to feel comfortable and get down to business" (Belsten 1996, 172). The need to build trust was, and is, a crucial foundation for building a stronger organization. As recounted by an ARSG member, "I sit in these meetings and I used to see the federal government and state government as very much obstructionist. Now I hear their very legitimate concerns. They want to do the right thing.... There's more working together" (Belsten 1996, 172–173). Additionally, the presence of trust leads to tangible savings in terms of time and efficiency in how things get done. "I think this process is starting to take on a life of its own. It's built up a lot of trust. Solutions are locally generated. And I know I can pick up the phone and talk with anyone in the group between meetings" (Belsten 1996, 174).

Over time, the trust within the group has resulted in the ability of its members to progress to a collective *understanding* of the problems they face, how these problems could be addressed and prioritized, and ultimately how they might be resolved. As one stakeholder commented, "It's a much more complicated issue than I think people initially realized. You do have to spend a great deal of time studying all the options before you can take any steps, finalize any solutions" (Belsten 1996, 172). From their initial meetings in 1994, the group gained better understanding of state water quality management activities, standards and regulations as well as what would be required to undertake a "voluntary" approach to standard setting and cleanup. Additional understanding of the nature of the problem has been facilitated by joint data gathering processes and research (Belsten 1996). A core group of approximately 30 stakeholders meet monthly to share their understanding about the state's water quality control standards and regulations, as well as the new knowledge they gain about factors contributing to the contamination. Minutes from each monthly meeting are sent out to all stakeholders and interested parties to ensure that those who could not be present are kept informed. Overall, the outcome of these meetings has been a greater comprehension of implications for setting specific water quality standards, greater appreciation of environmental technologies and cleanup strategies, and a more thorough awareness of the long-term consequences of the standards, the technologies and the cleanup.

Elicitation of *values* is implicit in the contact that comes through trust-building activities, as is the promotion of joint understanding. Through meetings and working groups, different entities have been able to express their concerns and preferences and have them taken seriously by the other stakeholders. In contrast to FOC, where external linkages promote the elicitation of the values of the broader community, ASRG has focused on learning and respecting the values of stakeholders within the core group.

Open and Closed Circles of Resources in CBEM Initiatives

As the case studies suggest, Friends of the Cheat and the Animas River Stakeholders Group were formed to address specific issues regarding watershed remediation. Both organizations were newly established and had no previous experience working on community-based environmental management initiatives. FOC was started by community members who had strong connections to the local community and its natural resources while the founding members of ARSG were selected by the Colorado Water Quality Control Division. The focus and structures of the organizations led to each having a distinct approach to attracting, working with, and maintaining organizational resource streams. These differences in structure and resources influenced the types of outcomes that resulted from the CBEM process. In FOC's case, building an organization from the bottom up contributed to the interdependency that developed between human and network resources. The FOC network was developed through the initiatives of the organizational founder and other founding members. Their commitment and networking skills made it possible to attract a diverse and representative group of board members to the organization. While formalization can impair some groups, it helped FOC establish clear communication patterns and a level of decentralization that has fostered input, reinforced ties to the local community, and promoted partnerships with agencies. Diversity of interests, the sincere desire to broaden the organization's network, ease of access and communication, and the efforts of staff and board members to build understanding and interest in restoration of the river, promoted the legitimacy of FOC. With its legitimacy established, the group has been able to secure financial as well as technical resources from funders and agencies within their ever-broadening network.

As Figure 1 suggests, the founding mission and bottom-up approach to organizing gave rise to activities that fostered what can be termed as an "open circle of resources." In other words, the founding orientation and grassroots nature of the initiative required that members work to build ties to the community and other individuals and organizations relevant to their mission. Human resources and energy led to connections with other organizations and agencies. Structural features that promoted decentralization and diversity reinforced these networks. The organization gained legitimacy by building further ties to the community and to agencies. Recognition then helped FOC attract financial and technical resources. In essence, FOC was able to take advantage of its existing, but limited resources (human, network, structural, legitimacy) and leverage these to attract additional resources (technical, financial, experiential, legitimacy, network) that were and are necessary for the group to achieve its ultimate objectives.

The substantive and social outcomes from the FOC initiative are tied to the way that the organization has managed and worked to expand its resources. The substantive outcomes of water quality studies and reclamation projects are a direct result of the financial and technical resources that were gained through the group's network resources. Yet, if FOC did not have legitimacy, it would have had a difficult time sustaining its network and obtaining financial and technical support. As the circle of resources expands and as the organization is recognized as a legitimate entity that can take action on behalf of the local community, FOC increases its social outcomes. Actions such as watershed remediation and educational initiatives have demonstrated a commitment to the community.

Networking and ongoing interaction and communication with community members have fostered understanding, trust, and awareness of local values.

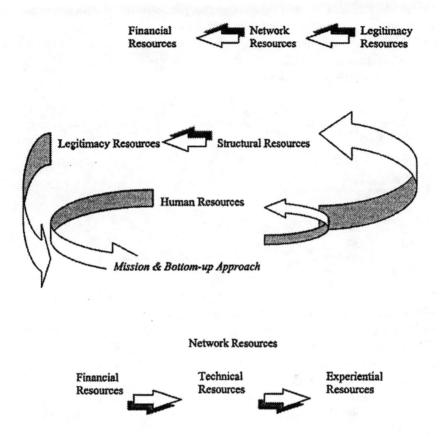

ARSG was founded as a top-down initiative by WQCD with the goal of determining water quality standards. The initial structure and intent established a distinct organizational trajectory and relationship to resources. In contrast to FOC, where human resources were central, the core of ARSG is the relationship between networks and financial and technical resources. The members of ARSG were selected by the Colorado Center for Environmental Management, and this group formed a tight network that has been focused on task completion. EPA provided the group with sufficient financial resources to create a level of stability that made it possible to hire staff members. Because of the closed nature of the network, the legitimacy of ARSG has been questioned within the local community. While network ties to EPA and WQCD have made it possible for the group to secure additional technical and financial resources, it has not been successful in establishing tight connections to the local community, nor has it sought to extend its efforts to include groups external to it. Nonetheless, this has not appeared to hamper ARSG's ability to achieve its goals.

Figure 2: Closed Circle of Resources for ARSG

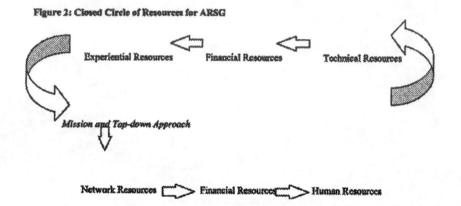

Like FOC, ARSG's outcomes are closely intertwined with its resources. ARSG's ability to conduct stream studies, undertake the use-attainability analysis, and engage in reclamation projects are a direct result of the financial and technical resources that have been made available to it by EPA. Because ARSG's relationships have been limited to interactions with members of a closed network, it has been successful in promoting understanding, trust, and appreciation of values among its own group, but has been less successful in promoting these social outcomes with groups external to it.

While FOC has been successful in generating bonding networks among its members as well as bridging networks with communities and organizations peripheral to the group, ARSG has established bonding networks among its immediate members. Both types of networks are and continue to be imperative to the outcomes achieved by these different groups. In the case of FOC, the bottom-up nature of the organization required that it build bridges to other organizations and agencies in order for its mission to be successful. With resource streams established, ARSG had to generate bonds that would foster internal trust and communication among group members so that the organization could accomplish its goals.

Initiating and Managing Different Types of CBEM Programs

These two case studies suggest that there are at least two different models of CBEM — those that are driven from within the community in a bottom-up manner, and those that are driven by agencies in a top-down manner. The case studies also suggest that the initial motivation and approach to organizing a CBEM effort may influence resource generation and the outcomes that are derived from these endeavors. While both bottom-up and top-down approaches helped in the process of AMD remediation and stream restoration, the link between project structure, resource availability and management, and outcomes, suggests that different types of initiatives may be more or less desirable, depending on the focus of the effort and the long- and short-range goals of the initiative.

Community members who had a deep concern for the river and the local community founded FOC as a bottom-up effort. Thus, the founder and initial member were known to the community. This helped the organization and its mandate to gain acceptance and legitimacy. While the group had to work to develop ties to government agencies, the high level of commitment and enthusiasm helped generate network affiliations that contributed to the organization's ability to secure financial and technical resources as well as cultivate further network ties and legitimacy. ARSG was developed through a top-down process with the mandate of establishing regulatory protocols. In many respects, this initiative reflects the agency culture from which it came and manifests an extension of the regulatory regime. The initiating structure and mandate ensured that the group had adequate financial and technical resources from the outset. Because financial, technical and structural stability were present, members did not need to develop external networks or gain local legitimacy.

The cases further suggest that achieving substantive and social outcomes may be related to the resources that an organization has available and the efforts that organizational members make to sustain and expand resource availability. Both cases indicate that the availability of staff, financial support, and technical expertise promote the realization of substantive goals. What differs is the type of networks that are formed and the social outcomes that flow from these networks. FOC's ability to legitimize itself as a community group was essential to securing additional resources. This forced it to build both bonding and bridging networks to achieve its mission. ARSG did not need to legitimize itself as a community-driven entity to secure additional resources. Consequently, it needed to build a

bonding network among the disparate groups that were brought together
to achieve the designation of water quality standards.

The role for government agencies, nonprofits and other funding entities also is different in the two cases. In the FOC case, external entities
played a supportive role in assisting FOC in achieving its mission. When
an initiative requires local support and commitment, it may be helpful for
agencies to collaborate with existing community organizations, those that
have gained legitimacy, by providing technical and financial resources. For
example, watershed management and remediation and community education are long-term initiatives that require the ongoing participation of
community members. If skillfully developed, these agency-community
organization partnerships have the potential to develop into self-sustaining collaborative ventures. Given the broad nature of FOC's effort, the
presence of a spontaneous and self-sustaining community-driven effort
may provide a greater chance of successfully restoring the Cheat River to
ecological health than a top-down effort.

In the ARSG case, external entities played a formative role in the
process and supplied structural, technical and financial resources to get
the effort started. Since then ARSG has taken on a life of its own and is
now driven by the group and less so by one agency or organization. Given
the narrower nature of ARSG's mission, this approach made sense. The
"thinness" of community around the issue of water quality standards in
San Juan County meant that a more organic, bottom-up effort was unlikely
to occur. When there are highly focused, short-term objectives, top-down
organizations appear to be the way to go. Although they may not have the
level of acceptance or be able to achieve the same degree of social outcomes as more grassroots-based endeavors, the steady stream of resources
and tight structure are useful for establishing, say, water quality standards
or the development of protocols for contaminant reduction.

This chapter examined only two case studies. Although the evidence
is limited, the findings help build our collective understanding of how
CBEM initiatives emerge, function, and achieve their goals. Nonetheless,
more research is needed on both top-down and bottom-up CBEM efforts
to afford greater insight into how they secure and use resources to achieve
their goals. The descriptions of CBEM in this chapter accentuate the
extremes of a continuum that ranges from top-down to bottom-up; however, they do not explore the many in-between variations of approach that
are currently being employed. While the cases provide preliminary evidence about some of the conditional factors that influence the type of
CBEM efforts undertaken as well as the resources that are important to
such efforts, more data are needed to advance our understanding. We also

need to continue to enhance our understanding of what constitutes success in CBEM. The demarcation between substantive and social outcomes that is presented in this chapter can serve as a framework for analysis while providing a foundation for additional research. Finally, we need to continue to work on understanding how resources are tied to different outcomes and the interdependencies of these complicated relationships. There is a danger that efforts to categorize and summarize the CBEM phenomenon will constrain the creativity that is currently emerging from these initiatives. Our observations need to express the richness embodied in these efforts without being overly reductionist or prescriptive. By being true to the complexity of the CBEM phenomenon we can gain a better understanding of how this new management approach can thrive in the future and how projects can be structured to offer innovative and enduring solutions to different environmental problems.

Endnotes

1. The pH value of a solution is a measure of acidity based upon a logarithmic scale with numbers lower on the scale representing an increase in the amount of acidity. For example, a pH of 6 is ten times more acidic than a pH of 7.

2. Under section 319, state, territories, and tribes can receive grants to support a wide variety of activities including technical assistance, financial assistance, education, training, technology transfer, demonstration projects, and monitoring to assist the success of specific nonpoint source implementation projects.

3. The Regional Geographic Initiative program is intended to support "place based" projects.

4. AMD is responsible for 50 percent of the streams in West Virginia not meeting water quality standards (EPA, undated brochure).

5. The Cheat River was again named as one of the most endangered rivers in 1996.

6. The AML program is a national fund administered by the federal OSM. A 15-cent tax is levied on every ton of deep-mined coal and 35 cents for each ton of surface coal mined. Allocations from the AML fund are made to state and tribal agencies through the congressional budgetary process.

7. ASCI funds cooperative agreements between OSM and nonprofit groups for local acid mine drainage programs (OSM, undated brochure).

8. WQCC is the agency in charge of implementing the Clean Water Act (CWA) and the Safe Drinking Water Act (SDWA). In accordance with the CWA and the SDWA, each state sets water quality standards that are subject to approval by the EPA.

9. For the first few years the EPA funded ARSG through the Rocky Moun-

tain Headwaters Mining Waste Initiative. Since then, EPA 319 funds have been a crucial source of funding.

10. All of these remediation projects are funded with EPA 319 funds.

References

American Rivers. 1996. American Rivers Announces Continent's Most Endangered Rivers of 1996. *http://www.amrivers.org/most.html.*

Animas River Stakeholder Group. 1999a. Background and General Information. *http://www.waterinfo.org/arsg/arsg.htm.*

Animas River Stakeholder Group. 1999b. History and Stakeholder Process. *http://www.waterinfo.org/arsg/history.html.*

Animas River Stakeholder Group. 1999c. Meeting Summary. *http://www.waterinfo.org/arsg/mtgsummary.html.*

Bassage, David. 1995a. Executive Director, Friends of the Cheat. In-person interview with Toddi A. Steelman. January 7, 1995. Bruceton, West Virginia.

Bassage, David. 1995b. Friends of Cheat Outlines Goals. *American Whitewater* 25 (2): 30.

Bassage, David. 1999a. Executive Director, Friends of the Cheat. In-person interview with Toddi A. Steelman. June, 1999. Kingwood, West Virginia.

Bassage, David. 1999b. E-mail correspondence with Toddi A. Steelman. October 13, 1999.

Bassage, David. 1999c. Stream of Consciousness. Friends of the Cheat Newsletter. July 1999.

Bassage, David. 2000. Executive Director, Friends of the Cheat. In-person interview with Toddi A. Steelman. May, 2000. Kingwood, West Virginia.

Belsten, Laura. 1996. *Community Collaboration in Environmental Decision Making.* Ph.D dissertation. University of Denver.

Besierle, Thomas C. 1999. Using Social Goals to Evaluate Public Participation in Environmental Decisions. *Policy Studies Review* 16 (3/4): 75–103.

Blair, Rob. 1996. *The Western San Juan Mountains: Their Geology, Ecology and Human History.* Niwot, CO.: University of Colorado Press.

Bosso, Christopher J. 1994. After the Movement: Environmental Activism in the 1990s. In *Environmental Policy in the 1990s, second edition,* edited by N. J. Vig and M. E. Kraft. Washington, DC: CQ Press.

Broetzman, Gary. 1996. *Animas River Collaborative Watershed Project: 1995 Status Report.* Denver, CO: Colorado Center for Environmental Management.

Bryant, Gary. 1996. Letter from Gary Bryant (EPA Region III) to Dave Bassage. February 1, 1996.

Chottiner, Lee. 1995. Cheat River Endangered: Makes National List, Ranks 8th Among Top 10. *Dominion Post,* 19 April.

Cutler, M. Rupert. 1995. Old Players with New Power: The Non-governmental Organizations. In *A New Century for Natural Resources Management,* edited by R. L. Knight and S. F. Bates. Washington, DC: Island Press.

Davis, Heather Nann. 1996. Cleanup Money Only Goes So Far. *Dominion Post*, 26 February.

DeBonis, Jeff. 1995. Natural Resource Agencies: Questioning the Paradigm. In *A New Century for Natural Resources Management*, edited by R. L. Knight and S. F. Bates. Washington, DC: Island Press.

Dunlap, Riley E., and Angela G. Mertig. 1992. *American Environmentalism: The US Environmental Movement 1970–90*. Washington, DC: Taylor and Francis.

Friends of the Cheat. 1999a. Friends of the Cheat. Available from *http://www.cheat.org/index.html*. Accessed September 26, 1999.

Friends of the Cheat. 1999b. Masthead. *FOC Newsletter*. July 1999.

Friends of the Cheat. 1999c. Total Maximum Daily Loads. *FOC Newsletter*. April 1999: 13.

Frodeman, Robert. 1999. A Sense of the Whole: Understanding Acid Mine Drainage in the West. Paper presented at the Natural Resources Law Center Continuing Education Workshop. April 1999. Denver, Colorado.

Gittell, Ross, and A. Vidal. 1998. *Community Organizing: Building Social Capital as a Development Strategy*. Thousand Oaks, CA: Sage Publications.

Gray, Barbara. 1985. Conditions Facilitating Interorganizational Collaboration. *Human Relations* 38 (10): 911–936.

Hays, Samuel. 1959. *Conservation and the Gospel of Efficiency: The Progressive Conservation Movement, 1890–1920*. New York, NY: Atheneum.

Haywood, Cori. 2000. Acting Executive Director Friends of the Cheat. In-person interview with Toddi A. Steelman. September. Kingwood, WV.

John, Dewitt. 1996. *Civic Environmentalism*. Washington, DC: Congressional Quarterly Press.

John, Dewitt, and M. Mlay. 1998. Community-Based Environmental Protection: How Federal and State Agencies Can Encourage Civic Environmentalism. Working paper. Washington, DC: National Academy of Public Administration.

Kaufman, H. 1969. Administrative Decentralization and Political Power. *Public Administration Review* 29 (1): 3–15.

Kempton, Willett, James S. Boster, and Jennifer A. Hartley. 1995. *Environmental Values in American Culture*. Boston, MA: MIT Press.

Kenney, Doug S. 1997. *Resource Management at the Watershed Level: An Assessment of the Changing Federal Role in the Emerging Era of Community-Based Watershed Management*. Boulder, CO. Natural Resources Law Center: Research Report # 15 (March 15).

Kenney, Doug. 1999. Are Community-Based Watershed Groups Really Effective? *Chronicle of Community*. Winter.

Kenney, Doug S., and W. B. Lord. 1999. *Analysis of Institutional Innovation in the Natural Resources and Environmental Realm: The Emergence of Alternative Problem-Solving Strategies in the American West*. Research Report RR-21. Boulder, CO: Natural Resources Law Center, University of Colorado School of Law.

Koontz, Tomas M., and Elizabeth Moore. 2000. Collaborative Environmental

Management: Fitting Stakeholders to Objectives. Paper presented at the 8th Annual ISSRM Conference, Bellingham, WA.

Korfmacher, Katrina. 2000. What's the Point of Partnering?: A Case Study of Eco-System Management in the Darby Watershed. *American Behavioral Scientist* 44 (4): in press.

McAllister, Sean. 1999. The Confluence of a River and a Community: An Experiment with Community-based Watershed Management in Southwestern Colorado. Paper for Advanced Natural Resources Seminar on San Juan Basin, University of Colorado Law School.

McGinnis, Michael Vincent. 1999. Making the Watershed Connection. *Policy Studies Journal* 27 (3): 497–501.

Meidinger, E. E. 1997. Organization and Legal Challenges for Ecosystem Management. In *Creating a Forestry for the 21st Century*, edited by K. Kohm and J. F Franklin. Washington, DC: Island Press.

Mineral Policy Center. 1999. Environmental Impacts of Mining. *http://www.mineralpolicy.org/Environment.html*.

Nelson, Lisa S., and Louis F. Weschler. 1998. Institutional Readiness for Integrated Watershed Management: The Case of the Maumee River. *The Social Science Journal* 35 (4): 565–576.

Office of Surface Mining and Environmental Protection Agency. 1995a. 1995 Progress Report: Statement of Mutual Intent Strategic Plan for the Restoration and Protection of Streams and Watersheds Polluted by Acid Mine Drainage from Abandoned Coal Mines. November 15, 1995.

Office of Surface Mining and Environmental Protection Agency. 1995b. Restoration and Protection of Streams and Watersheds Polluted by Acid Mine Drainage from Abandoned Coal Mines: Statement of Mutual Intent. February 9, 1995.

Office of Surface Mining Reclamation and Enforcement. 1996. Annual Evaluation Report for the Regulatory and Abandoned Mine Land Reclamation Programs Administered by the State of West Virginia for the Evaluation Year 1995. January.

Office of Surface Mining Reclamation and Enforcement. 1999. OSM Funds Two West Virginia Appalachian Clean Stream Projects Under New Watershed Cooperative Agreement Program. Press Release, September 30.

Office of Surface Mining Reclamation and Enforcement. Undated brochure. Appalachian Clean Streams Initiative. On file with author.

Parker, Vawter 1995. Natural Resources Management by Litigation. In *A New Century for Natural Resources Management*, edited by R. L. Knight and S. F. Bates. Washington, DC: Island Press.

Pickett, S. T. A., and Richard S. Ostfeld. 1995. The Shifting Paradigm of Ecology. In *A New Century for Natural Resources Management*, edited by R. L. Knight and S. F. Bates. Washington, DC: Island Press.

Poffenberg, Mark. 1998. *Communities and Forest Management in the United States and Canada*. Berkeley, CA: Working Group on Community Involvement in Forest Management.

Press, Daniel. 1998. Local Environmental Policy Capacity: A Framework for Research. *Natural Resources Journal* 38 (1): 29–52.

Selin, Steve, and Deborah Chavez. 1995. Developing a Collaborative Model for Environmental Planning and Management. *Environmental Management* 19 (2): 189–195.

Shannon, M. A., and A. R. Antypas. 1997. Open Institutions: Uncertainty and Ambiguity in 21st Century Forestry. In *Creating a Forestry for the 21st Century,* edited by K. Kohm and J. F. Franklin. Washington, DC: Island Press.

Simon, Bill. 1999. E-mail correspondence with Toddi A. Steelman. September 28, 1999.

Slovic, Paul. 1987. Perception of Risk. *Science* 236: 280–285.

Snyder, Jim. 1995. The Muddy Creek Story. *Friends of Cheat Newsletter.* May 6, 1995.

Steelman, Toddi A. 2001. Elite and Participatory Policy Making: Finding Balance in a Case of National Forest Management. *Policy Studies Journal* (forthcoming).

U.S. Environmental Protection Agency. 1995. *Human Health and Environmental Damages from Mining and Mineral Processing Wastes: Technical background document supporting the supplemental proposed rule applying Phase IV land disposal restrictions to newly identified mineral processing wastes.* http://www.epa.gov//epaoswer/other/mining/minedoc/damage/metadam.txt.

U.S. Environmental Protection Agency. 1997. *People, Places and Partnerships: A Progress Report on Community-based Environmental Protection.* EPA-100-R-97-0003. Washington, DC: US EPA.

U.S. Environmental Protection Agency. 2000. Coal Mining Point Source Category: Amendments to Effluent Limitations Guidelines and New Source Performance Standards. Available from *http://www.epa.gov/fedrgstr/EPA-/WATER/2000/April/Day-11/w8533.html.* Accessed on September 15, 2000.

U.S. Environmental Protection Agency. Undated brochure. *EPA Region III Coal Mine Drainage Initiative.* On file with author.

U.S. Geographic Survey. 1997. Mine Drainage and the Environment. *http://easternweb.er.usgs.gov/eastern/environment/drainage.html.*

Webler, Thomas, and Seth Tuler. 1999. Integrating Technical Analysis with Deliberation in Regional Watershed Management Planning: Applying the National Research Council Approach. Policy Studies Journal 27 (3): 530–543.

West Virginia Rivers Coalition. 1997. Stream Partners Act Funds Many New Initiatives. *Headwaters: Quarterly Newsletter of the West Virginia Rivers Coalition* 7 (1): 6.

Wiles, Brent. 1999. WV Department of Environmental Protection inspector and supervisor. In-person interview with Toddi A. Steelman, Kingwood, WV. June 25, 1999.

Wood, Donna J., and Barbara Gray. 1991. Toward a Comprehensive Theory of Collaboration. *Journal of Applied Behavioral Science* 27 (2): 139–162.

Wondolleck, Julia, and Steve Yaffee. 2000. *Making Collaboration Work: Lessons from Innovation in Natural Resource Management.* Covelo, CA: Island Press.

Yaffee, Steve L., and Julia M. Wondolleck. 1997. Building Bridges Across Agency Boundaries. In *Creating a Forestry for the 21st Century,* edited by K. Kohm and J. F. Franklin. Washington, DC: Island Press.

Yaffee, Steve L., Ali F. Phillips, Irene C. Frantz, Paul W. Hardy, Sussanne M. Maleki, and Barber Thorpe. 1996. *Ecosystem Management in the United States: An Assessment of Current Experience,* Washington, DC: Island Press.

Yosie, T. F., and T. D. Hebst. 1998. *Using Stakeholder Processes in Environmental Decisionmaking: An Evaluation of Lessons Learned, Key Issues, and Future Challenges.* Ruder Finn Washington and ICF Incorporated, September.

Index